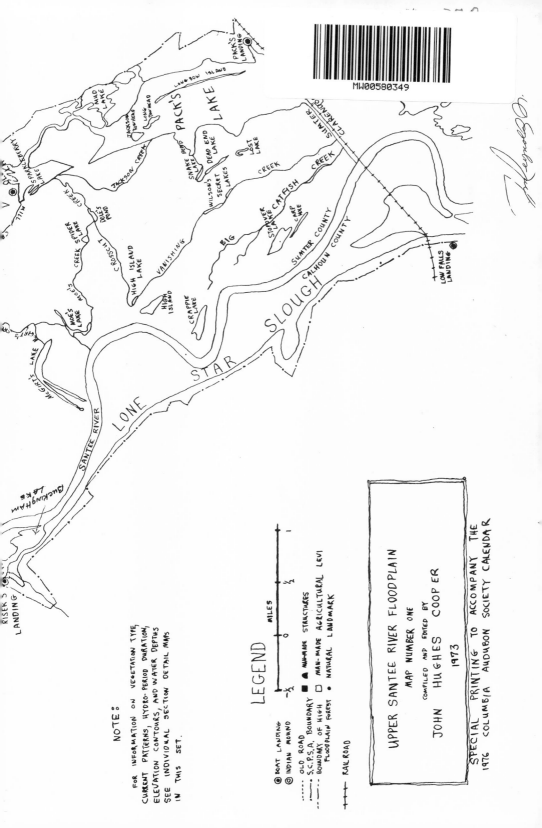

NOTE:

FOR INFORMATION ON VEGETATION TYPE, CURRENT PATTERNS, HYDRO-PERIOD DURATION, ELEVATION CONTOURS, AND WATER DEPTHS SEE INDIVIDUAL SECTION DETAIL MAPS IN THIS SET.

LEGEND

MILES

½    0    ½    1

⊙ BOAT LANDING
⊙ INDIAN MOUND
······· OLD ROAD
----- S.C.P.S.A. BOUNDARY
---- BOUNDARY OF HIGH FLOODPLAIN FOREST
■ MAN-MADE STRUCTURES
□ MAN-MADE AGRICULTURAL LEVI
● NATURAL LANDMARK
+-+-+ RAILROAD

UPPER SANTEE RIVER FLOODPLAIN

MAP NUMBER ONE

COMPILED AND EDITED BY

JOHN HUGHES COOPER

1973

SPECIAL PRINTING TO ACCOMPANY THE 1976 COLUMBIA AUDUBON SOCIETY CALENDAR

ARB
FROM
ACB SR.

# SUNRISE ON THE SANTEE

# SUNRISE
# ON THE SANTEE

*A Memoir of Waterfowling
in South Carolina*

Julius M. Reynolds, Jr.

UNIVERSITY OF SOUTH CAROLINA PRESS

© 2002 University of South Carolina

Published in Columbia, South Carolina, by the
University of South Carolina Press

Manufactured in the United States of America

06  05  04  03  02    5  4  3  2  1

Library of Congress Cataloging-in-Publication Data

Reynolds, Julius M., 1933–
    Sunrise on the Santee : a memoir of waterfowling in South Carolina /
Julius M. Reynolds, Jr.
        p. cm.
    ISBN 1-57003-454-0 (cloth : alk. paper)
    1. Waterfowl shooting—South Carolina—Santee River Region—Anecdotes.
2. Fishing—South Carolina—Santee River Region—Anecdotes. 3. Reynolds,
Julius M., 1933–  I. Title.
SK331 .R49 2002
799.2'44'097578—dc21                                             2001007080

Map of the Santee Delta provided by the Columbia Audubon Society; used with
permission of its author, John Hughes Cooper.
All photos are by the author.

*In special love and memory of my*
*Uncle Johnnie Zeigler*
*whose ways in the swamp became my ways*

# CONTENTS

# ILLUSTRATIONS

# Preface

*Sunrise on the Santee* is the story of my life and experiences as a hunter and fisherman on Lake Marion and Lake Moultrie from the time of my student years in Sumter, South Carolina, to adulthood, when I lived near the Santee Cooper lakes. It also covers some of my coastal saltwater marsh hunting during the time I lived in Walterboro, South Carolina.

I roamed the lakes hunting mostly ducks—duck hunting had became my favorite sport when my Uncle Johnnie Zeigler of Eastover, South Carolina, first took me into the Wateree Swamp to hunt with him. His reputation as a master huntsman spread afar, and he willingly shared his knowledge of the swamps with me.

The Santee Cooper lakes are mostly open water, with the exception of about 12,000 acres in the upper, swampy region of Lake Marion. It was there that I spent more than forty years hunting its many oak ridges, cypress flats, streams, and lakes, all of which were subject to flooding during the South Carolina duck seasons. The area from the confluence of the Wateree and Congaree Rivers to the Rimini train trestle was the "big swamp" to me. It was, and is today, very different from the rest of the 170,000 acres that make up the two Santee Cooper lakes, which take their names from the Revolutionary War generals Francis Marion (known as the Swamp Fox) and William Moultrie.

Waterfowling is more than a hobby or seasonal recreational pursuit. Waterfowling is a lifestyle, a passion shared with an unwavering desire to greet the dawn in the water-world of ducks and geese.

Waterfowling is getting up earlier than the world does to meet the inky darkness before first light. It's getting to the boat landing before the late arrivals do. It's thankfulness for the shocking cold and for the brisk wind as you step out of your car. It's the scary ride across choppy but usually familiar waters on the way to a favorite hunting blind.

It's boats, decoys, guns and duck calls, your favorite hunting partner who's always on time, and your loyal retriever that leads the way through the wind and waves by eagerly standing in the foremost point of your boat.

It's the dog's cold nose as he nestles under your legs as both of you antic-ipate the excitement that comes with the dawn.

It's sitting in the darkness that slowly gives way to the conquering light. It's sipping hot coffee from the thermos bottle you just opened and sensing the aroma and its warmth to come. It's sharing some with your hunting partner to help warm his chill as you await those first rays of sun-shine that chase away the early morning darkness. Soon the eastern sky will take on its orange tint, and another sunrise on the Santee will be born.

Waterfowling has a neverending season each year, as we never lose sight of our sport. When we're not hunting we're making plans and prepa-rations for the next opening day. We sometimes wonder why we go to so much effort, scanning catalogs with all the new equipment that come in the mail, screening each new item to see if it fits our needs and our pock-etbooks. Once committed, it's not really why we hunt, rather that we do.

# ACKNOWLEDGMENTS

I wish to thank my wife, Carolyn, for her devotion to my completion of this memoir, and for staying up late those many nights when the swamp detained me a little too long. I also am grateful to my mother and father, who so many years ago fostered my boyhood interests in the outdoors; to my son, Jay, who has loved the Great Santee as I have; and to my daughter, Liz, who shares our family's love of nature. Moreover, I wish to thank my sister, Betty, for her love of God's small creatures and the many orphaned ones she has nurtured, and my brother, John, for the many happy hours spent together in the swamps.

At the University of South Carolina Press, I extend my appreciation to Mr. Alexander Moore, acquisitions editor, for his support and encouragement throughout this effort.

To my longtime hunting companions, John W. Jackson and Robert M. Thompkins, who shared many of my memorable experiences, I express my gratitude, as well as to the State of South Carolina for making possible my personal playground, the Santee Cooper lakes.

# SUNRISE ON THE SANTEE

# 1

## THAT SPECIAL PLACE

As I write these words, the year is 2000, and I'm approaching my sixty-seventh birthday. Looking back at all the areas I've hunted, I recall goose hunting in Canada and Illinois, duck hunting in Nebraska and Louisiana, and over the last few years some special hunts in Arkansas. Trips to all of these top hunting spots were enjoyable. I remember the fellowship and I cherish those friendships made. But of all the duck hunting in those out-of-state places and other areas of South Carolina, the Santee lakes and swamp are where my heart is. They comprise that special place to me.

Today, compared to other states, the hunting there is as poor as it is in most of the Atlantic Flyway, but for many years the Santee was tops. Sportsmen didn't have to go out of state to hunt. Our swamps, rivers, and salt marshes were home to a myriad of ducks each winter. Our refuge system on the Santee lakes held in excess of 100,000 ducks. And many ducks frequented private wetlands around our state. Duck hunting was a popular sport on the Santee, and only in the last few years has it faded. But still, the big swamp at the headwaters of Lake Marion holds a special meaning for me. I've always loved the earthy aroma coming from the muddy banks of its many creeks and flats.

The Santee and I shared our early years, and I grew up with the lake's popularity and reputation as a sporting paradise. I began fishing it when I was eight years old, and later I hunted ducks with my Uncle Johnnie in the Wateree Swamp just above the great Santee Swamp. I was a freshman in high school when he first took me in his boat and into his world of duck hunting. Fifty years later I love it as I did when I was a boy; and over all those years, I have drunk heavily from the wonders it created. I've seen multitudes of ducks visit the Santee to frolic in its waters and to eat the acorns from the swamp's ridges. I've watched them leave on the moon each March, knowing that they would again come my way. My respect for them as visitors enhanced my understanding of migration, a mystery only they and their kind truly know. They came on tired wings for years, and we would meet in the big swamp.

On my many visits, I've observed the animals that love the swamp and live there in an eclectic community. From the small to the large, all have allowed me a look at their wildness and their natural contentment. I once watched a wild hog teaching her small babies how to root the swamp floor in search of that day's meal. I've seen a racoon, after following his tracks on the creek's edge, opening clams with almost human adeptness. I've seen wild turkeys fly across in front of my boat in search of the acorns the great oaks had offered. I've been led in merry chase by otters in their playful way. I've seen squirrels, whose treetop homes are the very source of their nourishment, gathering the early season acorns. They travel the tops of the great oaks as though every limb leads to a new adventure. I've seen deer drink from the cool swamp creeks and disappear as quickly as they came. And late in the day I've heard the eerie hoots of the great owls, as if telling me, "It's time to go home." They seldom communicate, but their "hoot, hoot, to-hoo" echoes through the tall woods, and from afar another will sometimes answer in agreement. Sharing these secrets with the wild swamp dwellers helped make the Santee that special place for me.

# 2

## LEARNING TO LOVE
## THE OUTDOORS

Being born in Sumter, South Carolina, enhanced my chances of learning to fish and hunt. My father and his father were almost legendary fishermen in Sumter and Lee Counties; and Mother grew up loving the outdoors on the Zeigler farm near Eastover, South Carolina. We were surrounded with numerous ponds, rivers, swamps, and lakes in Sumter and Richland Counties, and lived just two hours from the seashore. All this afforded me the opportunity to learn to love the outdoors. Through a system of damming and flooding the great Santee Cooper lakes were becoming a reality and were finished when I was eight years old. Daddy and Granddaddy Reynolds were enthusiastic fishermen, and I guess it kind of rubbed off, especially when I started fishing with my father as a youngster. Listening to Daddy's tales of his father's redbreast fishing in the Black River was always appealing, and his tale of catching a giant catfish as a young boy really got my heart racing. But it wasn't until I helped him dig earthworms and earned my place on a trip that I really fell in love with fishing.

My mother's younger brother, Uncle Johnnie, would later introduce me to hunting, which ultimately became my favorite sport. I've often been asked which I love more, hunting or fishing. I could only answer that question by saying I could never go fishing and pull myself away from hunting when the ducks were flying! My early hunting experiences consisted of roaming Grandmother's farmland and shooting field sparrows with my BB gun. My Uncle Clyde would let me shoot his little Winchester .22 rifle on occasion at whatever we could find. I never got to know my mother's father, as he died when I was about three years old, but he left to my grandmother and her four children the family farm of about one hundred acres where my love of the outdoors began.

Learning to fish with my daddy was my first outdoor love. We frequently fished what Daddy called "flood-gate holes." They were black water creeks or streams that normally flowed through ponds and were created when the pond's dam and overflow system fed water back into the original creek bed. Many flood-gate holes we fished had gristmills located there. In those days (1935–45), these mills played an important part in grinding corn for human consumption, and when a farm family brought their corn to be ground into cornmeal, the water flowing through the mill and into the creek bed would increase the fishing activity down below. The flow created a lot of white foam on the water, and the fish downstream were attracted by fresh water rich with oxygen. Daddy always began his "lead-lining" near the foam in deep water. My first recollection of this early fishing was in Richland County at the flood-gate hole at Weston's Pond, near Eastover. There was a big pond there that we didn't have permission to fish, but anyone could fish the flood-gate hole below the dam. The gristmill there was operated by an elderly man named Dave. Saturday was our day to go to Weston's and see Dave. Usually we were visiting my grandmother Zeigler at that time. Daddy and I would dig our earthworms behind Grandmother's chicken house. There always seemed to be a great deal there! Digging bait was something I learned to do early on, as Daddy always wanted plenty of worms. He knew exactly how to care for them in our bait bucket, which was usually an old lard can with wire for a handle—not too much water on the black dirt, and, definitely, never leave the bait bucket in the sun!

We caught mostly small fish at Weston's Pond, but they were "game" and I cut my fishin' teeth on small bream, sun perch, and warmouth (Daddy called 'em mollies). We always loved to go mollie fishing. They seemed to be plentiful and easy to catch. As I remember, a mollie is the only fish that would bite twice, most often even after being pulled to the surface and missed. We caught long stringers of good-sized mollies from Weston's.

Let me describe our tackle for flood-gate fishing. Daddy's father was a superb redbreast fisherman, and he used long cane poles (bamboo) and black braided line. Monofilament had not been born yet, and braided line seemed just right. Daddy continued where Granddaddy left off—the cane pole and braided line. We liked a long pole, about ten or eleven feet, and, of course, as light as we could find. We wound the line on the cane about a third of its length and fastened it with a loop knot on the tip. Just in case the tip broke, we could still hold onto the fish. We very seldom used a cork, but rather two split-lead shot about three inches up from the hook and clamped onto the line using a pair of pliers. We fished this tight line with a size six hook. Daddy used only one earthworm for his bait and hooked the worm only once, in the middle of the worm's length. The worm could move freely with this hooking, and the mollies loved a wiggly worm. When the cane poles were scarce at the store, we often cut our own from a cane patch in the country. We would cut off all the limbs, attach a brick to one end, and hang the green cane to dry, usually from a tall tree. Armed with this kind of tackle, I enjoyed fishing with Daddy for many years of my childhood.

Weston's Pond near Eastover, Second Mill in Sumter, and the old Congaree riverbed in Richland County were our steady fishing holes. We never fished in a boat, but always from the bank, and usually in the same spot over and over again. Later on we fished the Santee Cooper lakes from the bank and caught stringers of fish that were unbelievable. We did use a cork there, and it was cut from a bottle stopper. Granddaddy Reynolds, who we called Papa, always happened to have some new ones for us when we visited him in Bishopville, South Carolina. He usually made up our lines using the black line, little corks he had cut, and turkey-feather quills stuck through the cork to hold it in place. Something extra he did that I never saw anyone else do was to rub beeswax on his black braided line. It was a preservative, he said, and seemed to extend the life of the line. He would always have a little ball of beeswax and would rub the full length of the line a couple of times. His prowess as a fisherman was widely known throughout Lee County and the Black River area where redbreast fishing was king. Daddy had learned the "lead line technique" as a youngster while fishing the Black River. "You have to be sharp to catch a redbreast," Papa always said. "The bream and other flat fish are easy."

I will never forget the Saturdays at Weston's Pond and the Old Congaree riverbed. On the way to the Congaree, we often checked the shallow ditches beside the road leaving Eastover. Here we would find small crayfish (crawfish), and with our dip net we took many from the shallow water roadside ditches. They made excellent bait for crappie and bass. Daddy and I often took along my Uncle Ellis, who lived in Columbia. He loved to fish, and, like most of us, was a fisherman of habit. He often fished the same spot trip after trip and usually didn't want anybody dropping a line near his. And, as a young boy, I often got too close for comfort. One Saturday

at the Congaree I happened to get my line in first and very near Uncle
Ellis's favorite spot. Before I knew it, I had two large crappie on the bank.
At the time, I didn't know what I had done that ruined my uncle's day, but
as I remember it now, he didn't catch a fish that day despite all his patience.
Daddy just laughed and said I ought to have more respect for my elders.
But we all caught our share of fish over the years, as there seemed to be
plenty for everyone at the Congaree.

During my boyhood, the great Santee Cooper project got under way
in 1939 and was completed in 1942. Lakes Marion and Moultrie were filling and soon became the talk of the fishing world, at least around South
Carolina. A great many fish were being caught, and as I recall there was
no limit on what you could catch. "Santee," as we called it, was formed
when the Santee River was dammed in Clarendon County.

# 3

## GRANDMOTHER'S FARM

When hunting became my favorite sport and the lure of the woods overcame my early love of fishing, I had only the BB guns, or air rifles, that youngsters began with; and most young boys had one in those days. My father, who had lost his left eye to an air rifle as a child, never embraced hunting like he did fishing. My early interest in hunting came from my mother's side, particularly from her brother, Johnnie Zeigler of Eastover, South Carolina, and my other uncle, Clyde Lowder, who had married my mother's younger sister, Madeline. My grandparents on Mother's side owned a farm just outside of Eastover, and it was there that my early trodding of the fields and woods began. I remember so well those cold Christmastimes when I would chase field sparrows across the frozen and wet plowed-up cotton fields in front of Grandmother Zeigler's big, two-story house that had been my mother's childhood home.

Those sparrows led me a merry chase many times; and, when I stayed in the fields too long, my hands would get so cold I could not even cock the lever on my BB gun. Grandmother would put a pan of water on the old wood stove and heat it just right. She'd put my hands in it for a few seconds at a time until the feeling returned.

During those years, I soon discovered other guns in the house. Grandmother's Colt .32 revolver was kept on the mantle, high out of the reach of her young grandchildren. It had been my grandfather's when he oversaw many laborers on the farm and in his lumber business. I remember Mother mentioning that many of Granddaddy's coat pockets were worn out from carrying that pistol. And Uncle Clyde's single-shot Winchester .22 rifle stayed behind his bedroom door.

Guns appeared to me, at that age, to be something people had for protection. My first shot with the Winchester .22 rifle was during a summer visit to Grandmother's. Uncle Clyde taught me how to load and shoot it *only* up in the trees. Ammunition was very scarce during the forties due to World War II which ended in 1945. Just after the end of the war, Uncle Clyde and Aunt Madeline opened a small country store by remodeling one of the six or seven tenant houses on the farm. Those houses were where the farm hands lived and raised their families. Aunt Maggie, as I called her, sold rifle and shotgun ammunition in her store. A box of .22 caliber shorts was, as I recall, about thirty-five cents for fifty cartridges. Daddy would buy a box or two for me, and sometimes he would join in the shooting of sparrows around the farm.

I worked in the fields with the farm hands picking cotton during my summer visits to the farm. This is my earliest remembrance of making money. Grandmother paid a penny for each pound of cotton picked. She always let me put a brick or two in my burlap bag just before weighing time. Also, Aunt Maggie let me help her in the store. I could drink all the Cokes and RC colas that I wanted and eat all the crackers I could hold. Crackers in those days were bought with pennies. They were packaged in very large pasteboard boxes, and many sold two for a penny. Aunt Maggie knew just how many a few cents would buy. Some of the young field hands would come in with maybe fifteen cents. This would buy two RC colas, the largest bottled drinks at that time, and a small paper bag of crackers. Pennies meant something in those days. All soft drinks were five cents then.

At Christmas when I was a teenager, I would get six or seven boxes of .22 cartridges as gifts. Uncle Clyde would let me shoot those in the Winchester. Christmas at Grandmother's always included large Christmas trees. I'll never forget the huge piles of presents under them, for Christmas was always a gathering of the whole family.

As I grew taller, I eventually was treated to driving Grandmother's old 1934 Chevrolet. I was still not a teenager, but one day she showed me how to start the old car and how to back it out the garage on the side of one of the farm's barns. I was never afraid of her car, even though she cautioned me about its dangers every time I drove it. Eventually, I graduated from riding mules to driving my grandmother around the farm and into Eastover for groceries. She trusted my early driving even though I was years away from the driving age.

My love for the outdoors grew each summer when Mother would take my sister and me to the farm. Mother was born in nearby Ft. Motte, South Carolina, but grew up on the Eastover farm. She was a true country girl who loved the farm life. When she took my sister and me to the farm, usually we would stay a week or two. She took pride in showing us where she had grown up and all about country living. Family was everything to her and even into their senior years she and Daddy visited her sisters and brother frequently. I think Daddy had a tough time convincing Mother to settle in Sumter.

All my uncles and aunts seemed to love the family children, and loving them in return was a highlight of my childhood. I relished being around Grandmother Zeigler's farm and having fun with my family. My cousins, Marie, Jean, and Callie, were always visiting. The farm was where we all gathered on many weekends. Aunt Lucille and Uncle Ellis drove over from Columbia on Sundays to join the family at Grandmother's huge dinner table. There was always plenty of food. Uncle Johnnie and Aunt Lula would drive over from where they lived in the Eastover community, just a few miles from the farm. After dinner Uncle Johnnie always talked about the hunting he was doing in the Wateree Swamp near Eastover. As I grew and learned to handle the family rifles, he recognized the the love to hunt was also running through my blood. In the years that followed, he shared his knowledge of the woods with me.

I loved and treasured Grandmother Zeigler because she was so much like my mother, and she was always eager to help me learn about the outdoor farm life.

The grandchildren often made a game of exploring around the big two-story Zeigler home. Several buildings were behind the house, including the stable, which we called "the lot," where the mules stayed when not being worked in the fields. A large tool shed offered protection from the elements for shovels and hoes, rakes, plows, and other implements I could not recognize as a youngster. Of course, the smokehouse was used for curing meat, and in the chicken house Grandmother's reliable hens kept her fully supplied with fresh eggs. And as was usual in those days, a well-worn path lead to a small house that was off by itself. Many times I walked the path to Grandmother's little "outhouse." It was a popular spot!

Grandmother's farm had the largest well pump I ever saw. The family's water supply came from a deep well by pumping the long handle repeatedly while filling numerous buckets each day. For convenience a hanger for holding the buckets as they filled was made into the spout. A five-gallon bucket of water is heavy! I remember helping Charlie, Grandmother's dedicated farm hand, carry those buckets into the kitchen and place them on a table. A dipper was kept handy for filling our glasses with the cool, refreshing drink.

The kitchen was a center of activity each day as Grandmother's wood stove cooked the delectable dishes she prepared. She was a cook who had no equal in those days, and the only help she accepted was that a constant supply of wood for the stove be kept nearby. I have never understood how she withstood all that extra heat during the summer months, except that she did keep a large block of ice in the old-timey, wooden icebox. We grand-children enjoyed standing close whenver one of the adults chipped off a bowl of ice because small chips would fly out from the chipping-block and they felt wonderful on our warm skin!

Grandmother's cooking would be the envy of today's chefs. Two spe-cialties that she made for me were liver pudding and cucumber pickles. Both were heavily seasoned with red peppers from her garden. Sometimes, when she sent me to gather tomatoes and cucumbers from the garden, I would take along a salt shaker and an old, dull knife and just help myself! They were oh-so-good! Often when Grandmother was planning to serve chicken for a family gathering on a Sunday, she would go outside, scatter shelled corn around her feet, and select one or two. After catching her "picks," she would feel the plumpness of the breasts. I was just amazed at how she did things, particularly when seeing her prepare these chickens for cooking. My mother always said no one could cook like her mother, and she was right most of the time.

Aunt Madeline, my mother's younger sister, was a unique person in many ways. She treated me like I was her own son, and I thought she was really special. It was always evident that she loved her family and each member was important to her, and she was beloved in turn by her family. Even the animals on the farm seemed to sense that they need have no fear of her, for they would follow her around the yard the minute she came out of the house. All of the smaller animals were her "pets," and they were numerous! During my childhood, she had peacocks, guinea fowl, bantam chickens and other chickens, turkeys, and a few cats. Uncle Clyde's bird dogs were always kept in their kennels due to many autos passing the farm, and he attended to their needs. Usually Aunt Madeline's pets crowded around her so many at a time that she had to choose her steps carefully. Later on, a family of goats was added, whose home was across the farm-to-market paved road, down by the creek that ran through the woods. At one time they also had a beautiful horse named Lady, which I was never permitted to ride, as they felt she was too spirited. I've always felt that my sister, Betty, took her love of animals from Aunt Madeline. They were very close.

Aunt Madeline and Uncle Clyde were well known in the Eastover area: she for her enormous collection of pitchers from all over the world, her talents for using materials and objects around the home and farm to make unusual decorative arrangements, as well as for her love of nature; he for his well-trained bird dogs that afforded him endless invitations to quail hunts in the area, and for the enjoyable dove shoots which he hosted on the big farm. Aunt Madeline very fittingly named the farm Happy Acres.

Located on the crest of a hill and surrounded by many acres of open farmland, Grandmother's home was somewhat of a landmark in the East-over community, and in the 1980s was included among South Carolina's historic homes.

Aunt Madeline and Uncle Clyde were the last family members to occupy the old homeplace—they were living there in 1989 when Hurricane Hugo's fierce winds roared up the South Carolina coastline and through the midlands. Hugo's hundred-mile-per-hour winds raced over the large field in front of the house and ripped away the entire roof. The storm came at night as my aunt and uncle lay in bed, enduring the rains that poured in on them. They knew from the frightful sounds they were hearing that this was a most severe storm, and believed they would not survive until daylight. Their lives were spared, and the next morning they became aware of the extensive damage the hurricane had wrought. Though most walls remained, a chimney had fallen into the dining room, windows across the front of the house had been blown out, everything inside the home was rain soaked, and several of the huge old oak trees had been felled all about the yard.

The home was repaired, but Aunt Madeline and Uncle Clyde never lived in it again, instead choosing to live across the road in the small clubhouse that they had used for entertaining, not very far from Aunt Madeline's beloved goats. The little goat family and the clubhouse had been protected by the woods from Hugo's wrath.

Uncle Clyde continues to live in his clubhouse even though Aunt Madeline passed away years ago. I'm sure that his fond memories of the old homeplace live with him to this day.

The Reynolds side of our family were city dwellers in Bishopville, South Carolina. They were fishermen for sure, as my Grandfather Reynolds led his sons in the sport. When I was old enough to hold a fishing pole of some description, Daddy would take me with him. I don't recall ever fishing with Daddy's brother, Uncle Sheldon, or his sons, Toby and Anthony. But I do remember an unusual time when we used some fatback tied on a string and pole to catch big crayfish from a ditch that ran behind their home in Bishopville. We certainly had fun together when I visited them during my adolescent years.

# 4

# THE SANTEE COOPER CREATED

Little did I realize in my young years that the project known as Santee Cooper would create a sportsman's paradise. Of course, this was a by-product of the creation of a hydroelectric project that had been a dream as early as 1920, many years before I was born. In 1934, the South Carolina Public Service Authority was created by Governor Ibra C. Blackwood. The purpose of the project was to provide electricity to the many rural areas of South Carolina still dark. At that time, private utilities did not provide electricity to such sparsely populated areas. These were the days of the Great Depression, and the project would provide inexpensive electricity to light the darkened homes located throughout thirty-five of the state's counties.

Lakes Marion and Moultrie were to be created by the flow of water from an enormous watershed above. Rivers whose waters flowed southward were the Broad, Catawba, Wateree, and Congaree. These brought the necessary water to the lake areas. Actually, the confluence of the Wateree and Congaree Rivers creates the Santee River, which begins what became the upper part of the Santee Cooper project; it includes about twelve thousand acres which ultimately became my favorite hunting area.

The project was massive, to say the least. At the peak of construction, more than twelve thousand people were employed in the clearing of more than 225 square miles of swamplands located in five counties. More than forty million cubic yards of earth were removed to create the lakes. Construction included forty-two miles of dams and dikes, a seven-mile diversion canal, a powerhouse, and a seventy-five-foot lock on Lake Moultrie.

Information in this section is taken from "Fifty Years: Improving the Quality of Life in South Carolina," Santee Cooper 1984 Annual Report (Moncks Corner, S.C.: Santee Cooper, 1984).

When construction began, workers from every county in the state were taken off relief payrolls and put to work. The entire project was done by men, mules, and muscle. Many separate tracts of land were purchased by the Public Service Authority; over nine hundred families were resettled; more than forty-nine million board feet of timber were cut and removed from the Santee Swamp alone. Lake Moultrie was completely clear-cut, but Lake Marion was not, due to the demand for the completion of the project. Hydroelectric power was needed because of the threat of World War II. President Franklin D. Roosevelt declared Santee Cooper a national defense project in 1941, and the Lake Marion clearing was stopped. Thousands of acres of timber were left standing and even today some of those flooded trees remain. On May 15, 1941, the mighty Santee River was stopped on its surge to the sea, and each day an average of twelve billion gallons of water began to fill what is now the two lakes. By February of 1942, 160,000 acres were flooded. Less than three years after the clearing had begun, hydroelectric power was delivered to the first Santee Cooper customer. I was eight years old at that time. So I guess that makes me a little older than the Santee. But really we were born about the same time—and we became buddies for life!

Many plantation owners in Georgetown and Charleston Counties, down below the huge Santee Cooper project, were not pleased when the fresh water that previously flowed freely down the Santee and Cooper Rivers was stopped. The fresh water had kept much of the coastal saltwater from intruding further inland and into their property.

One of the most notable plantation owners was Archibald Rutledge, who loved his Hampton Plantation on the great Santee, and strongly objected to the creation of the Santee Cooper project. It forever changed the freshwater environment of his beloved homeland. Reading Mr. Rutledge's writings and descriptions of his life-long adventures on the game-abundant river kindled my desire to write about my era many years after his death. Mr. Rutledge, who was named poet laureate of South Carolina by legislative action in 1934, had an innate ability to write eloquently about the wildlife that had shared his many years of roaming the vast wetlands and swamps.

Most of my wife's relatives were born in Clarendon County, which bordered the coming Lake Marion, and lived there prior to the project itself. They were mostly farmers, making a modest living in that area. My wife's uncle, A. D. Hemingway, lived in nearby Davis Station and hunted and fished in the Santee Swamp. His favorite sport was coon hunting, and he made good money selling coon hides from the big swamp. I have many times talked with A. D. about what the swamp was like before it became a lake. His adventures and trips into the swamp were many. It took so long to get into his favorite areas, he would just stay several days. There were numerous huge trees with hollows in them that he used for shelter when it rained. He hunted areas known as Cut-0 Lake and Gator Hole. One tale he told frequently was about the black bears that appeared in the Davis Station area shortly after the water rose in 1941. Like most folks in Clarendon County, A. D. was saddened by the cutting of the timber that was home to all the animals of the Santee Swamp. And likewise, the Santee project changed the lives of many folks who lived there.

I never hunted with A. D., who also loved to hunt deer, but his brother, Clair Hemingway, took me quail hunting several times around 1958 and 1959. We hunted the shoreline areas now known as Goat Island and Taw Caw Creek. There were no houses around the water's edge, and we roamed anywhere we wanted. Clair had a stripped-down DeSoto with a dog box on the back. In fact, the vehicle had no body—just seats somehow mounted on the frame. Clair had put wide tires on it, and we never feared getting stuck. The quail were plentiful, and sometimes after our hunt, Clair would take me to an area near Taw Caw Creek to shoot the late-in-the-day doves on their way from watering to roosting. The shoreline we hunted back then is now a highly developed area with many houses, a large marina, and a golf course.

# 5

# EARLY DUCK HUNTING

My memory of exactly when I began shooting a shotgun is kind of vague, but I do know it was over fifty years ago. Daddy took me down to Burns Hardware in Sumter during my early high school years and bought a Mossberg .410-gauge shotgun for me. It was the smallest shotgun made and its recoil was light, but it held three shells and had detachable screw-on chokes. I remember showing it to my Aunt Madeline, and she bought one just like it.

Learning to handle the little gun was done mostly in Sumter, at a nearby dry savannah on the Pinewood Road. This wetland was close to town, and it frequently filled with rainwater. But it was during the dry spells that I learned to shoot meadow larks as they flushed in front of me. The larks gave me the opportunity for shots going in all directions, and soon I was ready to try my newfound talent on the local bobwhite quail. However, my first game birds to fall to the .410 were doves that sat on the power line that ran across the savannah. A ditch was close by, and I took advantage of it by crawling along and up to the doves. I wasn't a good enough shot to bag one on the wing.

My grandmother Reynolds knew a family who owned a sizeable piece of property on the Pinewood Road about six or seven miles from Sumter. It was there that I killed my first quail "on the rise." Daddy would give me a dollar to buy a pocketful of shells, and I was ready to go hunting. After school there was plenty of time to walk up a covey or two, and several of my school buddies went along. We never did take many quail from one covey, mainly because they were too fast and too smart for us.

Daddy knew a dog trainer in Sumter, and through him I was given an old and stubborn pointer. He was already named Rex and had seen his best hunting days, but he still loved to roam the woods and fields with me and we became a good team. He would sometimes break his point before I could get to him, but I was proud to have him. After Rex, I had two setters. My Uncle Clyde always had bird-dog puppies. His favorite sport was quail hunting, and his kennels always held several trained pointers and setters. It was from him that puppies came my way. There was Rebel, a white setter, and Trumpet, a black and white setter. They were fine hunters that I enjoyed throughout high school and college. Daddy named the black and white setter because as I was learning to play the trumpet in the high school band, he would howl along. I always wondered whether the neighbors thought Trumpet sounded better than I did!

----

The Santee lakes are located about thirty miles south of Sumter and below Manning, South Carolina. Between the two cities and connecting them is a swamp most locals called Pocalla Swamp, though the actual name is Poco-taligo Swamp. It had been logged-out probably in the forties, which opened it up considerably but clogged up its creeks, slowing the water flow. A lot of grassy areas took over, and many ducks would fly up from the Santee area. Most of them came from the Santee National Refuge near Summerton, South Carolina. Pocalla Swamp was very difficult to get into and hunt because the adjacent landowners had their roads chained off and their land posted against trespassing. One of my high school friends, Tommy Brown, lived near the Dingle's Mill area just outside Sumter, and his parents' land adjoined the swamp. It was here I learned that many ducks frequented Pocalla around Christmastime and New Year's. Tommy and I, along with another adventurous friend, Ernest Schwach, hunted the edge of the swamp. We would even camp out on weekends. We had no hip boots or waders, so we got wet many times venturing far enough out to get a shot or two. It's a wonder we didn't stay sick all winter!

After high school and during my four years at Clemson, I gained access to the swamp in several places. A friend, Fletcher Williams, and I hunted farther from Sumter and very near the Clarendon County line. It was here that I really learned just how much the ducks loved Pocalla. The swamp seemed alive with mallards, teal, and wood ducks. All the duck hunters around knew this area was tops, but it was so difficult to wade out far enough, that only we youngsters tried. The swamp was a mud hole, and many logs and limbs had been left from the long-ago logging activities. Another problem with Pocalla was that it held the largest concentration of snakes I'd ever seen. In early winter they were still active and everywhere. The old remaining logging tramroads were the only dry land areas in the swamp and harbored cottonmouth moccasins galore! Several years later, I talked to some of the old loggers who had helped in the cutting. They confirmed that they had "never seen anything like the snakes in that swamp." Labor was difficult to hire during that time, as nobody wanted to tackle the cottonmouths. In years to come, some of my most memorable hunts occurred in Pocalla Swamp. Nothing ever equaled the last week of the 1966 season. But that's another tale I'll write about later.

While attending Clemson, I was able to keep my shotgun at the quartermaster's unit, and it was easy to get to when I stayed up there on weekends. I had now graduated to a 16-gauge Ithaca pump Daddy bought from the Western Auto in Sumter. It was quite an improvement over the .410-gauge I began with. Clemson had much land bordering the campus that also bordered the Seneca River, which flowed less than a half-mile from my barracks (at that time Clemson was a military college). I enjoyed roaming the territory near the river and passing away the weekend there when I couldn't get home.

My music activities sometimes kept me away from my hometown. I played trumpet not only in Clemson's Tiger Band but also in two different dance bands, and managed to make a few dollars along the way. The big band scene was the music of the day, and our groups played engagements all over the Carolinas and Georgia. Finally, I got together enough money to put a down payment on an engagement ring for my future wife, Carolyn, my high school sweetheart whom I began dating again while at Clemson. We were in the same class at Edmunds High School in Sumter, and after graduation, Carolyn got a secretarial job at Shaw Air Force Base near Sumter. I went on to Clemson and spent the four longest years of my life there!

When I bought that pretty little diamond from Clemson Jewelers, I had no idea how I was going to keep it safe. But somehow I managed to hold onto it. It became my constant companion, even when I walked the river bottoms or the banks of the Seneca River. I remember taking it out of my pocket many times and daydreaming about how and when I was going to give it to Carolyn. It finally happened at Christmastime in 1955, and we were married June 15, 1956, just twelve days after my graduation from Clemson.

The Seneca River held a few surprises for me that I picked up while hunting the bottoms. Quite often I would flush small groups of mallard ducks from the river's eddy pockets. I never could get a shot at any, and anyway, if I had knocked one down, it probably would have fallen in the river and been carried downstream. I was telling Ned Huggins from Johnsonville, South Carolina, about the ducks on the river, and he said, to my surprise, that he had a small wooden riverboat he kept up at school. Ned was a hunter, but didn't have his shotgun at Clemson. But that didn't matter as long as he had that boat. We made plans to float the river one afternoon just to see what success we could have. We would put the boat in right behind the Clemson campus and float down to what was called the "cherry crossing," a spot where a bridge spanned the river. The float would take about three hours, and a friend of Ned's would pick us up with Ned's car and the boat trailer.

Ned's riverboat was easy to paddle and steer in the river's current using one paddle. He was a talented paddler, which tickled me 'cause I got to do most of the shootin'! We would pack mud from the riverbank in the V-bow of the boat and stick brushy limbs in the mud. The small boat looked like a log with limbs to the mallards. A mallard is usually a cautious bird, but they didn't spook and jump from the eddy pockets until we were close enough for a shot. We would try to stay near the inside river bends, for here the water flowed more slowly and created a sort of resting and feeding place for the ducks. We routinely spotted the unaware mallards a long way off before putting the 16-gauge to work. Ned's paddle never touched the side of the boat or made any undue or audible ripples in the water. We spoke very quietly or said nothing at all during the drift. If the ducks got up in an unexpected direction, Ned had a knack for turning the boat just right and just in time for me to have a fair chance.

The riverbank and bottoms held many oak trees, and the shallow river allowed the ducks to feed on the oaks' acorns. Ned and I took many mallards from the river, and occasionally we even cut classes when we felt the urge to shoot a few. Between the river hunts at Clemson and the Pocalla Swamp hunts back in Sumter, I managed to keep up my love for duck hunting all through my college years.

The fall of 1954, I was about halfway through my schooling at Clemson, and most weekends I tried to catch a ride home with students who had their own cars. As a freshman, I didn't have the privilege of going home whenever I wanted to. But, as I remember, it was while I was at home during the Christmas holidays that I visited my uncle and aunt in

Eastover. Uncle Clyde and I loved to talk hunting, and would confer about his pointers and setters. Quail hunting was his favorite, and occasionally he would ask me to come over from Sumter and join him on a hunt. He had an army-surplus Jeep that he had converted into a little hunting buggy so he could follow the dogs across the fields and around the bottoms. I enjoyed the quail hunting with him, as he was really set up with the Jeep and plenty of land to hunt.

But on one particular visit he said, "Well, I recently got a taste of your favorite sport—duck hunting." He and one of his quail-hunting buddies had gotten wind of a bunch of ducks being on the Santee and had hunted a couple of days at Santee State Park, near Elloree, South Carolina. He described the area where they'd hunted, which was across from the park and on the other side of the Santee River channel that makes its way through the upper lake, Lake Marion. He said the water was very low, and that they had just walked out to the mud flats and stood around the dead trees and stumps. He said, though, that he didn't really like duck hunting, as he had to constantly be "looking up," and he didn't have to do that with quail. Uncle Clyde didn't have to tell me much more to excite my interest, only that they had seen a lot of ducks, and he thought all of 'em were mallards.

Following the visit with Uncle Clyde, I called my friend, Dumont Bordeaux, who was also home from Clemson. Dumont's family had a boat and motor that were seldom used. Their green and white colors weren't the best for hunting, but we were happy to be able to use the rig and made preparations to check out the state park the next day. The Bordeaux family boat sat on an old trailer whose hitch was different from anything I'd seen. The connection to the towing vehicle was by a bolt instead of a coupler-type hitch. Our trip from Sumter to the park carried us over some bumpy roads, particularly over the rough dirt road to the park's boat landing. About a quarter of a mile from our destination, we realized the boat was no longer following us down the dirt road! We had no idea how far back it had come loose, but remembering when the paved road ended, we figured that's where it might be.

Upon arriving at that point, we couldn't see the rig anywhere, so we kept going back along the wooded paved road leading into the park, and, finally, there it was. It had left the road and proceeded out into the woods. We could not, to save us, figure why we had not heard it hit the pavement. A tree had stopped everything, and the boat was way forward on the little trailer. We checked for damage and noticed that underneath the bow had been ground down quite a bit. The paved road saw to that. We managed to hook up again and went on to the lake. Fortunately, the boat did not leak when we launched it!

I could not believe that Santee was so low in water. It was almost dry from the Santee State Park landing all the way to the Santee River channel. We managed to launch the boat in a small but deep body of water known as Boat Lake, which connected to a creek that wound its way out to the river. This was the first time either of us had launched a boat on the Elloree side of the Santee. Now, forty-five years later, I relate the former low-water conditions to younger residents. Of course, it's hard for them to believe that the lake level got so low in 1954. Low lake levels reveal many unknown features of the bottom, and in later years I used those to good advantage when fishing that same area.

We managed to work our way out of Boat Lake, and after going through a couple of what looked like very old bridge pilings in the creek, we entered the main riverbed.

Not having hunted or fished on the state park side of the lake, we had no idea which way to go, and paused where the creek ended at the river. I did know which way Persanti Island was, and could see across the river toward it. So we decided to idle down toward that way for a mile or so. Arriving near a creek mouth on the left and near what is now known as Stave Island, we turned in to a rather sizeable creek with exposed banks on both sides. I learned later it was the entrance to Durgan's Creek, which flowed into the Santee at Stave Island, land that normally was under water. Durgan's proved to be a main creek channel that paralleled the Clarendon County side of the lake. The area on this rare low-water level had left scattered small pools of water on both sides of the creek. As we motored on up the creek, ducks began flying up from the small, secluded pools. The ducks, disturbed by our distant motor noise, took leave only to settle back down in other waters and on up the creek. It looked like we had really found a spot that the mallards liked.

Leaving the green and white boat near some logs that helped to hide it, we walked along the muddy but solid exposed lake bottom away from Dumont's boat. It was midmorning, and by normal hunting standards the duck flight would be over. But we soon saw small flocks of ducks coming up the lake from the refuge area several miles below us. We split up about fifty yards apart and hid behind some convenient stumps between several small shallow pools. The pools seemed to be a rest area for the ducks, as I could not identify any food source there. As long as we remained motionless against the old stumps and roots, the ducks would get lower and lower as they gathered overhead. In those days I was a very poor duck caller; so the only call I used was a simple lonesome hen quack, and very few at that. Since we had no decoys with us that day, we soon realized that we would have to take whatever shots we could at passing ducks. Dumont was the first to get a decent chance at a mallard, and he made a great shot. The flock flared my way, and I managed to cripple a hen mallard that splashed down just a few yards away. I chased the duck immediately and made the killing shot on the water. Dumont had waded out and picked up another mallard hen. It was a good start; however, the shots had alarmed the ducks in the surrounding ponds, and everywhere we looked ducks were leaving. From the number of ducks using the flats around us, we figured we had located our hunting spot for the remainder of our holidays at home.

During the latter part of the 1954 duck season, I spent all my available holidays and weekends hunting the same Durgan's Creek section of Lake Marion, and the water level remained very low. However, I entered the lake from the Clarendon County side using an old landing called Hickory Top. It was off the beaten path and not too far from the little farm community of Rimini. The landing was located just off Durgan's Creek, and small wooden swamp boats could be rented for one dollar per day. As I remember, the owner's name was Grayson, and we became acquaintances during that season.

We continued to use Dumont's boat, and on many trips we would put in at Hickory Top, work our way down Durgan's, and end up in a huge lake. We later found out it was Brown's Lake, and it appeared to be very deep and was the largest body of open water we could find at that time. After visiting this spot several times, we learned it was a very large duck roost. Nearly every time we were there, ducks of all kinds would come in to spend the night. The lake bank had been dry for quite a spell, and we could walk it for long stretches. There was much cover along the bank, and we made good use of it as blinds. At Brown's Lake the mallards always came in high, but many other ducks such as teal, wood ducks, and mergansers flew low and were our better targets. We never stayed too late here, as we traveled only by small flashlights on the way out. High intensity spotlights known as Q-beams had not yet been invented.

One particular early morning trip to Brown's Lake, I decided to explore the dry area beyond it. Dumont had staked out a favorite spot, a little pool of water where we had flushed fifty or so ducks the day before. We had put a few decoys out, and he was prepared to sit on those until I got back. Leaving the lake and making my way toward the Santee State Park side of Lake Marion, I picked my way through the sucking mud, high and dry ridges, and through many dead trees. The area was indeed a dead forest, made by flooding when the Santee lakes were formed. The gnarled tops of the once giant cypress trees became markers that I could identify on my walk back to Brown's Lake. Many ducks were using the seclusion of the dead-timbered area. I was hoping that I would get a shot at a rising mallard, or that one would swim close enough for a water shot. Surprisingly, I had the place to myself. I saw no footprints that weren't mine. The ducks had not been spooked previously, and they seemed to sense that the mud flats and tall dead timber held safety for them.

I hadn't taken a bird on my venture yet, and it wasn't until I retraced my steps that, luckily, I got the chance I was hoping for. But before heading back toward Brown's Lake, I realized that I had made my way all the way to the Santee River channel in front of Santee State Park! Nobody would believe today that a person could walk all the way from Brown's Lake to the river channel with just a pair of hip boots on. Such exceptionally low water levels as occurred in 1954 have not happened again in my nearly fifty years of duck hunting the Santee. Even so, I must have endured more than a mile of mud to get to the river, and that far back.

The trek back across the shallow water flats and through the tall but dead cypress trees was tiring, as I had not stopped to rest. Fatigue, even for a twenty-one-year-old, prompted me to rest a bit near a rather dense stand of cypress. The shallow water that I crossed fed what looked to be a small lake. It was here, as I rested, that several small groups of teal buzzed the area and over the log where I was sitting half-hidden. They seemed interested in taking refuge in the trees nearby, and did. No sooner than a few minutes after they settled in, I noticed bigger ducks swimming out to meet them. Why I hadn't spooked them as I crossed the shallow end of their pond, I'll never know, but they seemed oblivious to my being there. They took a turn toward the shallow water and me, and came, follow-the-leader style, so that the right shot on the water would bag several at one time. I was able to turn behind my cover in order to make the shot and not be noticed. My 16-gauge with number six shot fired only once, but there were three ducks that didn't take off afterward. I had bagged two very large black ducks and one of the little green-winged teal. Uncle Johnnie had taught me, years before, how to make a shot like that. "You must aim below the ducks so the shot will rake the water," he always said. And through the years of hunting on foot in other Santee Swamp flats, I used this method of on-the-water shooting over and over.

I had not heard any shooting from the Brown's Lake area where I had left Dumont and didn't think he'd had much luck. I had left him several hours earlier with the decoys, and when I returned to where he was sup-posed to be, he was nowhere to be seen. But I was happy to see the boat still tied to our usual tree. As I approached the waiting boat, there was Dumont, asleep in the bottom of the boat with his head resting on the float cushion and his feet propped on the front seat. He said his day had been slow but restful. The ducks had not returned to the spot and the decoys. He always teased me about my success and luck that day, and I always told him that luck is where opportunity and preparation cross. He would just laugh!

One of our weekend hunts found several of us camped out on the San-tee riverbank across from the state park. A couple of friends from Clemson had joined us. They were upstate duck hunters, and having heard Dumont and me brag about the great Santee, accepted our invitation to hunt with us. Hunting the Santee would be quite different from the small beaver-pond hunts they were used to.

The lake was still very low, which allowed us to pitch small tents on the bank of the river. The sunrise the first morning brought nothing but clouds, and later on a steady drizzle. We were all disappointed with the rainy, cold morning, but we decided to hunt the Durgan's Creek area where it joined the river channel. All of us were Clemson cadets, and several of us had brought along our supposedly trusty rain coats that we used in inclement weather at school.

It was on this trip that I bagged my first canvasback duck and, due to my so-called raincoat, lost my resistance to catching a cold. Later, we called 1954 the year of the leaky raincoat, and decided that duck hunting wasn't much good in rainy weather! Nevertheless, we hunted in wet weather for two days, and it seemed I could never get warm, even at night. Inside the tents became a soggy mess. Outside conditions were terrible, and the ducks weren't cooperating either. I became ill from that cold and wet exposure, and for years to come I always got sick from hunting in similar conditions. Only in the last few years have I been able to handle a drizzle and cold weather, but today's waterproof, warm garments are much improved. My son, Jay, would later say when viewing a rainy weather forecast, "Looks like a Gore-Tex day."

June of 1956 was very special. I was awarded my degree in Animal Husbandry from Clemson, and June 15 was Carolyn's and my wedding day. During my last two years at Clemson, I could hardly bear to be away from her. We just seemed to be right for each other, and at last our separation was over. The Gardners, Carolyn's family, and the Reynolds family had been acquaintances for many years. And now we were kin. The two families sent us off on our honeymoon trip. We said we would be gone until the money ran out, and after going down one side of Florida's coastline and back up the other, our pocketbooks were about empty! We were gone eight days and had seen some of Florida's most beautiful scenery. We took movies of the spots we visited, and, of course, anywhere there was sand and sea the movie camera was pointed out the window of Carolyn's little '49 Plymouth. Those movies are treasures today, and we dust them off frequently and laugh at how young we were then. The movies became a habit, and as our family grew, and at special family gatherings, we frequently brought out the camera.

Shortly after Carolyn and I were married, in fact the very next month, I was inducted into the United States Air Force. It was off to Lackland Air Force Base in Texas for four weeks of basic training, four weeks I would just as soon forget, as they began in July and ended in August, 1956. The Texas summer is a scorcher, and with little shade in the San Antonio area, I felt that I was fortunate to endure the weeks there. The only good thing I remember about Lackland was leaving.

I had been assigned to the band at Lackland and did play a little with the Lackland Air Force Base Band. My music background at Clemson with the trumpet and another audition landed me a place in the Eighth Air Force Band at Schilling Air Force Base in Salina, Kansas. So, after I returned to Sumter, Carolyn and I loaded her Plymouth with our very few possessions, and fifteen hundred miles later arrived in Salina. We were fortunate to find a small upstairs apartment in the city about five miles from the base. The apartment was just what we needed, as it was furnished and the rent was reasonable.

The summers there were very hot, but we spent a good many weekends fishing and picnicking at Lake Kanapolis. I got along just fine as a trumpeter in the band, except when we were called on to fly around the Midwest playing special performances. I made ten flights with the band, and at least half of them were scary, to say the least. Two of these resulted in our donning parachutes in preparation for possibly abandoning the aircraft.

Our apartment was located about two blocks from Salina's main business district and very near the Plains Hotel. The Plains was owned and managed by a seasoned duck hunter who had long since stored his decoys. Al Norton became a real friend and hunting companion during my eighteen months in the air force. Al's love for duck hunting hadn't equaled mine for several years, but he showed a renewed desire to tell me about the productive hunts at a place he called "the bottoms." I learned that he was referring to Cheyenne Bottoms near Great Bend, Kansas. Many times he would brag about how the ducks loved the area and about the great hunts he had there. Also, there was a private club he hunted occasionally, located next to Cheyenne Bottoms. It was known as the Mallard Club. That area was closed to public hunting. With Al's influence, I decided to check out the bottoms for myself. So, one Saturday I made the eighty-mile trip and much to my delight found a hunting opportunity the likes of which I had never seen. Here was public duck hunting for one dollar per day. Cheyenne Bottoms, as I remember, had five different pools, four of which were open to hunting. The fifth and middle pool was a sanctuary. The area was probably named for the Indians who lived there years before, and was a huge wetland that held water during wet times. But in low rainfall periods it didn't serve the needs of the great flocks of ducks traveling the Central Flyway. I was never sure just which agency was given credit for improving this bottomland and was responsible for what I was seeing. I was told water was diverted from the Arkansas River through a canal and into Cheyenne Bottoms. This solved the need for consistent water levels and aquatic vegetation to attract and hold thousands of ducks and other water birds that loved shallow water. Before the area was flooded, dikes were made that divided the pools and could be driven on. A couple of hundred concrete sunken blinds were put in the huntable pools. I don't remember just when the project was completed, but it was years before my arrival.

In order to hunt the bottoms, duck hunters were required to stop at the administration building, pay a dollar, and pick up a key to the sunken blind of their choice. On the wall there was a large map of the five pools from which you selected your blind. From the roads on top of the dikes, all the sunken blinds looked like small islands about twenty feet in diameter. Dirt from the pool clearing was used to create each of the little islands. Foliage had been planted on each island around the top of the sunken blind so as to disguise everything. Each pit had a metal top which kept much of the rainwater out and was locked. The hunter would unlock the top and hide it in the foliage. Some real thought and planning made Cheyenne Bottoms a pleasure to hunt. The blinds were all placed in a row. From the dike, the first row was a three-hundred-yard wade. The second row was six hundred yards away, and the third row, which I never hunted, was nine hundred yards from the dikes. Small signs even marked where you could walk off the dike into no more than two and a half to three feet of water. And the water depth was the same all the way to your chosen blind. I never owned waders in those early years, as hip boots were adequate and were my favorite anyway.

During my military stay in Salina, I took advantage of the bottoms as much as I could. The duck seasons have always been so short, and having to learn where to go in strange places made the season that much shorter. But going to this new place just seemed right. There always seemed to be birds present and eager to come to my call and my decoys. I eventually took several Kansas friends on hunts there. We were always successful, and the trip from Salina was made shorter when expectations were high.

I soon had the new-gun fever, as my high school Ithaca pump had an improved cylinder barrel which was right only for close range shooting; but Cheyenne Bottoms was different than previous hunting grounds, and I figured I'd do better with a semiautomatic and a modified choke. My Ithaca was a 16-gauge and, as I remember, I always preferred the 16- over the 12-gauge guns, mainly because they had less recoil and were lighter. I was a slender fellow most of my life, and I felt that the 12-gauge was too much gun.

There was a very nice sporting goods store on the main street in Salina. It's where I had acquired my dozen rubber decoys. The brand was Deeks, and I enjoyed using them in various settings. They would inflate by holding them by their heads and simply dropping them into the water. I had looked at their shotguns before and always thought it would be nice to own what Browning Arms Co. called a Sweet 16. Carolyn had, in anticipation of receiving some civil service retirement money, said she would buy me a new gun with some of what she received, and would buy for herself a new Singer sewing machine. To this very day we still have both, and they have given us good service over all these years.

I compared the Sweet 16 to the 12-gauge again, but as usual stayed with the smaller gun. It just seemed to handle better, and the 16-gauge receiver had a smaller hump than the twelve. None of the Sweet 16 models in stock had a ventilated rib, but the gun could be sent to Simmons Gun Specialties in Kansas City, Missouri, for a lightweight rib to be added to the 28-inch modified barrel. I agreed to do that, and expected the delivery in about two weeks. Browning guns, at that time, were not discounted in price. They were considered fair-trade items. The list price on the Sweet 16 or the Light 12 was $137.75, including vent-ribbed barrel. Money was very scarce in those days, and the gun was certainly a special purchase. Carolyn was pleased that she could buy another high-priced toy for her hunting husband, despite the fact our son was to be born soon. I eventually had my initials engraved on the receiver. And even today, the Sweet 16 occupies the first slot in my gun cabinet, forty-two years later!

Al Norton was always eager to see our harvest, and he would come over my way to see the evidence of my tall tales. After several of my trips to his old hunting grounds, and seeing the big greenheaded mallards we bagged, he knocked on my door late one afternoon, and, much to my surprise, he was carrying a new 12-gauge Browning semiautomatic. Al was in his sixties, but was young at heart. He said, "Let's break this new gun in next Saturday." It pleased me to know I was going to help him do something he really loved to do, so we made plans. Al's old decoys, long since packed away, were still in great shape. He was pleased when we unpacked them, as they hadn't seen water in years. Al said we would leave early just to insure getting the blind I had found productive. In his garage was his new Hudson, all shiny black. The Hudson auto was very popular in the fifties. "We'll drive my car," he said, "as it's got a bigger trunk."

Come Saturday, we struck out for Cheyenne Bottoms for our hunt. The weather forecast sounded like a duck day was in the making as the prediction was for cold with wind. Kansas can be very cold in winter, and we both wondered if we had the clothes to handle that day—face masks, Gore-Tex waterproof garments, and insulated clothing were not available yet.

Arriving at the entrance in plenty of time, and surprised at the few cars already there, we hurried inside to reserve the blind of our choice. My lucky spot was still open, and we paid our dollar for the day's hunt. We noticed that the wind was blowing from the northwest and the temperature seemed to have dropped since we left home two hours earlier. The Hudson took us out to the crossing off the dike. Since we were early, we enjoyed the car's heater and wished we could take it inside the blind with us. We could see the headlights of other vehicles making their way slowly atop the dikes. Saturday normally drew a good bunch to the bottoms. I think most knew the weather this day was just right to make the ducks move.

Giving ourselves enough time, we unloaded Al's old decoys, which filled two sacks, and, along with our shotguns, began our wade out to the blinds on the second row. We took it slow, as I didn't know what kind of shape Al's legs were in, but he kept up. We found the A-blind three hundred yards out, and took aim on the six-hundred-yard B-blind. The sun was just breaking, and the coming light helped us locate our target.

The little ducks that fly close to the water had just begun to move as we reached our island. I unlocked the concrete blind and hid the top, as usual, in what cover remained around the rim of the blind. Al took the guns and got down out of the wind. I proceeded to wade out and place the decoys upwind from the blind, putting them about twenty yards away. I left an opening among the decoys, hoping this would lead the birds to within our gun range.

Finishing that task and getting back to Al, who had been watching the weather as much as the working ducks, I climbed down beside him. Al had already loaded the 12-gauge and was ready as two teal ducks lit in the decoys. It was time to shoot, but we had hoped for mallards or the like. Little teal were not on our menu this day. Three shells were anxiously forced into my 16-gauge, and it was just minutes before a pair of mallards were listening to my close calls. As they made their turn into the now stronger and northerly wind, we took 'em on the pass and before they got their feet wet. I played retriever for the day, and waded out to get our first birds before the wind took them out of sight. As I recall, the limit was three ducks back then, and we didn't think it would take long to limit out.

Ducks seemed to be flying everywhere and kept me calling constantly. But, due to the wind, only a few could hear. It was moving decoys that lured the birds close. Al managed another drake mallard that came right in, and a few minutes later we decoyed a small flock. As we got to our feet and did our best to get our barrels pointed, the flock caught the wind and was quickly leaving with the now stronger northerner. It took our six shells to bring down two. I took off in a fast wade, throwing water all over the front of my hunting pants and coat. Gathering this pair and heading back against the wind with wet hands and frozen face, I realized the weather was getting to be too much, especially being six hundred yards out in the marsh. I said to Al, "I'm about frozen." He replied, "Me, too." My mouth and face were so cold that I could not blow a decent note on the duck call. And in minutes, the call was frozen and useless. We made the wise decision to pick up the old decoys, which had once again done the job in fooling their live brethren. Just as I was about to climb out of the blind, a very fast and large redheaded duck skimmed the decoys. He passed Al's side of the blind and came around for his approach. Al made a swing-through sort of shot and folded the duck cleanly. It floated close and I retrieved it. Much to our liking, it proved to be a very large drake canvasback. Since all my duck hunting had taken place in South Carolina which had few canvasbacks, it was the first drake I had seen up close. Al was elated, and we were pleased to have finished our limit in such a short time. But the weather was getting rough.

Picking up and bagging the decoys was pure misery. Everything seemed to be frozen. The temperature must have fallen far below freezing about sunrise, and now ice was forming on the shallow water of Cheyenne Bottoms. Just a skim to start with, but it didn't take long for Al and me to realize we might be in for big trouble. And we were! My hands were hurting like never before. My little cotton gloves were useless, as I couldn't get them on; they had gotten wet on the way out earlier. Somehow we managed to tie our handkerchiefs over our faces, and started the wade back to the dike we had left a couple of hours before. The shallow water was now frozen, and as far as we could see, the whole of Cheyenne Bottoms was rapidly freezing over. Here we were, six hundred yards between us and the dike, and ice the entire way. I was amazed to see a body of water freeze so quickly. I led the way, breaking ice that was up to a quarter of an inch thick. Al was really struggling, and I knew it. I had to make a path for him, and did so using my hip boots to break through. Al had his new shotgun, and I had two bags of frozen decoys and my shotgun. We had put the six ducks in the decoy bag. I was afraid the ice would cut my hip boots, but little by little I broke our way to the three-hundred-yard A-blind, and we stopped a short while to rest. Al's hands had long since lost their strength. I pushed his shotgun through the game-pocket openings in his hunting coat, and we started on the last three hundred yards to where the Hudson awaited our arrival. The ice was thicker now, and my supreme effort produced cramps in my legs. Progress was painful, but the car kept getting closer and closer. Stopping for rest was out of the question, as we felt that the ice would thicken every minute. We kept going, the decoys and ducks dragging behind, until we finally felt the safety of the dike beneath our very cold feet.

The first thing was to get the Hudson running and the heater on full blast. With the wind and cold outside, Al and I just sat in the car and tried to get our hands working. Neither of us had experienced anything near this bad before. How could the water freeze so fast? We feared the dike would be iced and turning around to get out would be hazardous. The Hudson's wide tires helped with the traction problem, and we carefully made our way back to headquarters to turn in our key.

When I look back on that hunt, I am reminded that duck-killing weather can truly be man-killing weather. Al had hunted here many times, but none so demanding and dangerous. My two winters in Kansas produced the coldest weather I had ever experienced—quite different from South Carolina.

———————

During our stay in Kansas, our son was born—in November 1957 on a cold and snowy day. I remember very well driving in the snow and hoping to get Carolyn to the hospital in time. Perhaps by being born in cold weather, his love for the cold and the hunting that comes with it was born too. Little did I know that he would come to love to fish and hunt to the extent his father did. For the past thirty years, he and I have enjoyed the outdoors together on the Santee Cooper lakes. I passed on most all the knowledge that my years had allowed me to accumulate, and he added much to that as the area changed with time.

Shortly after J. M., III, was born, my mother and my younger brother made the trip to Salina, and Carolyn and I thought it was great they were able to come and be with us during this special time in our lives. We began calling our son Jay, since so many called me J. M., and my father was known as Julius. My father did not come on this trip, as he had his insurance business to run. He had come during the previous summer, along with all the other family members, and all of us had done a lot of sightseeing. That summer of 1957 in Kansas seemed as hot to us as the following winter was cold during my duck hunting excursions!

My brother, John, was nine years old at that time, and fifteen years my junior. He was a young sportsman learning from Daddy and me. When the trip was planned, I mentioned to Mother to let John bring his .410-gauge shotgun as we might have a chance to hunt. My brother, even at the age of nine, was already learning to hit birds on the wing with the little gun, and I was hoping I could take him to the bottoms for a duck hunt. However, getting him out to one of the blinds was a problem I hadn't yet solved.

I knew a sergeant in Special Services on the base, and he helped solve our problem. He said some small one-man life rafts had accumulated at Special Services, and perhaps we could use one. Of course, it had to be blown up, and the old carbon dioxide cartridges were unusable. So we tried blowing up the little yellow raft using lung power. It didn't take too long with both of us working at it.

We planned an early morning hunt at Cheyenne Bottoms, and our plan worked beautifully. I put John and his .410 shotgun and our decoys in the raft, and floated him out to an A-blind, three hundred yards from the dike. We partially deflated the raft and pulled it down into the pit blind with us. As usual, the wind was active, and my dozen Deek decoys looked enticing around the blind. I really didn't expect my little brother to kill a duck, but hoped he would get to see what a real duck hunt over decoys was all about. Looking out toward the refuge area, and becoming aware that the sun was starting to offer a little light, we strained to see if anything would come our way. As on previous trips, ducks moved early at the bottoms, and this morning was no exception.

John was warming up his gun on some fast-moving teal that skimmed the decoys. I kept telling him to get the barrel moving and swing the barrel in front of the swift little teal. He did just that and rolled one out of a small flock. He was real tickled at that, but not as much as I, considering the teal duck is about as hard to hit as anything that flies. Here was a young boy nine years old, shooting the smallest shotgun made at one of the most difficult targets, and doing well, as we collected several more before the morning was over.

When our mother heard the story, she said we must be "just foolin'," but when John showed her the ducks, she said, "How am I ever going to get him back to South Carolina?" This hunt, I do believe, was the outdoor experience that propelled my brother toward becoming a terrific wing shooter around Sumter, South Carolina. He has the little .410 even today, and I'm sure it holds a special place in his gun cabinet and in his memory, for it accounted for his first duck, one of many we would bring home together.

The two duck seasons I spent in Kansas, I couldn't stay away from Cheyenne Bottoms. I was fortunate to hear about it from Al Norton and I wanted my wife, Carolyn, to see my find. We were expecting our first child in a couple of weeks, and she wasn't sure about going the eighty miles or so from the Salina hospital. I assured her of a smooth ride, and if she had signs of trouble we would make the journey back immediately. So we decided to fix a lunch and take it with us, and not get such an early start. It was nearly daylight when we left our little apartment and headed west, out of Salina. I had described the huge wetland to her many times, but I wanted to show her just what it was all about.

As we turned south off I-70 and onto Highway 156, the sunrise seemed to be in a hurry, and we were still a long way from my hunting spot. We began to notice V-formations of big ducks. They were traveling all right, and I suspected what we were seeing was a migration from Nebraska. I told Carolyn I'd bet they were headed to the bottoms. There were many southbound ducks, and all headed in the direction we were going. Something was pushing them, and it must have been changing weather above us.

When we arrived to pick up my key and pay my dollar at the administration building, I hurried back to Carolyn who had the car's motor and heater still running. We drove down the dikes and around to an area I had chosen, and I could see large flocks of ducks coming straight in as if they were tired from their long flight. To say I was excited was an understatement. Carolyn was getting to see a very active and huge wetland filling up with big ducks. I couldn't wait to get out to the A-blind I had chosen. After parking our little Plymouth on the dike at the marked access into the shallow marsh, I quickly put on my hip boots and hunting coat and gathered up the Deeks I had always used when hunting the bottoms.

It didn't take long for me to realize I had chosen a hot spot. Mallards were falling in as I waded out to the blind. Hurriedly, I unlocked the blind cover and hid it in the grass behind the blind and loaded the Sweet 16 with Super-X sixes. I knew Carolyn could see everything going on, and was seeing exactly what duck hunting was all about.

The mallards were still falling in, and I began to call to the closer ones. They were still trying to decide just what was going on around my sunken pit blind. The shooting was easy and fast. I collected my four greenheads in no time and was soon picking up the little rubber Deek decoys that had fooled their counterparts again. The big mallards were all new arrivals to the Bottoms, and, even while I was gathering the decoys, they continued lighting nearby. The Deeks could be folded up easily, then the string and weight wrapped into a small package. The dozen fitted in the game pocket of my hunting coat nicely.

Carolyn saw me wading back toward the car and knew I had been successful—gun in one hand and a handful of ducks in the other. She had the car running and the heater on. With the hip boots, the hunting coat, my shotgun, and the greenheads in the trunk, I jumped in to join her and my soon-to-be-born son. From the time I left the car, waded to the blind, put out decoys, shot a limit of ducks, picked up decoys, waded back to the dike, shed my hunting coat and hip boots, and climbed behind the steering wheel, the entire time taken was a total of forty-five minutes. It was a picture-perfect hunt I'll never forget. Our unborn son said he was impressed, too!

I spent eighteen months at a Strategic Air Command base known at that time as Smokey Hill Air Force Base, later renamed Schilling Air Force Base. The big B-47 and B-52 aircraft used the long runways. And, much to my surprise, the runways seemed to attract jack rabbits. On some days you could see a dozen or more eating grass nearby. I later learned that chasing Kansas jack rabbits with greyhound dogs was popular in local sporting circles. Sounded like fun, but I never had the opportunity to share in the sport.

———————

I did, however, take advantage of the base's bombing range. It was seldom used for any practice bombing while I was stationed there. I don't recall just how I came upon a map of the range, but I did and kept it in my car. The map indicated there were many small ponds scattered over the area.

Although no one had said they hunted there, I did some checking and found out that I could hunt the ponds on Saturdays because no bombing practice ever occurred then.

The map proved to be very accurate and led me to the ponds, some very small and some perhaps five acres in size. After parking the car away from a pond, I would sneak behind the pond dam and slowly peer over to see if any ducks were sitting close enough to shoot. Many times the ponds held nothing, but sometimes after checking several I would find a few ducks loafing and undisturbed. There were all kinds, including shovelers, teal, mallards, and gadwalls. Being patient and staying low behind the dam would produce opportunities to shoot the surprised ducks. My first shot was usually at two or more close together on the water; then as they flushed, I might knock down another couple before they got out of the 16's range. I provided many friends at the base with ducks from the bombing range ponds. Carolyn and I never learned to cook them to our liking.

In the fall of 1957, when my mother and brother were visiting us, I took my brother John on a bombing-range hunt. John and his .410 shotgun were eager to go, and we were up early, as usual; we had hunted Cheyenne Bottoms the week before. The weather was very cold and windy, and I wondered whether the ponds would have open water so early in the day. We found several that did, and ducks were using the larger ponds that morning. We decided we wouldn't shoot anything but mallards that day. Smaller ducks were on some ponds, but we found only one that had mallards.

The pond was very small, and there was only one pair sitting close to the middle, a big greenhead and probably his mate. Getting a shot would be difficult, and we waited a long time hoping they would swim closer. Finally, we made our move from behind the dam, which was our usual method, and both the Sweet 16 and John's .410 blazed away at the surprised pair. Neither was able to fly, so we reloaded and finished the job.

Ice around the perimeter of the pond kept the ducks from floating in to shore. My brother asked how we would bring them in, and I said, "There's only one way to retrieve the pair, and that's to go get 'em." The water was frozen about fifteen or twenty feet out from the edge, but didn't seem thick. We searched around and found a sizeable limb to use for my first-time adventure into icy water. I remembered Mother telling us about her brother, Uncle Johnnie, stripping off and swimming for the ducks he had downed in the Wateree Swamp in South Carolina. I figured that if he could handle a swim, I could handle just a short wade. I didn't think the water was very deep.

I told John to take both guns and go back to the car, start it up, and turn the heater on full blast, and I would be in as soon as I made the retrieve. He headed for the car, and I stripped off the hip boots, took off my pants, and picked up the stick to aid my attempt. Thank goodness the little pond was not very deep and I didn't get over my waist in the icy water. It took only a minute or two to make it to where the ducks lay and back. I was right that the ice was not thick, but the water was, undoubtedly, the coldest I'd ever been in. While putting my pants back on, I saw that my legs were flushed red as a mallard's legs from the cold. Now I knew why their feet were always so red!

John had the heater on, and we laughed at what I had done; I told him the next turn was his, only he needed to be a few years older.

# 6

# BACK TO SOUTH CAROLINA

Early in 1958 I received an honorable discharge from the United States Air Force, and Carolyn and I returned from Schilling Air Force Base in Salina, Kansas, to our hometown of Sumter, South Carolina.

While at Clemson I had majored in Animal Husbandry, so I returned there for several job interviews, but found nothing to my liking in that field as only jobs requiring a lot of traveling seemed to be available.

My father had been in the life insurance business for most of his adult life and when he suggested that I might give that a try I agreed, since Daddy loved his work so much. My "trial period" has lasted over forty years!

I was hired by Liberty Life Insurance Company as an agent in Manning, South Carolina, which is just a few miles from Lake Marion, the upper lake of the Santee Cooper system. The Manning route encompassed areas all around the lake and familiarized me with places I had frequented in my high school years while fishing and hunting.

Fish camps and boat landings were numerous around Lake Marion at that time, and a few homes. The fishing was fabulous and Daddy and I soon picked up our favorite sport again, favoring Lake Marion's Wyboo Creek which was only about thirty-five miles from Sumter. We loved trolling for bass and striped bass in Wyboo Creek. Striped bass, called rockfish by South Carolina fishermen, were becoming plentiful, and every spring Wyboo Creek held its share of "rocks" ranging in weight from five to twenty-five pounds. To insure Daddy's and my continued enjoyment of trolling for bass, I purchased my first outboard motor, a 7½ horsepower Johnson from Carolina Hardware in Sumter.

After I began duck hunting the Santee lakes, the stumps and my regular use in the swamps prompted that I trade motors at the end of each season. Only during the last thirteen years have I run any brand other than

Johnson. The two boats I currently own are powered by Yamaha out-boards, a 150-horsepower model and a 25-horsepower model.

When trolling with Daddy, we rented a wooden boat nearly every Saturday from Joe's Place, a landing on Wyboo Creek. Joe's rental fee was only one dollar per day! He also offered for the fishermen a good selection of lures, live minnows, crickets, and almost anything one would need for a day of fishing on the lake. Joe was a splendid sportsman and always accommodated Daddy and me in any way that he could.

It was in Wyboo Creek that I caught my first really large rockfish. It happened on a slow fishing day when Carolyn caught her first "rock." Her fish weighed about five pounds and, of course, she was proud of her catch. She and I were trolling with identical white bucktails with pork rind trailers when, as lady luck would have it, the big fish bit my lure. The fish almost stopped the boat when he struck, and I immediately cut the Johnson off. The brute tired after a few minutes and I was able to net him. Carolyn made the remark that her's looked like a minnow compared to mine. We have photos of our catches on that day.

We hurried back toward Joe's Place as I was anxious to weigh my prize. Passing under the big power line that crossed Wyboo, we quickly beached the wooden boat. Joe's helper, Herman, who worked the landing for him, greeted us with his usual enthusiasm. Now, Herman was indeed one-of-a-kind! Everybody who visited Joe's Place appreciated his helpful-ness and admired his wit. You could, on any day, ask Herman whether the fish were biting that day and he would say, "They bitin', but some days better than others." Or, you might ask, "Herman, what's bitin' today?" and Herman would reply, "Crappies, carp, bream, bass, rockfish, eels, cat-fish, and mosquitoes." And with that he would heave a big laugh—that contagious laugh that made everybody happy just to be on the Santee. As my daddy would say, "He was quite a character."

When Herman saw Carolyn and me lugging our rockfish up the hill to the scale, he said, while putting on a big smile and laughing every breath, "Mis'er Reynolds, anybody say they caught that fish ain't tellin' the truth." He couldn't wait to hoist the big one onto the scale that hung out front of Joe's. When Joe saw what was going on, he hurried out of his shop to see my fish. The scale stopped just short of twenty pounds, and Joe exclaimed, "That's a nice one!" I had heard that favorite expression of his many times before, but this time it was extra special!

As Carolyn and I went back out for more trolling, Joe told Herman to tell everybody going out to fish, "Tell 'em to watch out for that hole up there where Reynolds pulled that fish out, somebody might just fall in it!"

Daddy and I caught so many fish in Wyboo Creek and Potato Creek, which by water was about four miles away from Joe's, that on Saturday mornings several boats would be waiting at Joe's to follow us, particularly to our favorite spring fishing spots in Potato Creek. This was a great area for catching spawning crappie in the live willow bushes. We used live minnows and fished right down beside the willow bushes. The crappies were there every year as long as the willows were. Of course, as time passed and the boats continuously broke down the willows, the fishing deteriorated.

One of our several productive trolling runs was an underwater point near the mouth of Potato Creek and close to Myers' Landing. Largemouth bass in the seven-and-eight-pound range seemed to like being among the larger rockfish. Daddy and I used green and white plugs made by Bomber to catch both. When trolled, the Bomber, which looked and swam like a crayfish, would run about fifteen feet deep and when approaching the long, deep point would dig the bottom and trigger a strike. We took pictures of the huge strings of fish we took from that point, and Daddy showed them to many disbelievers over the years.

In the fall of 1958 several friends and I began our education of the big swamp and an old swamp landing known locally as Sparkleberry. Joe Drose had spent hours telling me about the area, but we had yet to make a trip there together.

The road leading to the very primitive entrance to the great Santee Swamp was a narrow, dirt, field road that was always in poor condition as it wasn't maintained by the county. Leaving Sumter we traveled through Pinewood to a paved road that connected Rimini with the Manchester State Forest, a favorite public dove hunting area that we hunted during the September seasons. After turning off this paved road we passed several tenant houses beside the narrow field road where old cars were parked in the front yards indicating the road normally was passable. Driving down the field road and through a fenced-in pasture we would come to a steep, red-clay hill, and that was the worst part of getting to the swamp. The small pasture was owned by L. L. Kolb of Pinewood, and it was said that he could not legally close off the road through his property since it had been open for many years.

Traveling the dirt road and crossing the pasture were easy. But going down that red-clay hill on what was mistakenly called a road was something else! The hill was fairly steep and the red clay when wet was as slick as goose grease. We always dreaded that hill, but it was the only way into the swamp. Getting back up the hill, usually at night, was almost impossible if the hill was wet. In rainy periods the wash-outs and deep ruts caused the car to almost drag along.

Hunters and fishermen of today's generation would not believe how difficult it was to get to Sparkleberry when I first heard about it. No launching ramp, floodlight, or parking lot—just a swampy, eerie place used by dedicated and determined sportsmen for entering the upper, upper section of Lake Marion. But what a duck hunting area for a young hunter who had the stamina and enthusiasm for it! Of course, some hunters frequented the upper Santee only in search of deer and squirrels.

Recently my wife and I found our way over to the Sumter side of the lake and to Sparkleberry, forty-three years after I shot my first duck there. As you might expect after forty-three years and with many, many sportsmen going there to hunt and fish, a well-kept, red-clay and gravel road now runs all the way to a double concrete boat ramp at the swamp's edge. Parking is now organized on a nice area that has been cleared of trees. The treacherous hill road is no longer used and is barely recognizable from the parking lot. Of all those who used the old road, I feel that I am one of the few who might remember it ever existed. Forty-three years ago almost everyone left their boats at Sparkleberry from season to season. Now there are no boats chained to the cypress and willow trees that edge the small swampy flat.

After learning the best way to the swamp I, eventually, got to know Mr. L. L. Kolb who owned and operated a service station/country store in Pinewood. Mr. Kolb and I spent many hours together and he gave my friends and me his blessings for passage through his land and shared his extensive knowledge of the Santee Swamp with me. He had kept a small boat at Sparkleberry half a lifetime and had hunted from that point mostly in the Mill Creek area, where he harvested many ducks. Hunting there was convenient for him as it was close to the Sumter County side.

My hunting buddies at that time were Dumont Bordeaux and my brother-in-law, Frank Kalish. Dumont and I had hunted and fished together while attending Edmunds High School in Sumter and while we were at Clemson. He had acquired an old 5-horsepower Johnson, but neither of us had a boat suitable for the big swamp. We checked around at the local marine dealers for one that we could leave down at the swamp's edge and that was big enough for the three of us. Luckily we found an old semi-vee bottom, wooden boat that had been fiberglassed on the bottom and up the sides several inches. This swamp craft we found at McLain Marine & Equipment right in our hometown of Sumter.

I knew the owner's son, Jack McLain, from school days, and after some sweet talking like, "Jack you'll never sell that old boat," and, "It's been on your lot for ages and the grass has grown so high around it you probably didn't even remember you had it," he replied, "How's twenty-five dollars sound, along with five big old swamp ducks?" Since all of us were just getting started in our jobs and didn't have much spare money, we jumped at the deal! That same afternoon we hauled the fourteen-footer over to Dumont's. During the next few weeks and before the 1958 duck season began, we made a few repairs on the seats and strengthened the transom and put on two coats of "swamp-brown" paint. We were happy and excited about the coming season now that we had a "rig" to use for exploring the big swamp. The boat didn't leak, and we knew the fiberglass on the bottom would protect it from all those stumps, logs, and cypress knees we were sure to encounter. We were ready!

# 7

# Johnnie Zeigler, the Quietest Man in the Woods

When looking back over my hunting years, I can truly say no one has influenced my love of hunting as did my uncle, Johnnie Zeigler. To my mother, he was "Bubba," and she told me of his game hunting while they were growing up on the Zeigler farm near Eastover, South Carolina. Mother always portrayed him as being hardened to the winter weather and loving the fall and the cold of hunting season. I only wish she were here now to help me recollect some of the good old times.

Bubba also drove the mule and wagon that took Mother and my two aunts to school each morning. I do remember their tales of bad roads and harsh weather, but they managed to get an education despite the long early morning rides to the schoolhouse.

Uncle Johnnie grew up very near the Wateree River Swamp, and began hunting and fishing there as a youngster. He spent most of his life in that one section of South Carolina. It was said that no one knew the Wateree Swamp as well as he did. I recall some of his longtime friends saying the game wardens would ask for his help in finding someone who was lost in the Wateree, and he would willingly help them. His reputation as a hunter spread as he grew older, and sportsmen from all over sought his knowledge. At one time, I think he made his living selling catfish that he caught from the river. Landowners of the Wateree swamp gave him permission to hunt their property, and he would return their favors with a better understanding of how to hunt their own land. He was huntmaster for many deer drives on their lands.

In knowing and admiring him over my years, I felt his life was one of simplicity. He spent his days loving his wife and their three daughters, their home, and the Eastover Baptist Church, all the while enjoying "his" wonderful Wateree River and swamp. Aunt Lula would say, "No one loves the outdoors like Johnnie."

Bubba spent many days and some nights in the swamplands of the Wateree. I recall that on one of our hunting trips he showed me the swamp shelter he had built to have just in case he was caught by bad weather, or, perhaps, wanted to spend the night listening to the swamp animals around him. He had carried lumber in his boat and had shaped and screened in a shelter that he could sleep in. He built it on strong legs about four feet off the swamp floor, with only one long, narrow room and overhanging eaves to keep out the rain. The screened-in side allowed him a view of his beloved swamp. His little shelter was never damaged by others, as most knew it belonged to their friend.

Mother told me of an incident that happened one autumn afternoon when Bubba sat down beside a tree near the river. The warm sun caused him to doze off for a short while, and when he awoke, something most unusual had happened. A tapered, black tail, which he immediately recognized as belonging to a snake, was protruding from his pant leg. He could not feel the snake against his leg because of the long underwear he had worn that day. When he eased to his feet, the black tail and the rest of the snake slid down and out of his pants. The nonpoisonous blacksnake went on its way!

There were not many boats on the river years ago, and wildlife could be seen more readily. There was a particularly large alligator that my uncle had seen many times as it lay high and dry, sunning on the river's bank. Uncle Johnnie believed the gator had taken many deer from the swamp as he lay in ambush, and he had tried to end the demon's habit several times. The huge gator would always slide back into the river as Uncle Johnnie approached in his boat. One day would be different, as my uncle sneaked through the swamp quietly and found the gator in his usual spot. The heavy buckshot load from his 12-gauge ended the gator's long career of reducing the swamp's deer population!

I remember seeing a picture of that gator, and it was so big that it hung out the back of an old pickup truck. At that time, it was the largest South Carolina alligator I had ever seen, and probably one of the largest in the Wateree swamp.

Uncle Johnnie's dog was a small black and white terrier, and during the warm summer months it was his constant companion on the river. Pee

Wee joined his master on nearly every trip, frequently accompanying him into the swamp and through the swamp trails. During the South Carolina summers, the swamps are full of mosquitoes and snakes, and one must be careful where one steps. On such a summer day, Pee Wee was leading Uncle Johnnie through one of the numerous swamp trails, when suddenly he yelped and jumped backward in fear. Uncle Johnnie immediately saw that a cottonmouth moccasin had struck at Pee Wee, and the snake was still standing his ground. Pee Wee limped back to his master, who could see the bite marks on the dog's leg. When telling this story, Bubba always said he believed that his little dog had saved him from the snake's bite, since he was leading their way through the swamp. Despite the dog's small size, he survived the snake's wrath and continued to follow Uncle Johnnie on his trips to the river swamp.

My earliest recollection of hunting with Uncle Johnnie is during my high school years, 1948–52. Since I had outgrown my first shotgun, a .410-gauge, Daddy helped me get a new 16-gauge Ithaca pump gun my junior year, and I soon had serious hunting on my mind. I was ready for some of those ducks my uncle talked about that filled the creeks and acorn flats of the Wateree swamp. He always said the ducks would fly up from the Santee reserve near Summerton when the water was high and fill the great flats off the river that he knew so well. No matter how much corn they ate in the refuge, "Those ducks gonna come up," he said often. And he was always right. The mallards, black ducks, and wood ducks loved the Wateree area.

During those years, I would telephone Bubba in Eastover about taking me duck hunting. He would either say that conditions were not right, or just "come on." I knew then that the water was high, and he was going to show me some "sho-nuff" hunting. The thing that always puzzled me was that he said, "Be here about eight o'clock in the morning." Now I thought that was kind of late to be going duck hunting, but not for Bubba's ducks! In later years, I patterned some of my hunting philosophy after these late-hour starts.

Needless to say, a youngster going hunting the next morning doesn't get much sleep the night before. Of course, I always arrived in Eastover well before the appointed hour, and, as usual, Aunt Lula would be preparing breakfast. Uncle Johnnie was putting on layers of clothing and looking around for his hip boots. We never had any waders in those days, just hip boots. Uncle Johnnie said you couldn't beat the B. F. Goodrich Lite-N-Tuf boots, so I had a pair, too.

Aunt Lula cooked grits, eggs, and bacon for us, as she knew we wouldn't be eating much in the swamp. We did take a little lunch, occasionally. But we went to hunt, not eat; and, as I remember, we didn't take anything to drink. I do recall that on one trip the weather was hot, so I drank water from the Wateree River. I wouldn't do that today, but I sure did then, and I did not get sick from it!

Bubba kept his boats in the river so they would not leak. He made his own boats from boards that had been treated with creosote, and in order to prevent leaks, put them in the river so the boards would swell. He always kept a little can with which to scoop the rainwater, just in case. His riverboats were always made alike, about fifteen feet long, with low sides. They were not wide and could be controlled easily with a paddle. All had pointed bows and only two boards for seats. His 5-horsepower Johnson outboard motor got us up and down the river as fast as we needed to go.

One of his boats he kept in the Wateree River bordering Mr. John Cotton's land, and the other on Mr. Caldwell James's place. We used the one closest to the ducks at the time. Today, International Paper (formerly Union Camp) owns a big plant located on the John Cotton place, and Mr. Caldwell James's land now has a duck club or two. I wonder what Uncle Johnnie would say about his beloved swamp if he were living today. He always said to me, "Never tell where you hunt!"

It seems to me that we always went downstream from either landing, and we would check the willow shoals for ducks as we went. Occasionally, when the temperature had been at freezing for several days, we would paddle the river and jump ducks that were hiding in the willows. Bubba knew which ones would have ducks, and he knew just how to position the boat for me to get a shot. This was a lot of fun, but not nearly as productive as paddling the creeks. Many times we would leave the river, enter Sandy Creek which flowed down the swamp, and drift with the current.

In those days, it was illegal to mount an outboard motor on a boat while drifting and shooting ducks. The law is different today. Bubba would place the Johnson motor on the floor in the middle of the boat for good balance. We would not need it again until we reached the river. He would skillfully guide his homemade craft with a long, flat paddle he had made— always keeping to the inside of the creek bends in hopes of getting close enough to the ducks for a good shot. The wood ducks, commonly known in South Carolina as woodies or summer ducks, were numerous then, and the creeks were full, particularly on the inside bends. Bubba always called them "little ducks." To him the mallards and blacks were "big ducks."

Uncle Johnnie would quietly tease me when I would miss a shot, and sometimes he would back me up with his old single-shot 12-gauge. But talking was taboo when in the woods! We very seldom said anything, but used signals we knew and understood.

I remember very well when on one bend of the river there was a mallard hen sitting on a log in the middle of the creek. She didn't know what to do as we appeared around the bend and seemed frozen to the log. We got so close before she flushed that I missed her twice with my Ithaca 16-gauge. Bubba picked up his single-barrel, and as she got to the top of the trees, made one of the longest shots I ever saw. He motioned to me to retrieve the mallard while he guided the boat to the bank. It would tickle him that we worked so well as a team. He didn't have a son to carry hunting, so I've always enjoyed feeling I was his "huntin' son." I surely was a lucky boy to have him share his swamp with me.

We would drift on down Beech Creek and Little River and on into what Bubba called the Live River. He meant the Wateree River, of course. It would take all day to make the drift, particularly if we stopped to sneak-hunt a flat. Bubba had explained earlier that a flat is a low area, usually filled with cypress and gum trees, between two ridges. The South Carolina swamps such as the Wateree, Congaree, and Santee all seem to have many flats and ridges. The hardwood trees that grow on these ridges produce acorns that attract the ducks.

Once, before reaching the river, we heard mallards calling from a wooded area on a flat that Bubba knew very well. The overflow from Beech Creek had filled a space thick with great oaks. They had produced well that year, and the ducks were really on the acorns. We couldn't see them, but we knew they were there. We tied the boat to a tree, not making a sound, and I witnessed my first great sneak hunt. I had not done this before, and Bubba told me to step in his footprints as I followed. He chose his way skillfully, putting his feet down slowly and not disturbing anything. We were in luck that day, as the leaves on the swamp floor were damp from the creek overflow. I followed him step for step. The damp leaves didn't crackle, but the sticks were noisy. I did my best and said nothing.

Now sneaking up on ducks isn't easy, and getting close enough for a shot can be a time-consuming experience, quite a challenge. Ducks are extremely sharp, and their ability to survive depends on it. One careless moment, and they're in trouble. A duck's eyesight is excellent. Seeing bright colors or shades of bright colors sends them on their way. Also, a foreign-shaped object spooks them easily. Man is certainly foreign to their world, and his outline and his noise must be eliminated if he is to get close enough for a killing shot. And ducks hear quite well. Unfamiliar sounds, such as sticks or dry leaves being crushed underfoot, must be kept to a minimum.

I could not believe my eyes! The whole area was loaded with green-heads, tipping up and feeding on the acorns. There were so many I thought the swamp belonged to them! They would tip up to eat in the shallow water and then sort of beat the water with their wings, apparently trying to scatter the leaves. I had never seen several thousand ducks in a small area and just out in front of me. We crawled up behind a large fallen log that concealed us while we planned what to do next. The ducks were not aware of our presence as they continued their feeding. Finally, Bubba whispered that I should stay behind the log, and he would backtrack and try to get around and to the side of the ducks. I should stay ready to shoot, but not fire until he did. He crawled away, and soon was out of my sight. He told me later that he had crossed the little gut of water that was feeding the flat and sneaked out and around the mallards. As I waited, I could not help but rise up and look at what was going on. The green heads of the drakes were shining everywhere, and the hens were close at hand, smaller and less conspicuous. From my position, which was actually a small point of dry swamp out into the flat, I felt surrounded by the ducks. I was truly in their world for my first time. They never seemed to notice anything out of the norm and even swam on behind me looking for more acorns. It took Bubba a long time to gain the position he wanted, and I was determined not to spook his ducks.

The long silence ended when the first shot from Bubba's single-barrel sounded like a cannon. Wings were getting airborne in every direction. I struggled to my knees as the frantic ducks were clawing for altitude. To my amazement, hundreds were flying out directly toward and over me and through the huge trees. Bubba's 12-gauge had put them in my direction!

My shots were haphazard as I emptied my pump gun, but I quickly managed to cram two more shells into the Ithaca before all the ducks had passed over my head. From the five shots, three mallards lay on the shallow water around me. I couldn't wait to get my hands on them. Two greenheads lay close together, and a hen that had righted herself was swimming away toward some canes on the far bank. After awakening the whole swamp with my sloshing around, I caught up with her. I was thrilled I had three big ducks to show Uncle Johnnie.

Returning to my log and, hopefully, gaining a chance to rest a minute, I spied Uncle Johnnie making his way slowly and quietly across the shallow, feather-covered flat toward me. He was hardly making a ripple in the knee-deep water, a perfect example for me. He had always said, "No noise in the woods," and I was learning.

What a sight he was! In one hand was his trusty gun, and in the other was a load of big mallards, five of them. He was a man of few smiles, but this time he was smiling my way, indicating his approval that we had "done good." I could not comprehend just how he had managed to bag five ducks with a single-shot gun until he explained his shooting technique. He revealed that his first shot was made at two or more ducks close together on the water, assuring a multiple kill. He then unloaded the single-barrel, still mounted on his right shoulder, by opening the breech and allowing the fired shell to eject over his shoulder. He held two additional shells in his left hand and fed the empty chamber each time. Bubba said he had used this technique over and over since he was a youngster. Once the on-the-water shot was made, he then picked out single ducks leaving the flat. The single-barrel must have had a great shot pattern, since some of the shots were at long, shotgun ranges.

We sat on our log admiring the large mallards, and talked quietly about why the ducks were here and about the magnificent oak trees that have fed the ducks for generations. Bubba pointed out that many other residents of the swamp depended on the great oaks for their food, also: deer, squirrels, hogs, turkeys.

I recall Uncle Johnnie's smoking habits. He rolled his own cigarettes and always kept cigarette papers and a little sack of tobacco in his shirt pocket. He would dump tobacco from the little sack onto a cigarette paper held carefully by two fingers. If the wind was blowing, he turned his back to it and proceeded, rolling the paper to wrap the tobacco and licking the side with glue. When finished, he twisted both ends and lit it with a strike-anywhere match. He loved to smoke his homemade cigarettes, and did for many years. Smoking led to his ill health in later life, as emphysema finally took its toll.

Our usual trip would take us through Beech Creek, into Little River, and finally back to the Wateree River. Bubba would set the Johnson motor on the transom and tighten the clamping bracket. Then out into the current and back upriver. What a day we would have! I learned the ways of the swamp from him, and he seemed to enjoy taking opportunities to show me the dos and don'ts. He was proud of the swamp knowledge he had acquired from his many trips. He showed me Horseshoe Lake on one excursion, and I will always remember a shot he made with the single-barrel 12-gauge, killing three mallards with one blast.

We had sneaked into Horseshoe and spotted a few wood ducks right away. We passed those up in favor of finding some mallards or blacks. After a few minutes of watching from our vantage point behind a large cypress, we discovered a big greenhead mallard ahead of us, feeding up our side of the lake's floodwater. Bubba soon called my attention to two others following. Our strategy was to shoot two of them when the time was right. I was peering at them from the right side of the cypress and Bubba on the left. He whispered that we would shoot the drakes when they passed a small opening about thirty-five yards directly in front of us. I was obliged and shaking with excitement. The ducks never saw us as we readied our shotguns, and when Bubba cocked the hammer on his 12-gauge, my duck had swum behind a small stickup, obscuring my line of sight. Bubba wasted no time in making the most incredible shot I had ever seen. Sensing that I could not make my shot, he made short work of the three mallards, pulling the trigger at just the right moment, when all three were together. The load of number six shot turned all the mallards upside down. The amazing thing about the shot was that the hen in the trio was at least four feet or more away from the two drakes. Bubba's old single-barrel gun had covered the entire area where the ducks sat. Most hunters would have bagged one, maybe two, but Bubba had all three! I was amazed, but not Bubba. It's not the first time his gun made a hard shot look easy. His on-the-water technique was to aim his gun below the duck so that the small shot would ricochet off the water. Actually, he aimed about ten or twelve inches under the duck's body, thereby putting as much shot as possible into the neck and head areas. Number six size shot was just the ticket for this.

Another event that I have seen only once occurred one afternoon near an old oxbow lake. We had spent some time looking for deer tracks on the small, secluded island near the oxbow—something we did frequently—after working most of the day hunting ducks. But no tracks that day. Bubba opened the throttle of the little Johnson and headed upriver toward home. As I remember, we were on a straight stretch of river when a mallard hen flew over us from behind, and on upriver. When she was about a hundred yards beyond us, from out of nowhere a large hawk seemed to fall from the sky, passing with great speed and apparently striking the duck. I had never seen such an attack. The mallard folded her wings and fell from the sky into a willow shoal, evidently scared to death. She disappeared below the willows, and our best efforts to find or flush her were futile. We searched and probed the limbs with our paddle. Finally we gave up, realizing the mallard, in her attempt to survive, had submerged only to hold onto a limb until she felt all danger had passed.

As I look back to my early hunting in the Wateree, I remember many ideas that my uncle taught me, and many observations that he made, such as how to use the trees for navigation. "The trees are your friends," he instructed me. "Remember them well and they will keep you from getting lost." Many times we would stop on the river, and he would direct us to an acorn flat out in the swamp, using his trees as landmarks. I remember he always would walk away from the boat a few yards, then turn around to look back at the trees bordering the river where we had left the boat. "We'll remember those when coming back," he would say. And it always worked.

Another practice of his was to use the sun for keeping our direction. These two navigational aids afforded me many safe trips into other swamps, as well as the Wateree.

Duck hunting of all kinds became my favorite sport, but my early duck knowledge came from sneak hunting with Bubba. Duck habits and how they relate to food and habitat were first learned with him. Swamp ducks are primarily wood ducks, mallards, and black ducks. They love shallow water. He showed me why the ducks were using a particular flat or area; the way they muddied the shallow water flats in search of acorns; the right depth of water for tipping up; the way they scattered the leaves on the bottom by beating the water with their wings. I could never appreciate what the big mallards were doing until I saw it happen several times. Muddy flats near the great oaks were sure signs that ducks were feeding in that particular flat.

A tip he showed me for retrieving a downed duck in deep water has stuck with me since I was a boy. We had shot wood ducks in a deep creek that he called Clarkson's Old River, a creek that flowed from the Wateree River and on around a very flat area that was once used for farming. The water was too deep to wade to them without getting wet. Bubba always carried in his coat a length of cord, twenty to twenty-five feet long. The cord was tied neatly so that it could be unwound quickly. That day he found a stick from the swamp floor about three feet long and heavy enough to throw. It needed to float, and did. He tied the cord off-center on the stick, and holding the end of the line, threw the stick beyond the duck lying in deep water. Then, gently, he guided the stick toward the duck, as the off-center knot would cause the longer end of the stick to trail the short end, thereby forming a corner between the cord and the short end. He would work magic with this retrieving method. I saw him use it several times. To this day, his string and stick idea has kept my feet dry and saved many ducks from being left in deep creeks, and flats too deep to wade.

In all the Wateree swamplands we hunted, we cherished one area above all for our duck-hunting activities. Bubba called it the Clarkson Swamp. It bordered the river, and the area we hunted was probably two hundred acres or more. The Clarkson was surrounded by an old dam that was built to keep out water from Clarkson's Old River. An old map I later acquired referred to it as the Clark property, and from the map, looked to be the same area. We always walked from the river to get in the Clarkson, usually on what I remember to be an old logging road. We crossed the creek on a bridge and entered the huge flat where the dam and logging road met.

I'll never forget my first trip there with Uncle Johnnie. He had not described the place, except to the extent that the ducks loved it. After seeing it for myself, I could understand why. The huge flat contained some of the largest oak trees I had ever seen, and so many in one place. The massive canopy they had created had retarded the undergrowth of smaller trees and bushes to the extent that the swamp floor was virtually bare in most areas. There were some low-growing green canes, but mostly clear and hard ground covered with the oaks' small acorns. A couple of low areas were worn into the swamp floor by water from the Clarkson's Old River. But for the most part, the old dam was only broken in two spots that allowed overflow into the flat. Uncle Johnnie knew very well that during the years when the acorn crop was abundant and the water was high, the ducks would flock to the great flat. Every time I went with him, they would have already located the small acorns, their iridescent green heads being a dead giveaway.

There were, at times, several thousand mallards, black ducks, and wood ducks in the flat, all feeding on their favorite swamp food. There were so many they hardly noticed others being flushed by our intrusion. We would stay near the dam and hunt from it. Bubba knew just where to leave the dam without allowing the water to go over our hip boots, and we would move slowly into the green cane patches hoping to get close enough for a shot. Sometimes we would split up, going separate ways. I always knew when his old 12-gauge rocked the silence that rapid shooting was going to start. The air would be so full of ducks leaving that it was hard to swing on just one. The area was so big and the oak trees so tall that the ducks would sometimes fly around the flat and not go out and over the trees. Some would light again to resume feeding. We seldom ran them all out at one time.

We visited the Clarkson swamp many times during my youth. It was always a delight to go with Bubba and share the swamp with him. Even during his long bout with emphysema, we continued to hunt the ducks there. He would tell me to go ahead, that he would be along. His walking became limited, but never his desire to visit his river swamp and its wildlife. I knew he was hurting when he sat down frequently, but he never complained. On our last trips together, he would never leave the dam to wade the flats. He left that to me.

Johnnie Zeigler's life as a hunter of the Wateree Swamp ended in October of 1962. In my eyes, his prowess as an outdoorsman was unequaled. His ability to blend in with and understand nature was itself an accomplishment few attain. He grasped what man could take from the woods, and he never wasted what the swamp offered.

His hunting gun now graces a special place in my cabinet. Aunt Lula gave it to me along with the boat we had used on those cold December and January days. I'm glad he came along when the woods and wild things were plentiful. And I'm grateful and proud that he shared them with me. His way with the woods became my way. His influence on me sparked and enriched my enjoyment of the outdoors. I shall never forget him.

# 8

# SPARKLEBERRY

Like most hunters who use Sparkleberry as their entrance to the Santee Swamp, Dumont, Frank, and I kept our little swamp boat chained to a hefty cypress tree on the edge of a small and shallow flat. Most of the time the flat had several feet of water in the middle, but during dry periods the boat would be sitting on the muddy swamp floor. The boat had a strong eye bolt under the small deck and through the bow. We secured it with a stout chain and lock to the same tree most of the time. Dumont's little Johnson motor was easy to carry and mount on the transom.

To get out of the landing area, a ditch had been dug that sometimes had a little water, enough to drag the boat through to a large, shallow, and very stumpy flat known as John's Flat. John's Flat was the way into the swamp's twelve thousand acres of hardwood ridges and cypress flats, creeks, and lakes that my hunting buddies and I would enjoy for years to come. The little ditch apparently had been dug with shovels and a lot of back-breaking energy, since no machinery could have gotten into such a primitive spot. It was probably seven or eight feet wide, and when the water was up was deep enough to idle the small Johnson through. But with low water, boats had to be dragged through the mud. We would tie a rope to the bow eye and pull and push it through. What a fellow will do to shoot a duck!

During very low water levels, John's Flat's water level was only a foot or so deep, and with so many stumps left after being logged out, it became almost impossible to use. We have, on occasion, had to leave our boat in Sparkleberry Lake itself, which was about a half mile from the landing. The lake was very deep, and on low-water days had an exposed bank. Very few people ever knew the exact spot of the lake, and that an old road used to run all the way from the landing to the lake's edge. It was this road that we walked, carrying the 5-horsepower Johnson on our shoulders.

Taking turns toting the motor to the lake allowed Dumont, Frank, and me to hunt even on low water.

Sparkleberry Lake, like many swamp lakes, was really just a widened area of a creek. In the case of Sparkleberry Lake, it was the widest and deepest area of Mill Creek, which flowed almost the full length of the swamp on the Sumter County side. Just below the lake was an area that Mill Creek flowed through on the way down toward the Pack's Landing area. We called it Sparkleberry Cut-Down because of the huge stump field left from logging activities years before. Except for the creek bed running downstream and into the tall timber at the lower end, the cut-down was fairly shallow. It was open, with few trees, but had three additional shallow coves running toward the hill side.

In the first year or two of hunting ducks around Sparkleberry Lake, we found that the open area was very poor for decoying ducks of any kind. But the coves on the hill side attracted mallards and gadwalls and an occasional teal. It was in these coves that I killed my first gadwalls and learned that they would decoy easier than a mallard. On many occasions, just standing in the brush at the water's edge using a small decoy spread, we took many gadwalls that came to my Mallardtone call. I was not a good caller in those days, but a good quack or two helped.

The lower stretch of shallow water flowed through some thick bushes, quite close to the hill. I have seen this area teem with hundreds of mallards frolicking during the midmorning and middle of the day. It was too thick to put out decoys, but I did a little sneaking around and shot some as they flushed. And I wasn't beyond shooting a big greenhead on the water.

Several years later, during the Christmas holidays of 1961 or 1962, my brother John, who was still a youngster, and I located a concentration of widgeon very near the cut-down, but closer to Pack's Landing. The area was behind some bushy islands that separated this open area from the main part of the lake. It reminded me of an old rice field, but someone later told me it was called Mud Lake. It was shallow and grassy, and the wigeon loved the grass. It always puzzled me why certain kinds of ducks like one area over another, but I soon learned it was the food they preferred that attracted them to certain spots. Close by were the cut-down flats of Sparkleberry that drew mallards and gadwalls.

Despite being a young teenager, John handled a shotgun like a pro. We spooked the several hundred wigeon while entering the grassy flat, and that gave us enough time to put out our half-worn-out decoys and hide the boat. The spot we chose for the decoys allowed us to hide beside and within a low, bushy tree just a short distance from the half-dozen decoys. Our tree apparently had lost its top section of limbs which allowed John and me to shoot through the treetop. It was perfect cover, and the limbs made a comfortable seat while we waited. Even though wigeon don't quack like a mallard or most puddle ducks, they can be attracted by a mallard duck call.

We hunted this spot several days with nobody coming in on us, and took many limits of wigeon from the grassy flat. I remember so well Mother's cook, Rosa, saying, "Please don't bring any more home. My whole family has been picking them ducks for days." My brother's little 20-gauge bolt action shotgun and my Sweet 16 semiautomatic took their toll on the wigeon that Christmas.

During the '58 season, Dumont, Frank, and I spent nearly every weekend hunting and exploring more and more territory. The water level stayed low that year, but we kept looking for new places that held ducks. Leaving the landing and traveling down John's Flat, out to Mill Creek, and north through the flooded timber and swamp, we finally found Otter Flats. This area that opened up was probably a mile long and had several creeks that fed off in different directions. The lower creek to the left led to McGirt's Lake, the lower creek to the right led to Hog House Gut. Today, most duck hunters call that creek Snake Creek, and others called it Sumter Creek.

Running parallel and northerly to Hog House Gut was Fifty Fools' Creek. And, farther over toward the Sumter County hill, was Mill Creek which came up from Sparkleberry Lake. Hog House Gut, Fifty Fools' Creek, and Mill Creek intermingled through a great highland named Pine Island. All three were bordered by huge oak trees that produced a duck's favorite food—acorns. Many mallards, black ducks, and wood ducks wintered here and fed on the acorns in the flooded flats and edges of the creeks.

I, personally, explored these three creeks for several years, but found more ducks along Hog House Gut than the other creeks. I hunted in that area a lot by myself.

Going on upstream in Otter Flats was another creek on the right that led us up the western side of Pine Island. This was Pine Island Creek, located almost exactly in the center of the Santee Swamp. In fact, the swamp was five miles wide at that point, with over two miles of wetlands and ridges to the east and to the west. Pine Island Creek split the great swamp right down the center, and this creek was a thoroughfare for ducks flying up from the Summerton refuge down below. Through the years I hunted it many times, and it proved to be the luckiest section of the entire swamp.

But our first year of using the Johnson motor and our twenty-five-dollar swamp boat, we mainly hunted around McGirt's Lake. It would take us about forty-five minutes to make the trip from Sparkleberry Landing. We started out before daylight, using mostly regular-sized flashlights to light the way. Q-Beams and really good spotlights had not appeared on the market yet. We learned where every underwater stump and log "lived" on the way to McGirt's, and sometimes we could make the trip without shearing a pin in the little Johnson.

McGirt's Lake was quite big and deep with huge cypress trees and acorn-bearing oaks in the shallow flats around it. The top end of the lake was divided by a long line of cypress trees. The water was shallow enough to use hip boots. The divided flats were used by many wood ducks and, occasionally, some mallards. In the late afternoon, we would hide the boat among the cypress and scatter out to shoot the left fork of the lake. There were more acorn trees on that side, and since the water was shallow, the ducks came in to feed. Wood ducks were not easy to hit, but we always had plenty to shoot at.

Over the first weekend or two that we hunted McGirt's, I noticed that farther over into the swamp the woodies kept going down in one area. I realized that we could not get our boat into the woods, so I set out one afternoon to see how far I could go with just hip boots. Luckily, the cypress flats the ducks were using were shallow at certain points. Other places were probably waist deep. We had pretty well shot out the ducks in our earlier spot, and they were moving deeper into the area I was now scouting. It didn't take long to figure out just why they were piling into the flat I was standing in and beyond. Huge oaks bearing small acorns lined one side of the shallow flat. The area exploded with wood ducks as I was trying to cross to the oak tree side. There must have been a hundred or more in one fifty-yard stretch, going out through the huge trees in every direction. I didn't fire a shot, thinking we would be there the next morning before they arrived. And we were.

I was still shooting my Browning 16-gauge. Frank had borrowed his grandfather's 12-gauge double barrel, and Dumont had just bought a new Browning 12-gauge semiautomatic. We set up the next morning before daylight with plenty of shells. Frank and Dumont inched their way down the far side of the dark, eerie swamp and took a stand in a good opening in the trees. I stayed about seventy-five yards away and was leaning beside a cypress that I could hide behind, if needed. We had hardly gotten ready when the first ducks hit the dark water. It was still too dark to shoot safely, and anyway, you can't see a "black woody" in a black water flat that time of morning.

In those days we didn't pay much attention to "shootin'" times in the morning, and as soon as it was "seeing time," we awakened everything in the swamp with our three guns bellowing among the huge oak and cypress trees. If the ducks came in my end and I got to shooting, they would fly out toward Dumont and Frank. And the same thing would happen if they came in on their end. We must have shot a box of number sixes apiece at woodies coming and going. It was a hunt we wouldn't forget, that year.

It wasn't long before we began looking for the ducks we had downed. I didn't make any long shots and was pretty sure my birds could be found. I was sitting on a stump after picking up, and thinking that Dumont and Frank were taking a long time coming back my way. I knew they had burned some gunpowder to say the least, and had probably had trouble finding their ducks. But before long I saw them both coming down the far side of the little flat where I was sitting. Both were lugging a load of ducks and talking about the ones I should have downed, since the Sweet 16 was not idle that morning.

I had not yet crossed the flat in the particular spot where I was sitting, and did not know a log was lying near the bottom, so I could not warn them that a log lay where they were going to cross. Dumont was the first to wade out with his new Browning in one hand and a bunch of ducks in the other, and Frank came slowly behind him. Dumont was waving his kill around and showing them off when suddenly he was falling forward, having tripped over the log. Frank couldn't stop his fall, and Dumont went down gun-first into the December-cold water. He was mostly all under water, his new 12-gauge on the bottom, before Frank could get a hand on him. Bad luck like that should be a laughing matter, except when it happens in wintertime water. It was no joke, and Dumont was really disgusted that he had not been more aware of his footing.

We weren't far from our boat, so we went on to it before attempting to do something for a shivering Dumont. Frank and I got his hip boots off, then his soaked clothes; by this time, Dumont was shaking uncontrollably. He was very cold-natured and the drenching had put him in a bad way.

It was good that I had on layered clothing that morning, and Frank and I shared some dry clothes with Dumont. That didn't leave much on either of us! We put Dumont in the front of the boat and sat him on the floor, turned his back to the wind, and headed for the landing. For Dumont, we couldn't arrive soon enough. But the car heater soon had him in better shape. After we were halfway home, Frank and I had a good laugh with Dumont, accusing him of having a hangover that morning. We all agreed we had a terrific hunt with a "wet ending."

I had many hunts around McGirt's Lake that year, and one I especially recall was the afternoon I took my wife, Carolyn, to that same flat where Dumont had been "swimming." Although she had once, on a trip to Kansas, watched from the car as I took a limit of ducks, Carolyn had never actually been duck hunting with me, and she had an interest in seeing the big swamp.

I borrowed a pair of black hip boots for her to use, and what a sight she was in those! An afternoon hunt would be warmer, except for the ride out of the swamp, so she agreed to go. We stood together in shallow water beside a very large cypress. I had some good shooting, and she helped me mark the whereabouts of my downed birds. All I shot was a couple of ducks that afternoon, but it was enough for Carolyn. As she said, "Let's get out of this swamp before dark!" So I followed orders from "the boss," and we were soon on the way home to get our one-year-old son, who was with his grandmother. Many years later, I took our son to the very spot where his mother experienced her first and only Santee duck hunt.

During a slow weekend around McGirt's Lake hunting by myself, I explored the right fork at the top end of the lake. I managed to bring the twenty-five-dollar swamp boat, but I had a new 10-horsepower Johnson motor. It ran like a charm, and really would push our boat. The right slough ran a long ways out of McGirt's to a small opening at the edge of the tall cypresses. I remember someone had put a barrel high in one of the biggest cypresses, and was able to climb up to it using what appeared to be teeth from a cotton picker. They were driven into the huge tree far enough to support a climbing hunter. I never tried to climb it, and still don't know how the barrel was fastened to the tree. Over the years I observed several barrels scattered throughout the swamp that were used by hunters to shoot passing ducks. They were always high up and were quite effective.

The little opening was a really ducky-looking spot to put out decoys. I never did shoot any there, but while sitting in the cover one afternoon, I saw a good many mallards going down on the other side of a nearby ridge of willows. I did not know at the time that mallards were going in to what is known as Shirah Flats. I had never been that far in the big swamp before, but I had to find out more about where those ducks were going.

I beached the swamp boat on the willow ridge and walked down a piece to see if there was any way to get the boat into where I was seeing the ducks go down. There was never enough water anywhere on the ridge that my boat could be floated across. I could see several bodies of water and several rows of low bushes and small trees farther over.

Taking the 10-horsepower off the boat, I carried it the twenty yards or so to the water's edge on the other side of the then-dry ridge. Then I dragged the boat across and remounted the Johnson. It was the only way I could continue my progress into Shirah Flats. I didn't go far that afternoon, as the sun was just below the treetops, but the pothole-looking area beyond the ridge I'd just crossed had sufficient cover to camouflage our brown and muddy-colored boat. I ran it in at the end of the cover, so that if any ducks did come in I might get off a shot or two.

Planning to wait just a little while, as I was a long way into the swamp and by myself, my patience was rewarded when two big mallards appeared very low and came in after circling my hidden boat only once. I stood up at just the right time and splashed them both. It appeared that I had found a roosting area in the flats. Other ducks were going down farther over.

Darkness was about to catch me several miles up the swamp, and even though I felt like I could find my way back to McGirt's, it was my first trip up that far. I had a good three-cell flashlight with a big lens, so I put it to use about halfway back to McGirt's Lake. I felt fairly safe arriving there, as I had made the trip from McGirt's to Sparkleberry Landing many times.

As I made my way back, I kept my attention on landmark after landmark and took my time moving along with the 10-horsepower only at a fast idle. Arriving where McGirt's Creek meets the lower end of Otter Flats,

I turned downstream and headed through the flooded woods toward Mill Creek. This area was always tricky to navigate, and I noticed that the water seemed to be flowing faster than earlier that day. The three-cell light was brightening the way nicely when suddenly I brushed a bushy and low limb which not only hit me in the face, but knocked the flashlight from my hand. Luckily, it fell to the floor of the boat instead of being knocked out into the dark and deep swamp.

By the time I got things back under control and the motor out of gear, the fast-moving current had turned me around. At first I wasn't alarmed, but that big flooded area at night seemed to have forty different directions that all appeared right. It didn't seem like it took long to get the flashlight shining again, but by then the current had moved me a good ways off my usual trail. I took out my white handkerchief and tied it to a limb as a reference marker. I knew I couldn't be far off my trail, but the prospect of not getting back on it and becoming oriented again was scary. I would motor a little way from the handkerchief, hoping to find a landmark tree or stump, and then back to the handkerchief. I looked at the direction the water was flowing and figured that downstream had to be right. But downstream and thirty yards off the trail was still wrong. Finally, after turning upstream and doing a little zigzagging across the current, I recognized some trees that I always passed going from and coming to McGirt's Lake. I made another attempt toward downstream, and my landmarks, one after another, fell into place.

What a great feeling it was to know I was on my trail again! Soon I was at Mill Creek, and on to John's Flat. When I came to the little ditch that night, I was never so glad to pull a boat through the mud and to see familiar sites at the landing. I was safely back to Sparkleberry.

Over the many years of hunting the big swamp, I heard other hunters' tales about the dangers they encountered. There are many pitfalls lurking there, but in my opinion getting lost and turning a boat over or knocking a hole in its bottom are the two worst. I hit many logs or stumps with our boats, but never hard enough to do any damage. I was always careful along that line. But getting turned around and temporarily lost is something that happens to most who venture into a swamp as big as the Santee. I always seemed to have a good sense of direction, and I'm not sure how I acquired it. I often heeded the advice of my Uncle Johnnie, whose lessons about swamps always included the reminder to note the surrounding trees well.

One thing that can be confusing and will influence your navigation is fluctuating water levels. The water can cover your flats or your familiar stumps, and might create what seems like a creek channel, but is nothing more than high floodwater making its way downstream.

Some weekends at Sparkleberry, we would get off work midday and were able to hunt both Friday afternoon and Saturday. One such weekend, I took Dumont up to what I had found in Shirah Flats above McGirt's Lake. He was eager to see the new territory and to have a chance at some mallards. It was much easier to drag our boat across the little dry ridge when there were two of us, so I was glad I had company for this hunt.

The ducks were not moving in the early afternoon, so we decided to explore the area while nothing else looked promising. We came across a large bag of shelled corn that had been placed at water level, where the sizeable willow limbs entered the water. The burlap bag had been split open, and apparently was meant for the ducks to enjoy by swimming up to the bag and helping themselves to the corn. The water in Shirah was not extremely shallow, but was not flowing at its present level. We noticed duck feathers floating about the flat and felt that the ducks were using the area because of the corn and, of course, the nearby acorn trees. That afternoon we left Shirah Flats rather early and without firing a shot. We wanted to make plans to get back before dawn the next morning, and a good supper awaited us back at the landing.

Sometimes during these excursions, Daddy would let me use Mother's Ford station wagon, and we would go by a wood yard for a small load of firewood, just enough to have a small cooking fire for hamburgers or hotdogs. It was a kind of treat to have some warmth and hot food on our overnight weekends at Sparkleberry. There was really no wood available to be cut near the landing, and we were always too tired for that anyway.

The station wagon, supplied with our sleeping bags, was quite comfortable for two. So after our cookout, we would get to bed usually as early as eight or nine o'clock. Of course, this was always delayed by talking over our plans for the morning's hunt. And, after all, getting up at 4:30 A.M. and getting Dumont moving was a task! He was always slow to rise even though we had something special in mind. Being a poor sleeper, I usually didn't even need an alarm clock. We tried to leave the little flat that was home to our swamp boat before the Saturday crowd arrived. I used to remind my hunting partners that you can be late going fishing, but the ducks don't wait for anybody! Even on a cloudy morning they know when to leave their roosting place, and that's at daybreak.

The long trip up the swamp and on through McGirt's took at least an hour, as we always idled the outboard when the water was low. The only area on this route that we planed the boat was in McGirt's Lake itself.

Pulling the boat over the ridge, and making our way in the inky darkness of the swamp, we located the willow with the large sack of corn. We had selected our hunting spot the afternoon before and proceeded to put out the few decoys. The spot had cover just right for our little boat. There was some stabilizing debris under the boat, necessary for good shooting—something we always looked for, whether it was an underwater log or large limbs to wedge the boat between. We used cotton sheets to cover the motor and red gas tank, and to break the boat's outline. If we couldn't find an area where the boat would be steady enough, we would stand in the water. Our spot that morning seemed to be just right.

We appeared to be by ourselves in Shirah Flats that morning, a condition very lucky on a Saturday. As another sunrise on the Santee began, we were still by ourselves. I wondered just who or how many would be coming to check out the corn that was less than a hundred yards from our decoys.

A summer duck or two passed over, showing no interest in the area, but it wasn't long before we heard the lonesome, faint quack of a mallard. A flock of four or five flew low, headed up the swamp and, after circling a couple of times, appeared to have gone down several hundred yards above us in the direction of the main Santee River channel. Actually, Shirah Flats contained four or five sloughs running parallel to each other and separated by narrow ridges of land. Each flat after the largest one we were hunting grew smaller, with much cover, but was progressively nearer the river. Once, in later years, I explored the whole place on a higher water level, and found that I could go from one flat to the other, and the last one ran to within a few yards of the Santee riverbank. Mallards liked the security of the smaller and more densely covered sloughs. I had some productive jump shooting in those sloughs with never any sign of another hunter. I did discover a small wooden paddleboat far into these flats and very near the riverbank. It was quite old and appeared to be partially rotten. I believed it had been deserted many years before. Once, on floodwater conditions, my next-door neighbor Steve Morefield, who shared my love of duck hunting, and I floated and pulled my boat from Shirah Flats out to the river. As I remember, we came out across from Buckingham Lake and Landing, which is on the opposite side of the river.

As Dumont and I continued to scan the treetops that cold morning, we saw several pairs of mallards very low that would disappear in other areas of Shirah. Finally, a pair appeared to be headed for our decoys and listening to my calling on the Mallardtone call. They made a half-circle and came to the decoys against the wind. We splashed them easily with Dumont folding the hen as I shot the skying greenhead. My greenhead tumbled over and over as he lost altitude, and fell into a group of dead underbrush near the other side of our flat. I couldn't see him from my vantage point, but I had no doubts he was in that bushy spot. Picking up the hen very nearby, we turned toward where I'd seen the drake fall. Much to our surprise, the mallard was not there, but what we found was the duck's gizzard impaled on a stickup. I have shot down many ducks before and in all kinds of surroundings, but never seen anything like this. The gizzard remained with the mallard's long entrails still attached. The duck evidently had swum away and pulled out everything attached to his gizzard. I followed his feather trail away from the stickup, and soon found him about twenty yards down the ridge with his head resting on the dry bank. As we approached this handsome drake, I felt saddened for his demise.

During my long years of duck hunting, I have had mixed feelings about taking so many from the duck world. It's been over fifty years, as I write this, that I have hunted ducks. I've never missed a season, and I imagine a couple of thousand ducks have fallen to my gun. Every season those misgivings return, though the sport remains strongly within me. The challenge of the swamps, the cold, the mallards listening to my calls, my hunting companions, and the trip itself, keep me going.

As to the mystery of who had put the corn in Shirah Flats, early one morning a week or so after discovering it, we were set up again not far from the baited area. Our boat was covered, the decoys set, and we were awaiting sunrise. My hearing was good back then, and I could hear the birds quacking in the swamp, the wood ducks' whistles, and boat motors a long way off.

That morning, in the darkness, I heard what I thought was a small outboard getting closer. The sound appeared to be coming from the swampy section between us and the Santee River. We were set up in the largest of the flats, as usual. As the minutes ticked away, and that motor kept running, I became convinced that it was possibly headed our way. I knew the way through the several flats that lay between our flat and the river, and it sounded like whoever was coming knew it too. We concluded it just might be the party who had put out the sack of corn we had found at the base of the willow, and that there might be other sacks of corn in other places in the Shirah area. And it just might be the game warden! We laughed about being so foolish and negligent as to get fined for shooting in a baited area. But, if it was the warden, he probably would believe us about being away from the bait . . . as if that would save us some money!

It seemed that the small motor stopped just on the other side of the ridge in front of us. We listened, and we felt that party was listening too. The minutes went by without a sound. We kept watch in the direction of the last sound and never saw anyone. After about ten minutes, the little motor was started. Whoever it was remained invisible to us, but somehow he or they sensed that someone had stumbled upon their corn pile, and they weren't taking any chances. As we sat quietly, without making a sound, the party slowly made their way back the way they had come.

To this day, I don't know who had baited Shirah Flats. Even though I listened to many conversations of other swamp duck hunters, I never heard a clue as to who might have been on the other side of that ridge.

# 9

## Joe Drose, a Santee Hunter

Back in the '50's, I met Joe Drose, owner and operator of Joe's Place on Wyboo Creek, a popular area of Lake Marion. Joe was an avid fisherman and hunter, and helped all who came his way. His family all enjoyed being close to the waters of the Santee lakes, and his three sons were up-and-coming sportsmen like their daddy.

Over years of visiting Joe's Place and fishing out from there, I learned that Joe was an avid duck hunter who had roamed the lake and upper swampy areas long before I did. Now I had another duck-hunting buddy! Joe's knowledge of the lakes and swamps was amazing and he often shared it with me. I could have spent hours listening to him tell of hunting and fishing here and there and, particularly, about places I was familiar with. He was the first person to mention the big swamp to me. This was the area above Pack's Landing on upper Lake Marion near the farming community of Rimini. It was a long way from Wyboo Creek, but it would become the big swamp that I came to love as my duck hunting resumed in South Carolina.

Eventually, I hunted some of Santee's best areas with Joe. We always had fun around Jack's Creek, Cane Branch, Billup's Slough, Tupelo Flat, Persanti Island, the Super Hole and, of course, the Santee Swamp. Joe had hunted them all for years and treasured his experiences and memories. My recollections of him will always be fond ones.

Joe was unique in many ways. For instance, he loved Pepsi Colas and would always carry a twenty-four-bottle crate of Pepsis in his boat. He always told Herman, his loyal helper at his landing, to make sure the Pepsis were on every trip.

Joe's old Chevy pickup was just right for carrying his homemade duck boats to his favorite duck-hunting spots. And his little 5½-horse Evinrude was his favorite for getting around the backwater areas and swamps. The little motor had a two-blade weedless propeller that helped us get into shallow, weedy coves. It was amazing where the 5½ would go that larger motors couldn't. The propeller was the secret, as its blades were shaped and curved like a saber.

Joe knew that Jack's Creek and all its surrounding sloughs and branches would hold ducks. The Summerton refuge was nearby, and most days the ducks would leave it and spread out, but not far away. One of Joe's favorite techniques in this area, and one I adopted later on, was to flush whatever ducks were sitting in the coves and secluded spots, and if there were enough of them, he would set out a few decoys and hide in the natural cover. Joe's favorite duck gun was an old Remington 12-gauge semiautomatic with a 30-inch full-choked barrel, one he would lose years later when his boat overturned. He always used number four shot as we could use lead shot in those days. Joe was a fine shooter, and he could bring ducks down at great distances. My 16-gauge and I were no match for his skill and the big gun he shouldered. He knew that, and would let me have the first shot on many occasions. We didn't spend much time in a spot if the ducks did not return soon enough. We'd open a Pepsi and sip along, but if the ducks were not back by the time Joe had emptied two bottles, we would pick up and hit another spot.

Joe had a special way of opening his Pepsi Cola bottles. He would use the handle-end of his wooden boat paddle to pop the top. Holding the Pepsi in his left hand, he would position the paddle's handle under the edge of the bottle cap and with a motion of leverage with his right hand, snap the paddle's blade-end downward and pop went the bottle top. I had never seen this done before, and never again since hunting with Joe.

Joe stumped his lucky toe way back when he was setting up Joe's Place by hiring a black man named Herman. I believe his last name was Frazier, but he became known just by his first name to the regulars at the landing. Herman was about the friendliest fellow around, and Joe gave him his first job when he was a youngster. I don't think Herman finished grade school, but despite his education, he never lacked the understanding that people like to laugh. And laugh he did! Herman kept everybody in good spirits around Joe's Place not only during the busy fishing season but practically all the time. He made all Joe's customers happy with his good service, his wit, and loyalty to his work.

And when I went hunting with Joe Herman was always laughing and talking and telling jokes on himself and the clientele who visited there. He cheered up any bad situation, and folks loved to listen to Herman's tongue "just-a-waggin' away." He never seemed to get tired of it all and nobody else did either.

Joe and Herman made two small flat-bottom boats for use in the Santee swamp. Their bottoms were thick and stout to handle the stumps and cypress knees, and both could be put into Joe's pickup. Dr. D. O. Winter, of Sumter, South Carolina, loved to hunt the big swamp with Joe, and sometimes they would camp for several days deep into their favorite woods. I remember Joe was quite upset after one camping trip into the Santee Swamp when game wardens went through every piece of his and Dr. Winter's camping gear. Joe said they even unrolled their sleeping bags, searching for over-the-limit ducks. Joe was not a lawbreaker, and the wardens found that out.

Joe enhanced my knowledge of the Santee Swamp over the years. He familiarized me with areas like Catfish Creek, Otter Flats, Pine Island Creek, Broadwater Creek, and Broughton's Mound. Even though we didn't get to hunt all these places together, he relayed his knowledge so vividly I could not help but to learn from just listening. I remember asking him where in the world was the entrance to Pine Island Creek. He laughed and said, "I'll bet you've ridden by it many times, but those cypress trees have a way of keeping it hidden."

I shall always be indebted to Joe for his willingness to share his places with me. He most assuredly played a key role in the years of enjoyment I found in the swamps and sloughs of the Santee.

# *10*

## THE LOST WEEKEND

Being lost, or the more pleasant description, being turned around, is something that has probably happened to most swamp hunters, and is something that can happen easier than one thinks.

My first experience in being really lost happened one Friday afternoon with my brother-in-law, Frank. We had been lucky to have left Sumter about midday that weekend and had planned to hunt that afternoon some place close, and on Saturday move on up the swamp.

Arriving at Sparkleberry Landing in Mother's Ford station wagon, which was to be our shelter for the night, we hurried to get away in time to shoot what we called the afternoon feed flight, and later the roost flight. We had chosen an area off Mill Creek that we had scouted previously. The water level wasn't really high, but appeared to be on the rise. We knew that the acorn tree ridges several hundred yards to the north of Mill Creek would have water on them and that ducks should be using the area. Once before, I had a very productive hunt near the ridges, having taken four huge black ducks from a small pool of dark swamp water.

Leaving Sparkleberry and Mother's wagon, holding all our food and drinks, along with the sleeping bags that would await our return around first night, we struck out for the Mill Creek section of the swamp. The run took about twenty-five minutes. It was about four o'clock when we cut the motor and pulled the little swamp boat out into the floodwater and hid it, partially, in some brush. Finding our way back to it didn't seem to be a problem to either of us.

We were wearing our hip boots and had on our normal amount of warm clothes for walking the ridges. Both of us had small two-cell flashlights in our coats and a box of shells apiece. Frank was toting his big double-barreled 12-gauge and I had my Sweet 16, as usual. We took notice of the cloud cover on our walk away from the boat. I have always thought I had a sort of magic sense of direction and had used it many times going to and coming out of strange places. I certainly was not worried about finding the little boat later that afternoon.

Several hundred yards from where we had left the boat, we came to our first oak ridge. Crossing it, we found water in the flat of cypress trees, and quite a few wood ducks flushed from our noisy intrusion. We had walked maybe twenty to thirty minutes. Frank suggested we stick around to see if other woodies were using the flat near the acorn trees. Wanting to spread out, he walked on down a hundred yards or so from me, and in a minute or two I heard him fire both barrels of the 12-gauge. Woodies were flying out in all directions as Frank had unloaded on them while they were on the water. I didn't know how many he had killed at that time, but knowing Frank's ability with the big gun, I figured he had "put a hurtin'" on them.

The sun had long disappeared behind the cloudy sky, and as I leaned against a large cypress in shallow water, I noticed large flocks of woodies coming down the swamp, probably headed to the big roosting area in front of Pack's Landing. It was not unusual to see several thousand ducks going that way most any afternoon that I was in the big swamp.

Once in a while, I would see some low ducks hurtle down between the trees and into the watery area between Frank and me. I hadn't got a shot yet, but Frank began to burn powder, as the flat seemed to be where several big flocks had disappeared into the now darkened water. As late as it was, I figured I'd better move if I was going to get a shot. No sooner than saying that to myself, several woodies appeared over the low cypress and came into range. I put the Sweet 16 to work, and in five minutes or so bagged several as they came to the flat. Finding them became increasingly difficult with the fading light, and soon I was reaching for my flashlight. Wood ducks are very hard to find in black water flats, especially when darkness is falling. After finding a couple of downed birds, I realized dusk was upon us, and Frank had not come back to where we had split up. I really wasn't too concerned, as we weren't very far from the boat, but Frank was taking too long. By the time I saw his flashlight headed up the water's edge, it was almost dark. I got kind of fussy about him staying too long, but he was pleased he had been able to pick up a handful of woodies.

Dark in the swamp is particularly dark, as the trees shut out the last rays of sunlight much sooner than when you are in a clearing. I told Frank that we needed to get going, and now. There was a little light left, and we tried to get as far toward the boat as we could before the darkness overtook us. I felt that maybe we were about halfway to the hidden boat when complete darkness took over. I kept telling Frank that I felt like we needed to bear to the right a little more as we stumbled over nearly every log and into nearly every spiderweb in the swamp. I was trusting my "magic sense of direction" that I had always relied upon.

Frank didn't argue for another direction, so we kept on even though the flashlights weren't helping much. We decided to use mine and save his, just in case. I couldn't recognize any familiar landmarks, and soon we came to water. I figured it must be the same section of water where we had left our boat. But when we followed the water's edge, we found no boat. The water appeared deeper than we remembered, and was getting too deep for our hip boots. There seemed to be deep water all around us, and about that time I told Frank that I thought we were in trouble as I was completely turned around and my flashlight was now too dim to be of any help. We couldn't be far from our boat, due to the length of time we had walked. Still, water seemed to be everywhere even though we had walked through a lot of dry swamp on the way in just two hours before.

We tried to backtrack using Frank's light, and finding high ground was very difficult. In fact, dry ground looked nonexistent. If it had been during the daytime, I'm sure we could have found our way with ease, but it was pitch black dark. Both of us were getting tired, and it looked like we weren't going to find the boat. I was turned around, for sure, in the flooded and impenetrable Santee swamp. Frank said he had no idea which way to try next. Finally, we stumbled upon a bit of dry ridge and sat down to talk over our dilemma. To put it plainly, we were disgusted with ourselves for waiting so late to start the trek back to the boat, and now we were in a fix! We were tired, hungry, thirsty, and without the slightest notion which way the boat might be. We knew it couldn't be far, but with no light, it may as well have been ten miles. We just could not find the drier swamp we had walked through on the way in. But we did find the small dry ridge we were now resting on, and further investigation with Frank's rapidly dimming flashlight indicated it was bigger than we first believed. We even found some dry limbs and small logs with hopes of starting a fire. Frank was a smoker and, fortunately, had some dry matches. Years before, my Uncle Johnnie had taught me what to do when starting a fire in the swamp.

He always said, "Look for any limbs that are up off the swamp floor, ones that may have lodged in smaller trees as they fell. Dry wood is the key. Never select your wood from the swamp floor. It's always wet."

We gathered the dry limbs and broke them up into a small pile. Using our dry handkerchiefs underneath, we managed to start a small fire. We even raked up some leaves that would burn. The fire made things seem better in a small way, and we kept rounding up all the dry limbs and logs we could find. The flashlight batteries would gain a little strength after they were cut off for a while, allowing us to accumulate a good supply of wood for burning through the night. Staying on the little dry ridge and keeping the small fire ablaze seemed to be our best bet. We believed we had found enough wood to last the night. But the weather didn't cooperate— it started to rain, mostly just a drizzle, but we feared a hard rain would eventually put out our fire. The hard rain never developed, but the drizzle kept up all night.

We managed to keep the little fire going by paying close attention and not letting it get too low on wood. Our hunting clothes were not water repellent, and after several hours we really did need the fire.

The warmth was a big plus, and we felt the swamp animals would keep their distance too. At night in a swamp that big, you wonder just what lives there and roams the darkness. Frank and I imagined all sorts of things as we lay close to the fire. Our minds were certainly playing tricks on us! And, of course, we thought about all that good food back at the landing in Mother's station wagon.

That night was probably the most miserable I've spent outdoors that I can remember. It was even worse than the night many years before when as a boy scout I had participated in a "big camporee" that was held in a baseball stadium in Florence, South Carolina. Small pup tents were our shelter and, of course, we had our sleeping bags on the ground inside our little tents. During the night of the camporee, the weather turned rainy, then gradually got worse and worse as bucketsfull fell all night. The stadium eventually flooded, and the water almost floated the tents and everything in them. We had to retreat, and everyone sought shelter under the stands for the rest of the night. It was a miserable outdoor experience I had not forgotten, but here I was in the wild with all kinds of sounds coming from the darkness, and Frank wondering if any bears still lived in the swamp! Both of us knew that bears had lived there for many years before the great Santee Swamp was flooded. Our imaginations, coupled with spooky sounds coming from all directions, had us reaching for our shotguns and keeping them close. It was a very long, wet night.

---

We were several miles up the swamp from the Rimini train trestle, and I told Frank that when we heard the direction of the train crossing the swamp, we would know which way to go when light came. Finally, we heard the train we had hoped for. But instead of being directed toward Rimini, it sounded as though it ran all the way around us. Several trains came during the night and none of them ever gave us a hint as to which way was up the swamp or which way was down. I thought the train idea was a good one, but it proved to be of no help at all. Frank and I wondered just why the train sounded like it circled the swamp, but we didn't have a clue.

During the long, tense night, we got very little sleep wondering what would be our plan when daylight came. Finally, we agreed that we would get our bearings from the direction of the sunrise. But the weather remained cloudy throughout the night, foiling our plans again. The gray morning brought no recognizable sunrise in any direction, but rather seemed to come from all directions. What a letdown! Frank fussed about my not having brought a compass, and I fussed right back about why he hadn't brought one. My "built-in compass" that had worked so many times in the daylight when I'd never needed the real thing didn't work that night. I told Frank that before coming back into this swamp, the first thing new in my pocket would be a good compass with instructions for its use!

By daylight Saturday morning, we were thoroughly wet and pretty disgusted. But we had stayed safe all night and now, at last, we could get the heck out of the place. Still, the early morning light didn't tell us where we were or which way to go. We could hear the Saturday morning hunters running their boat motors, but they were going in all directions.

There comes a time when you're really lost that your mind just loses its ability to say, "Go this way," or, "Don't cross that flat!" I was at that point of not knowing which way to go, but we had to try some direction. The first thing we did was to leave our harvested ducks and travel as light as possible. We knew they would be eaten by hungry swamp creatures and, therefore, not wasted. It puzzled us that there was so much water and so little dry land where we were. We struck out in a random direction, hoping to catch a glimpse of anything that looked familiar.

It was about seven o'clock that morning when we discarded our ducks. A couple of hours later, we still had not made any progress on finding the boat or, really, finding anything we recognized. We crossed mud flats, cypress flats, and I even climbed several trees in hopes of recognizing something. Climbing trees hadn't been my forte since childhood, but it was worth a try.

By midday we were really and sho-nuff lost, and felt we must have been going in all the wrong directions. The shotguns were getting heavy enough to consider discarding them. My Sweet 16 must have gained twenty pounds, and I was glad it wasn't a twelve. The lack of food and water was taking its toll, even though we were young men in our mid-twenties.

We had crossed flat after flat, never realizing we must have been walking in circles. I'd always heard that was a common fallacy of being lost. One flat we were crossing seemed to have a good number of wood ducks flushing as we sloshed across. Then I noticed a couple of floating shotgun shells near the edge. Retrieving one of the spent shells, I realized it was a 16-gauge shell. Not many duck hunters used 16-gauge shotguns back then, and hardly any today.

As I scanned the area, I discovered there were several more shells very near a large cypress. Could this be where I was shooting the afternoon before? The shells looked like my gauge and my brand. I usually shot Western Super-X sixes. At that very instant, I realized the empty shells were surely the ones I had shot while standing beside the big cypress on the edge of the flat we had just crossed. My Uncle Johnnie was surely right when he said, "Trees are your friends, use them well."

The big cypress and my spent shells gathered my senses, and I said to Frank, "We're not lost anymore. Look, there, at my footprints; and these are my shells. Let's go find the boat and get the hell out of here. I'm hungry and I can taste those hamburgers we're gonna cook shortly."

Finding our little brown boat was easy now, as we both seemed to know the way through the swamp to the spot we had been searching for all morning. It was one o'clock Saturday afternoon when we reached our craft, unlocked the chain, and started the 10-horsepower Johnson. We were two wet and tired duck hunters, but as happy as we could be when, finally, we beached our boat back at Sparkleberry Landing. Mother's Ford wagon was a welcome sight.

# 11

## WATEREE DUCKS

In 1960, I accepted a transfer to Camden, South Carolina, from Liberty Life Insurance Company, a company I'd been working with since 1958. Actually, we rented a small house in Lugoff which is on the opposite side of the river from Camden. Camden is located on the Wateree River and very near Wateree Lake. The Wateree River flows south into the Santee River and is a main source of water, along with the Congaree River, for the Santee Cooper lakes. The Wateree River swamp is where I spent much time with my Uncle Johnnie and where he taught me how to hunt the swamps. Now I was many miles above his home in Eastover and the lakes themselves. Wateree Lake is quite large, and the swamp bordering the river is wide and extends many miles southward before reaching the Santee swamp at the headwaters of Lake Marion.

I soon learned where to fish and hunt. The fellows in the office there were always contributing their secrets to me and taking me with them. I had only one hunting season in the Lugoff area, but I have some fond memories of that time.

One unusual hunt I had involved a very small body of water in a hog pasture bordering the Wateree. I was searching for places to hunt ducks, and a policyholder of mine mentioned that ducks sometimes came in to his pasture to a small mud hole, or hog wallow. I couldn't imagine ducks sitting with hogs in the same mud hole. But, one Friday afternoon after work, I went by the farm and walked to the pasture. The hole of muddy water was probably forty yards long and not as wide, but sitting in one end of it were a dozen or so mallards. They, of course, promptly left. At first I couldn't figure why they were there, but after walking down to where they flushed, I saw why. The farmer was feeding his hogs with ear corn, and hogs being messy eaters, there was much corn around on the ground.

I was quite excited at the prospect of shooting some greenheads, but in surveying how I should go about it, realized that there was little or no cover in the pasture, particularly near the smelly hog wallow. But what there was, was broom sedge growing all around the pasture. These small patches of broom sedge could be put to good use. With Carolyn's help, we attached quite a bit of broom sedge to a burlap cotton sheet using needle and thread. The cotton sheet was big enough to cover me completely when lying down.

I was up early Saturday morning with my homemade camouflage and my 16-gauge, and I arrived at the pasture in plenty of time to check the wind direction and get set. I really didn't know what time of day the mallards used the area, or even if they would come back. But early morning is usually tops.

The sun was just waking up the world with the promise of a little daylight showing, when something flew low over the pasture. In those days, I could hear the duck wings and chatter. In later years, I lost that ability due to poor hearing that seems to run in our family. I had positioned myself facing the slight wind and was lying on my side with the sheet covering me. Ducks realize readily that something is different most of the time, and I didn't figure my camouflage would hold my concealment but a few minutes at best. But a few minutes was all I needed. A small flock backpedaled and lit in the middle of the little hog wallow before I could react.

They had not seen me, and I didn't move except to look out the corner of my eyes. Moments later, another larger bunch came across from the direction of the river and "slooshed" the water closer. Even as early as it was, I could make out that they were all big mallards, and it seemed every one of them sensed my presence. Their heads atop stretched necks all looked my way. My positioning had worked, and with a quick move to a sitting position, the sixteen spoke three times. The first shot was for the biggest greenheads I could see, and the next two were at the fleeting wings beating skyward in the very early dawn. There must have been twenty or so real surprised ducks that morning, of which four lay on the water. The others headed for the river with not a feather ruffled.

Of course, I was tickled that my plan had worked. The breeze eased the birds over to the edge where I easily gathered them, and after folding my broom straw-covered burlap and tying a string around the whole bundle, I headed across the pasture. Looking back toward the river, the sun was just beginning to show and I could see the wood ducks going to the acorn flats they love.

My friend, the farmer, had risen early and greeted me with a smile. With my thanks, I handed him three mallards, and I kept one. That big greenhead still graces my home, as I had him mounted. As I pass him from time to time, I remember when I would and could do most anything to get a shot like that. And that was forty years ago.

There was a creek that flowed into the Wateree River not far from our house in Lugoff. I believe the name of it was Twelve and Twenty Creek, and the wooded area bordering it had some small and shallow flats that held water when the creek flooded. I learned that wood ducks used this creek often. I used to follow a woods road down to the creek and would hunt the creek itself for woodies feeding on the acorns. Uncle Johnnie had taught me how to hunt ducks in the creeks and flats by sneaking along and "out-looking" the feeding ducks, or seeing them before they see you, something I did for years in the Santee Swamp.

Twelve and Twenty Creek had high banks which made it easier to "sneak." Some Saturdays, when in need of a close place to hunt, I would visit Twelve and Twenty Creek. Remembering other hunts in similar conditions, I began to explore the creek bank for oak trees. The oaks that year seemed to have lots of acorns, and I knew the ducks would find them if they were near the creek bank. One area I remember had several sizeable oaks near the creek bank, and some of their limbs hung over the water. I hunted the area several times and took a couple of woodies each trip. They soon became more cautious, and the slightest sound would start them swimming downstream at full speed.

The creek, as it made its way toward the Wateree River, made an abrupt horseshoe bend just below the ducks' favorite oak trees. One morning there must have been six or eight woodies feeding, as usual. I had crawled to the edge and could see the movement in the water, a telltale sign I always was alert to. But, anxious to see just how many were there, I made the mistake of getting too close. The wood ducks, always on the watch for danger, sensed something that started them on their way downstream. Several colorful drakes were leading the flock, and I felt they would make the horseshoe bend in a couple of minutes. Hoping they would, and that I could beat them at their own retreat, I hurried through the wooded area toward the downstream side of the creek bend. I positioned myself behind a tree large enough to hide me and waited to see if my hunch was right. My wait was short as the whole bunch was swimming as fast as they could, and with the current helping, they would soon be less than forty yards from where I was hidden.

The drakes had led the getaway and all had followed. To their surprise, I had outsmarted them, and made only one shot precisely when the three drakes were close. The load of number sixes took care of two in short order, leaving them on their backs with feet kicking toward the sky.

That winter turned out to be fairly cold, and my constant success on wood ducks at Twelve and Twenty kept me close to home most weekends. One Friday night, after looking at a cold weather forecast, I decided to hunt the area again. I knew the cold would have the ducks using the running water. What I didn't realize was that the shallow flats near the creek would freeze so quickly.

Arriving at the turnoff to the little woods road leading to my parking spot, I heard the icy mud puddles beneath my car's tires. Sure enough, there would be ice on the flats before I got to the creek bed, and this would make sneaking more difficult. I always dress for hunting before leaving home, even my hip boots, so I'm warm when I get out of the car. I never bought a pair of waders until much later in my hunting years. They were cumbersome and I always felt they were cold. For walking the woods and shallow flats, hip boots were my favorite.

I knew the area pretty well, even in the dark, and needed only a small flashlight to arrive at the little flat I always crossed en route to the oak tree area. It was still very early when I broke the ice on the edge and realized the night had been cold enough to freeze the entire flat. So I waited for some daylight before proceeding to the creek. I figured that, surely, the ducks would sense the flats were frozen and light in the running water of Twelve and Twenty Creek.

I always toted my 16-gauge Browning on my right arm and kept my hands in my coat pockets against the cold. The trigger guard was shaped just right for carrying the gun, as it didn't slip down over my arm and into the water or mud. As I stood in the icy flat and leaned against a cypress, out of nowhere and with practically no daylight to see by, a drake wood duck flew in and hit the frozen flat. I never saw him coming, except for a blur as he hit the ice. He slid across the icy flat and stopped, maybe six or seven feet from me. Neither one of us was expecting the other in that early light, so we just remained motionless. The tree I was leaning on and my dark clothing must have matched, so the duck stayed put. I noticed he began to shuffle his feet in the realization that he had definitely come to the wrong place, and as he turned away from me and attempted to walk on the ice, I managed to slowly move my hands to my gun, and with it at my side, moved the safety to off. With a calculated guess for aim, I pulled the trigger. The load caught the top of his head and a whole lot of icy water just in front of him.

I have since told this story many times, and none of my South Carolina duck-hunting acquaintances has ever experienced anything quite like this. And I never have since.

# 12

# A Cold Day
# on the Pee Dee

In 1961, Carolyn and our two children and I found ourselves in Florence, South Carolina. We had again accepted a transfer from Liberty Life. My position was the same as in Camden, that of staff manager. Florence was a larger office though, and I was supposed to gain some experience under the very successful manager there.

We had a tough time finding a suitable place to live and really didn't get settled for several months. Finally, we found a nice little house on Sewanee Drive and stayed there until my promotion to district manager of the Walterboro office in April of 1963.

During the two years in Florence, I shot a lot of doves on organized dove shoots, and improved my shooting skill with every season. I seemed to be on the way to better shooting while in Camden, and I continued improving in Florence. Dove shoots were easy to find, and I took in many during each season. But when duck season came around, the doves took a back seat. I was back and forth to the Santee lakes and swamp on weekends. Many times I invited other duck hunters to accompany me to my favorite spots in the swamps. Also, we hunted the Jack's Creek area frequently. Line Island, Billup's Slough, Cane Branch, Tupelo Flat, and Persanti Island were some other great spots we hunted.

During our stay in Florence, my Uncle Johnnie Zeigler died. I was heartbroken, as we had spent so much time together, with him giving freely of his knowledge of the swamp and his skills in locating the ducks and attaining the limits. Aunt Lula gave me his old 12-gauge shotgun and his boat, which I brought back to Florence. I had to keep water in the boat in order to keep the wood swollen and reduce the leaks. The boat didn't get much use, and in later years I gave it to my brother who put it in a pond in Sumter, South Carolina.

While I still had it, though, the old boat and I had one memorable hunt in Florence. The hunt occurred during a very cold spell that hit our area, when nighttime temperatures fell below ten degrees. The extreme cold lasted three days, and it was on that third day that I made my move.

The big Pee Dee River runs very near Florence, and I had heard several good reports about duck hunting in the lakes off the main river channel. A friend who had dove hunted with me many times wanted to go, but he had to get back for a meeting in the afternoon. We agreed a half day of cold would probably be enough, and so we made plans to get off for the morning.

The little swamp landing we knew about wasn't far from a lake off the channel. When we arrived about midmorning no one was at the landing, and no cars, either. That pleased us right off, and what we found after launching and going upstream pleased us too. After entering the lake, we couldn't believe what we were hearing. Ducks were quacking in the distant corner of the lake, and it sounded like a pile of them! We couldn't see what was going on since the lake curved, but we could hear all those quacks and felt that the lake was loaded with mallards. Most of the lake in front of us was frozen over, so we figured the ducks had come in the day before and had kept some water open by their constant paddling. What we discovered, after sneaking through the woods and staying well away from the water, was about twenty-five mallards holding some water open in the middle of the lake. They had done a good job of it and were well out from the bank and any cover that would allow us a chance of getting closer. They were simply too far for a shot on the water. We had no way of getting closer without spooking the rowdy bunch. They were having such a great time that we were amused just watching. However, to stand still very long in the severe cold and watch ducks we could not get to was not our intention, so we went back to the boat empty-handed.

My partner was already chilled to the bone, as he didn't have the heavy clothes a duck hunter needs. Soon he made it known that he could no longer stand the cold, so I took him back to the little landing and the car. He would take the boat trailer with him back to Florence and telephone my wife about picking me up later in the day. So he left for warmer surroundings, and I really wished that I had too. I wasn't sure what I'd do next and didn't think I could stand the cold very much longer.

I made the decision to spend the time before my wife came back on the running river. The water level was high, and I figured there would be some ducks in the cover near the banks and in the willow shoals. Uncle Johnnie and I had drifted the Wateree many times while hunting the shoals using the same technique. On a cold day like this one the ducks always took to the running water, and he knew it.

Slowing my little Johnson motor to an idle, I moved closer to the river's edge. Approaching a willow shoal just down the river, I shut off the motor and put my paddle to work steering the old boat nose-first with the current. My gun made ready and across my lap, I prepared myself for anything that might be sitting in the willows. At first I thought the willows were empty, but as I neared the last few trees mallards exploded and tried to get airborne through the thick limbs. My 16-gauge did its job, as usual, and a pair of mallards floated downstream.

The idea when floating the river was to be quiet and stay close to the inside bends. The eddy pockets behind the willow shoals usually held the ducks, and this was certainly true that day on the Pee Dee. I continued to float, and it seemed as if all the ducks from the river's frozen swampy areas had come to the running water. I had never seen so many, as nearly every willow shoal had ducks. Sometimes as many as twenty to thirty would flush as I approached. They were reluctant to leave their cover, and I passed up many opportunities at easy shots. I never saw another boat and heard none in the distance.

Within an hour my uncle's technique and the old boat had proved themselves again, for on the floor was another limit of greenheads, one of many the old boat transported out of my uncle's Wateree Swamp.

The ride back up the river was very cold, and I moved along slowly, savoring the day's success. I didn't see another person until I reached the out-of-the-way landing. Carolyn was waiting with the car and trailer, and I knew some welcome heat would soon thaw my frozen feet and hands. It had been a record cold day for me, but one to remember, for sure. That very cold day in Florence was the only occasion I ever hunted on the Pee Dee River.

# 13

## LOWCOUNTRY DUCKS

I was pleasantly surprised and, of course, pleased that in April of 1963 Liberty Life Insurance Company promoted me to district manager. This was something I had worked toward since my employment. Moving my family was always hard, but this move was what we had hoped for. Of course, we didn't know much about Walterboro, South Carolina, itself, or Colleton County, but I did know the office there had never been very productive, and the company wanted me to change that.

Also, I felt the Walterboro area would provide some fine opportunities for my two outdoor loves, hunting and fishing; I was getting back a little closer to my Santee Cooper. I never dreamed that the national pastime in Walterboro was hunting and fishing, and that they blew a whistle on Wednesday at noontime which meant "it's time to go." They even rolled up the sidewalk on Main Street when the whistle sounded. I soon found out that newcomers were readily accepted, and the fact that I quickly made it known that I loved their "national pastime" afforded me many invitations on hunts and fishing trips. One big problem, if you can call it a problem, was that there were so many good places to hunt and fish that deciding where to go became a chore. But the local sportsmen kept up with where the activity was.

At first, I didn't have much time for recreation because my immediate need was finding some new manpower in the form of new agents. It required some extensive effort to get the three people that I needed. The economy of Colleton County at that time was relatively poor, and it was said that over half the men working and living in Walterboro had jobs in Charleston, South Carolina. That meant they traveled over forty-five miles one way to get to work. After several weeks, I realized that the opinion of many was that one could not make a living in the insurance business in Walterboro.

The entire economy was poor due to the lack of industry. I had to change that notion with the first new agents I hired.

When I assumed my new duties in the Walterboro office, I found that the previous manager, who had been there for many years, had definitely let the office deteriorate, and getting it turned around would not be easy. I was fortunate in several ways to have an enthusiastic young man transferred in from our Georgetown office to be my assistant, or staff manager. Robert Thompkins had been a successful agent in Georgetown and knew the Liberty system quite well. He would be a great asset to our operation and was willing to work shoulder to shoulder with me in order to get our office on a productive basis. And another thing, he was an avid hunter and fisherman! He loved the outdoors as I did. We became great friends as we worked together. As usual with my friends, I eventually gave him a nickname. Robert became "Mr. T." after we began hunting together. I soon learned that he could handle his shotgun quite well.

We were introduced to some duck hunting areas around Colleton County, but we were more attracted to the salt marsh out of Bennett's Point, having learned about this from some of our policyholders who lived in that area.

There was an island near Bennett's Point known as Seabrook Island. There was no electricity or modern conveniences on the island despite the fact that a dozen or more families were living there. Their livelihood came from crabbing and fishing, and most of them had insurance coverage with Liberty Life. Robert and I had to take a boat over to the island monthly to collect premiums; there wasn't even a bridge. But this was a situation that we had inherited and it had to be changed, and it eventually was. However, going to Bennett's Point and going to Seabrook Island exposed to us some hunting areas that had no equal.

Another area that we hunted and enjoyed very much was below the steel bridge that crosses the Combahee River on Highway 17, near Gardens Corner, South Carolina. The duck hunting we did there was different from any I had ever done, but was very productive.

Just before moving to Walterboro from Florence, I bought a small boat, twelve feet long with a fish box in the middle. My outboard motor at that time was a 1960 5½-horsepower Johnson. I always used Johnson motors in those days because they were reliable, and I trusted them to bring me home under all conditions. Over the years, I purchased twenty-three Johnson motors and enjoyed most of them. Now though, I run Yamaha outboards as they seem to be one of the most reliable on today's market.

The twelve-footer was made by Carolina Boat Company in Lumberton, North Carolina. It cost me sixty-five dollars new and was shaped like your typical small pond boat, being widest in the middle and narrower at the back and front for easy paddling. The 5½-horse Johnson weighed sixty pounds and was just right for the little boat. With two aboard and equipment, it still moved along adequately, though it would not plane off, as it wasn't designed to. Previously, Daddy and I had used it some for small-water fishing, which he enjoyed. The fish box would fill with water, and it did a good job of keeping alive the small fish that we caught.

My first duck hunts on the Combahee River were during Thanksgiving week of 1963. I hunted by myself several times and used a few decoys in the edge of the river, with the boat hidden by the marsh grass. I never did bag any big ducks in the river, only divers such as ring-necked ducks, ruddy ducks, etc.

The good ducks, as I would call them, were all settled in the rice fields of the plantations, where duck food was plentiful. The old plantation fields where rice was grown many years before had been bought up by the wealthy folk for their duck hunting. All around the Combahee were old rice fields that held mallards, pintails, and wigeon. They very seldom left the fields except early each morning when some would fly toward the big saltwater marshes down the Combahee. Getting a chance at these ducks leaving the fields wasn't easy, as they left quite early. Usually I would arrive at the steel bridge before daylight and be on my way down the river as the new hunting day began. I enjoyed sunrises and was always eager to see the early-light flight. The Longbrow Plantation lights were usually on Saturday mornings, which meant some shooting would be forthcoming from their massive old rice fields and the ducks would be on the move.

After hiding my boat in the grassy river's edge, I would walk up on the plantation's dike for just a peek, being careful not to be seen. My favorite hiding spot on the dike featured a few low, thick bushes just on the marsh edge of their dike; and I had noticed this particular spot was close to the flight line for ducks leaving Longbrow. Some mornings, ducks would be low enough for a shot, but usually they were just out of range of my 16-gauge.

I had harvested a wood duck or two from behind these bushes, always being careful to shoot only once or twice each visit. I certainly didn't have money to pay for trespassing, so I stayed where I could quickly get back through the marsh grass to my boat; I even tried to pick up my empty shells each time.

Longbrow's fields always had ducks in those years and particularly seemed to attract a large flight of pintails. During my hunting years, I had not had many pintail opportunities and, to this day, I guess pintails would be close to the fewest of my duck harvest. I had taken many large mallards and blacks, but I had the desire to get a pintail to go with the big green-head that I had mounted in 1960. And it was from this Longbrow hiding place that I got the opportunity I had wished for.

In the early light I saw a flock of about twenty large ducks coming from the plantation property. At first, I wasn't sure what they were, and even if they would offer me a shot. As I peered from behind my bushes, the ducks were staying lower than flights I had seen on other Saturday mornings. Maybe, just maybe, if they passed over they would be close enough. On they came, and it now seemed that they were coming straight toward my spot, and they appeared to have the long, white look of pintails. Sure enough, they were big pintails and they were forming their flight formation as they came. Their leader was a big white drake, but they were gaining altitude as they recognized the river in front of them. My spirits sank. I figured they would be too high, as usual. The Sweet 16 would do only so much, and I hated to cripple beautiful ducks. But just as they came within a few yards of being almost straight over me, I could see that the lead bird was, indeed, a trophy. Almost instinctively, I mounted the 16, pulled out about five feet in front of him, and pulled the trigger, only once. The bird sort of flinched, but continued flying for a few seconds. Turning to watch him, I saw the big white bird slowly, but surely, lose altitude as he glided over the river. Had a lucky pellet hit him just right? He continued to glide, then folded and hit the wide-open river behind. My distant shot had been true, and I hurried through the marsh and to the boat. Coming close, I found the beautiful, but downed, pintail lying stretched out on the Combahee's black water. I was kind of sad that he had not been able to continue on with his flight mates, but one pellet had struck him under his chin. I paid J. M. Singleton's Taxidermy in Sumter twelve dollars to mount him for me, as Mr. Singleton had mounted my mallard in 1960 for ten dollars.

The mallard I took from the hog pasture just off the Wateree River in Camden and the Combahee pintail are the only ducks I've ever had mounted. They continue to grace my home in Orangeburg.

Later on, I learned that mallards and black ducks liked to frolic in the brackish water creeks that ran through the marshes surrounding the plantation property, and they seemed to seek refuge there when the plantations shot their fields heavily. It was in these small creeks that Mr. T. and I enjoyed paddling and drifting into the small backwaters where these big ducks would seek refuge. This technique I learned by myself when I realized the area below the steel bridge was affected by the tide. In fact, when fishing or hunting Colleton County's many freshwater streams, the tide, which affected them all, had to be considered before every trip.

At first, I saw ducks lighting out in a marshy area that I knew nothing about. So, my curiosity being active most of the time, particularly about ducks, I set out to find how I might get into the marsh areas bordering the big river. About a mile down the Combahee from the bridge where I launched my boat, I learned that most of the property on the right belonged to the DuPont family, and the property on the left, which was public marsh, belonged to Longbrow Plantation. I never learned who owned Longbrow. The river in that section took a long, slow bend to the right forming a very large horseshoe. Within that horseshoe lay more DuPont property. I took note that part of it was diked in, and I considered it private. I had always heard that if a creek ebbs and flows, entering it is not considered trespassing. There were several small creek openings on the right going down the river, and after a few trips, I decided to explore them with my little boat.

To my pleasant surprise, the little creeks, some twenty feet wide and some only wide enough to get the boat through, were loaded with mallards and black ducks. I would drift in with the tide when it was moving, and paddle some too. Being very quiet and patient, I surprised many flocks of big ducks in these very small, out-of-the-way creeks. My system was simple, but effective. I sat on the boat's fish box, my 16-gauge Browning lying across the front seat within easy reach, and proceeded slowly. Most of the time, I would know there were ducks in front of me because of the slightest ripples on the water. They would be feeding or just loafing up in the marsh grass, particularly around the intersections of other creeks. Often I was as close as twenty to thirty yards away when they flushed. My gun was fast and deadly as I took many mallards and blacks from the little creeks within that big river bend. I even picked up a few saltwater mink on the low tides while in those same creeks. A friend in Walterboro wanted those.

When I introduced Mr. T. to this method during our first year in Walterboro, we were just beginning to hunt together; it was our first of many duck seasons. Mr. T.'s personal shotgun was a 12-gauge 30-inch full-choke Browning semiautomatic, the big brother to my Sweet 16. He had been using it to shoot wood ducks as they crossed the trees in the swamps around Georgetown. It was not ideally suited for our close jump shooting, as it was heavier and had a tight shooting choke for long range. So we just used my 16-gauge and took turns paddling and shooting. The twelve-foot boat was just ideal for the protected marsh hunting.

After several trips hunting the marsh, Mr. T. and I had learned every foot of the big bend of the Combahee and had worked up a route through the many creeks that, eventually, came out on the opposite side. We would enter according to the tide flow, and sometimes the wind direction dictated which side we entered. We were the only hunters in the area, even though we hunted on Saturdays. It was great to have a place like this and not have to be concerned about other hunters being around the next bend. And, of course, we kept on exploring farther down the river. There were many more creeks down below and toward what was called the "Salt Break," but fewer big ducks. The marsh and creeks got larger and quite a bit more dangerous.

On one trip, after spending a lot of time down there, we saw a most unusual incident regarding a black duck. After visiting most of the area that day without much luck, we motored out of a small creek and into a larger one on the way home. We stopped to ponder where all the ducks had gone, and while discussing why the marsh seemed so empty, we noticed something floating our way. Whatever it was, was floating out with the tide and getting closer to us. Continuing to stare, we could not believe what we were seeing. It was clearly a large black mallard that had smartly climbed onto a board and was floating along, getting a restful ride down the creek. I guess I've seen some unusual and strange things in the wild, but never a black duck riding a board. Clever, to say the least. Mr. T. and I had a good laugh about that one.

Another incident to laugh about occurred on a foggy morning, going down the Combahee with my brother-in-law, Lanny Turner. Lanny lived in North Augusta, South Carolina, and had married my sister, Betty, a few years before. We had hunted ducks together several times in Pocotaligo Swamp, near Sumter. Most of the shooting there was pass-shooting wood ducks as they crossed the trees. Lanny was an excellent shot at long range and took many woodies from the swamp, along with me and my younger brother, John. We had also shot doves coming to water and to roost at his family's farm in Florence.

Lanny was a big person, and my twelve-foot boat was just large enough for him in the front. Seeing around him wasn't easy; I knew I had to be careful and avoid any adverse wind or water conditions we might confront. So we were proceeding down the river slowly, in the foggy early morning light, when I noticed something in the water in front of us. Getting a little closer, I could see that it was a deer swimming the river, and it was probably about halfway across. Lanny saw it right away and shouted, "It's a buck!" The deer season was in, but the law forbids molesting a deer while it is in the water. I asked Lanny if he would like to shoot and, if so, we would ride as close to him as we could at precisely the time the deer would be climbing the riverbank he was headed for.

Both of us had only shells for ducks, but Lanny's gun was a 12-gauge semiautomatic, handed down from his father. We both knew the old gun sometimes malfunctioned, but Lanny put three shells in it and was ready. The deer hit the bank at full speed and we were no more than twenty yards away when he did. I'm certain Lanny contracted "buck fever" about then, because every shot he made was over the deer's back. I really think only a couple of pellets from the old 12-gauge hit the deer. He disappeared into the marsh in seconds, apparently unhurt.

I teased Lanny so much that day about his great shooting that he bellowed out that he was tired of shooting that old gun and was going to buy a new one. And where could he find a bargain? I just happened to know a friend who had a practically new Browning 12-gauge semiautomatic, and I knew he wanted to sell it.

Lanny and I went to see the gun that night. It was exceptional in that the bluing on its metal surfaces was dark and deep, one of the prettiest I had seen on a Browning. The gun had nice wood and a Whiteline recoil pad on its stock. Also, a ventilated poly choke had been installed at the factory. Lanny fell in love with it and gave my friend one hundred dollars for it. On the way back to my house, Lanny began ribbing me about my just wanting to get him down to Walterboro to spend a bunch of money on a new gun. He still owns the gun and has never bought another. The Browning looks today the same as it did in 1963 when he carried it home.

My boat was definitely not safe in the open water, and we didn't take many chances when the wind was up. I had plenty of respect for the wind, especially once when by myself at the Salt Break area. I had found an open flooded area in front of a plantation house that was holding some ducks, and one morning I decided to do something different while hunting alone. I carried a dozen inflatable Deek decoys that I had bought while living in Kansas. Deeks would inflate when dropped on the water, and I had used them many times in protected water. But this open area proved to be their downfall.

I had put out all twelve in an open area near a spot where I could hide the boat. The marsh grass was tall enough to afford me good cover, and I had set up to wait for the big ducks that would come from the plantations shortly after daylight. My plans were to stay a short time and then hunt back upriver in my usual area. The wind wasn't bad early, but soon it freshened and came in directly from the big area below me. And in minutes the place was whitecapping. It didn't take long for me to unload the gun, put on my life jacket, and wonder just how I was going to go back upriver to safer conditions. The big creek and open area looked treacherous for my little boat. The sides were low, and I didn't have enough motor to get the boat up on top. Fortunately, the tide was fairly high, and I figured I might be able to ride in the river's protective marsh grass, which would break some of the rough water action.

By the time I readied myself for travel, I noticed my Deeks being blown over by the now stronger wind, which caused them to deflate. The Deeks were now being lost, as several had already sunk. Those that didn't sink were being blown across the five-foot-deep Salt Break toward bigger water. As I made an attempt to grab a couple, waves dumped into my low-sided stern. Realizing my peril, and becoming extremely worried, I turned the little boat and left the few decoys that hadn't gone down. The conditions were frightening, I must admit. I really didn't know whether I could stay afloat in such circumstances. But the 5½-horse Johnson never faltered as I bucked the whitecapping waves and road the edge of the grass that led back toward the river. I really don't know just how I managed to retreat like I did. My guardian angel must have been watching that morning and showed me the way.

I was several miles down the Combahee that morning and presumed I was by myself again. On the way back up the river, I rode the very edge of the marsh grass and sometimes in the grass itself, as out in the river the water was whitecapping like the Salt Break I had left. The propeller on the Johnson was a weedless design which was a blessing under those grassy conditions. A scared, tired, wet, cold, but thankful duck hunter ran the car's heater for a while before loading and heading home.

The duck season of 1963–64 was the only time I hunted the Combahee at the steel bridge, as the very next year every creek on the big horseshoe bend was diked off. I suppose it had been planned for some time by the owners. I was fortunate to have enjoyed the freedom when I did.

TOP: JMR's grandfather, W. S. Reynolds Sr. (standing), fishing for redbreast from the bank of the Black River near Bishopville, S.C., 1910. The man in the dugout canoe is unidentified.

Uncle Johnnie Zeigler (right) and Jim Harmon, both of Eastover, S.C., with 45-lb. striped bass (rockfish) caught from the Wateree River in the 1950s

LEFT: JMR and South Carolina governor Richard Riley proclaiming October 21, 1979, as Duck Calling Day in South Carolina

TOP: The Reynolds brothers, John (left) and J. M., with a nice catch from Lake Marion

Cajun, our chocolate Labrador, hiding out under camouflage netting

TOP: Cajun watches from a favorite cypress near Line Island on Lake Marion.

John Jackson, longtime hunting companion, with our limit of ringneck ducks

TOP: JMR (right) and Liberty Corporation CEO Francis Hipp, after their productive morning at the Santee Gun Club

JMR wins the Sneak Boat, a prize to remember, at the South Carolina Duck Calling Championship, 1978.

TOP: The houseboat—a home away from home—floats in a cypress thicket in upper Lake Marion.

Theodore, JMR's guide for the day, on a hunt at Santee Gun Club near McClellanville, S.C. Behind him are the marsh of Murphy Island and the canal leading to Hoyt Stand, Theodore's favorite pothole.

TOP: JMR's son Jay set up this open water blind on Lake Marion, not far from Santee State Park.

JMR's hunting buddies Jay and Drake

TOP: Foggy scene on the lake

JMR with friends in Arkansas, 1979

A happy twosome: JMR, and Drake enjoying another sniff of the ducks just retrieved

TOP: From Jay's blind, another sunrise over Persanti Island

Too early to shoot

TOP: View down Lake Marion from atop the houseboat

Low water in the Santee Swamp

TOP: Time out for Cajun

JMR (left) and Robert Thompkins, a longtime hunting partner, with a limit of mallards from Bank Creek, their favorite spot on Hutchinson Island near Bennett's Point

# 14

## St. Helena Sound

There's a little highway known locally as Green Pond Road that leaves Walterboro and runs southerly through the small farming communities of Ritter and Green Pond, and into Highway 17. A short mile or so from there is a narrow paved road that turns toward the coastal marshes and travels through picturesque woodlands belonging to wealthy plantation owners. Deer once roamed there more freely than any place I knew. They seemed to be carefree, and in the early morning hours would stand and look as my hunting partner and I made our way across creeks, marshes, and on to the Ashepoo River. Once, as we were crossing that river's bridge, a doe ran just in front of our car and across the bridge, only to disappear in the Bear Island marsh. It was a wild, woodsy road, and I traveled along it many times from 1963 to 1974. My hunting companion, for the most part, was my longtime friend, Robert Thompkins.

Each morning as we passed Bear Island, a state-owned public duck-hunting area, we were always pleased to see lights piercing the darkness across their marsh. Those lights suggested a duck hunt was planned for that day, and we knew that meant their hunt would move some ducks to the public salt marsh we were headed toward. Just a few miles past Bear Island the paved road ended, and a small dirt parking lot completed our early morning drive. We had arrived at Bennett's Point. There were a few small houses around the parking lot area occupied by the men and women who made their living on the salt water. Sometimes a shrimp boat was docked there, but in the early hours we were usually the only duck hunters at the landing. A fresh water pump was nearby from which the residents drew their water supply. It was a primitive corner of Colleton County.

The first time I ever put a boat in at Mosquito Creek was with a friend of mine, Joel Padgett. The landing on the creek was the only one at Bennett's

Point, but it was the entrance to some salt marshes that provided splendid but hazardous duck hunting.

The wide Ashepoo River met the creek at Bennett's Point and flowed down and around Hutchinson Island and then into St. Helena Sound. Hutchinson Island, very large and marshy, seemed to be a converging area for ducks leaving the various plantations' fields back inland. They flew over it on the way to the sound where, if water was not too rough, they would raft up until late in the day. I have seen them in such great numbers on the sound that it was as if one could walk across the water on their backs. Many thousands of mallards, black ducks, and pintails would visit the area on a duck day, when the cold and wind were just right.

Joel Padgett was my next door neighbor in Walterboro. We lived in Forest Hills on Shamrock Road. Both of us were young and trying to get a start in business. Joel grew up in Walterboro and loved to hunt. He was proficient with a shotgun, which he proved many times on dove shoots with me.

I recall one unusual dove shoot he and I enjoyed in the Bennett's Point area. The shoot was held on some of the D. D. Dodge property just across Mosquito Creek and was accessible by a small bridge at that time. Joel knew the Baldwin family who were caretakers of the massive Dodge acreage, and our invitation came through them. The big dove shoot was held on New Year's Day near the end of the South Carolina dove season, and usually the temperatures at that time of year were quite cold. But this New Year's was much warmer than usual and brought out quite a few sportsmen from the Walterboro area, many of whom I had met since moving there. Of course Joel knew nearly every eager shooter, and we exchanged duck-hunting tales while waiting for the go-ahead to enter the nearby corn-field that was being buzzed by flocks of full-grown, late-season doves. I couldn't help but wonder why everyone was being detained with that many birds already helping themselves to the spilled corn left on the field. My mind wandered to a similar shoot a year or so before where all the guests were enjoying a lowcountry barbeque dinner and, at the same time, the doves were filling their craws. When we finally did enter the field, hundreds of doves left and not the first one returned. I certainly hoped that wouldn't happen again this day, and it didn't.

The cornfield was enormous, and from the looks of things there wasn't a bad stand anywhere. The shoot sounded like a small war as the warm afternoon seemed to put the birds into high gear. Shotguns were swinging, and I'm sure the ammunition companies were smiling.

As the shooters filled their vests and limited out or ran out of shells, they left the field either proud of their shooting or repeatedly embarrassed by the little gray speedsters. I noticed a group gathering around a patrolman's car that I had seen parked previously. So when Joel came my way I inquired as to what might be going on. Joel said, "Let's go see." By the time we crossed the field there must have been two dozen folks around the patrol car. We were really inquisitive by then.

To our surprise, stretched out on the hood of that car was the largest rattlesnake I had ever seen, and right in the middle of his head was one large bullet hole. We learned that a well-known South Carolina highway patrolman who worked the Colleton County area had joined us on the shoot soon after his off-duty hours began. Cutter Ackerman was everybody's friend in that neck of the woods and quite a sportsman, too. Cutter had walked up on the big snake in our dove field and used his .38-caliber pistol quite accurately! He had brought the snake out and mounted it on the still-warm hood of his patrol car. As we all marveled at the snake's size, it continued to move as if it intended to crawl off the car's hood. Finally, one of the brave ones standing around said he wanted to measure the low-country monster and did so with a tape from the storage box on his pickup truck. The rattler was slightly over six feet long, including his long string of rattles. His body was as massive as a muscle-man's forearm, and his head looked to be nearly three inches wide.

To see snakes roaming their territory in midwinter is a rarity. We surmised that this warm day in January had brought the big fellow out of hibernation only to meet his fate in our cornfield. I have remembered to this day that in South Carolina snakes will become somewhat active on warm winter days.

One Friday night Joel came over and said that the plantations were shooting and we ought to be in the marsh the next morning. Of course, I didn't know which marsh he was referring to, but I didn't question that. Little did I know that this would be the beginning of many hunts on Hutchinson Island. Our hunt that day wasn't very successful, as Joel didn't really know the marsh too well in the dark. We never did find the spot in Two Sisters Creek that he was looking for. But he showed me how to hunt the marsh that day and how to use palmetto fans from the abundant native palmetto trees as blind material around the boat. Many ducks were flying that day, but to other spots in the marsh. Joel wasn't keen on going to a whole lot of trouble when hunting ducks, as his numerous connections with owners of private land afforded him much easier hunting. As I recall, we never hunted the marsh again together. We continued to shoot doves together though, and did have a terrific duck hunt in Sampson Island Creek a year later.

The next opportunity to hunt the salt marsh was with Marion Sams that same season. Marion and I had been acquaintances at Clemson College from 1952 to 1956. I remembered his home was in Walterboro and I looked him up when I was transferred there. Marion was doing quite well as an Exxon distributor for the county. He was a duck hunter since childhood, as his father had been caretaker of a large plantation in the lowcountry and had started him duck hunting while very young.

When we planned our trip, Marion agreed to take his boat. It was a fourteen-foot aluminum, with a 9.8-horsepower Mercury for power. It was certainly more boat than I had at the time, and Marion could carry it in the back of his pickup truck. Three of us would hunt that day, but I wasn't sure Robert and I could safely get down the Ashepoo River with Marion and his rather small and kind of low-sided boat, especially after we cut twelve or fifteen large palmetto fans on the way to the landing that morning. It would be quite a load.

Anyway, we slid the boat in at the government cut between the Ashepoo and Edisto Rivers. We reached that spot by going through some of D. D. Dodge property that adjoins Bennett's Point. This made our ride down the river much shorter. We hugged the riverbank all the way down its right side to the first creek we came to. It was named Long Ashepoo Creek and wasn't very large, but it ran a long way through the Hutchinson Island marsh and joined Two Sisters Creek. It was good to know that the two connected, as we found several good spots to hunt near where the creeks joined. In years to come, I once called and lit a hundred mallards in that junction.

The morning we hunted Long Ashepoo Creek, the wind was good and the tide was coming in as we arrived. We chose a spot where the creek widened and seemed just right to set our dozen or so decoys. After doing that, we pulled the boat up and onto the then-dry marsh and stuck the palmetto fans up around the boat in the thick mud. They made a great blind, and we were able to sit in the boat that morning. The dawn was coming, and we scanned the sky from between the palmetto fans every few seconds. It's always intrigued me that ducks seem to know when it's time to fly each morning, as they seem to be able to figure their lead time just right and arrive where they want to go at the crack of daylight.

Just at the point of light when we could see, large, dark shapes of ducks were overhead, and I began my lonesome hen quacks on my call. The lonesome hen call had worked many times in the earliest minutes of a new day. Before we could load our guns, ducks were circling close over our decoys. They wanted to join that lonesome hen they were hearing! We were set up just right for the ducks to come in against the wind and toward us in our hidden boat. The early shooting was easy, and we downed the eager mallards as they sailed in toward us. It was a terrific morning of decoy shooting and, as I remember, was the first morning Robert had shot mallards over decoys. We loaded the boat that morning, and I was amazed at how easy it was to call ducks in the marsh. I felt like a world champion, as nearly every duck would respond to my calling.

In the seasons that followed, we cut hundreds of palmetto fans from the government cut connecting the Ashepoo to Rock River. There they were easy to find and had long stems. We tried to be careful not to cut all the fans from a particular tree in hopes it would survive.

My two years in Walterboro were two to remember. Never had I lived where people loved to hunt and fish as they did there. During this time, I met and made some wonderful friends. Sportsmen like Ivey A. "Son" Smoak, an attorney; John R. Reynolds, an optometrist; Jimmy Gamble, a fertilizer salesman; and Dick Powell, also a salesman. And, of course, my neighbor Joel Padgett, a young attorney. These fellows and I loved to hunt, and that we did, not only while I lived in Walterboro, but for many years afterwards. John and Son were native to the area and were neighbors. One trait in their friendship was that they never drank their own liquor. If, after work, one wanted a social drink, he would always go next door to the other's house. It was crazy!

Even after I moved to Orangeburg in 1965, Son Smoak, over the next several years, invited me to spend several days each season in his home back in Walterboro. We would hunt my spots on Hutchinson Island instead of his easily accessible places that were private. He always said, "You can't beat the marsh."

On one particular hunt in the marsh, we had carried a small aluminum boat by pulling it behind John's big Glaspar. We used the little boat to get into the small creek and to put out the decoys. Less than an hour into our trip, rain set in. And did it rain! The marsh is not a comfortable place to be when it's cold and wet. We finally went back to the Glaspar and the three of us just sat in the rain with the aluminum boat turned upside down over us. We laughed at the whole bad decision to hunt that day. John's sly remark to Son and me was, "Remind me when we get back what a good time we had."

Most of the splendid marsh hunts I had were with Robert Thompkins. Both of us were struggling to keep our insurance office going, and we considered ourselves poor as snakes. One thing we were able to do was to take our vacations together during the last two weeks of duck season. How we managed that, I don't remember. We were the managers of the office and had seven agents to supervise. I do know that we would check on things as often as we could.

I was fortunate to meet an insurance adjuster who had an Arkansas Traveler aluminum boat for sale. He had acquired it from salvage and would take sixty-five dollars for it. The boat had been in an accident and had several bent places in the bow and side as a result of being thrown from its trailer suddenly. It looked like a fairly good boat that would be big enough to take the rough water around Colleton County. It was fourteen feet long, had eighteen-inch sides, and its thirty-six-inch bottom was fairly well braced in the floor. I couldn't tell by just looking whether or not it leaked water, but I felt that the 64-gauge aluminum could be repaired if it did. At this time, I still had the little 5½-horsepower Johnson. When Robert and I finally got the boat ready for hunting, we realized that using it in big water would call for a stronger motor. The old trailer I was using had been with me for some time and had been modified for my previous old boats, but it could be made to fit the Arkansas Traveler. Extra money with both of us was scarce, and we did all sorts of rigging to get by.

I managed to trade my 1960 Johnson for a 1959 10-horsepower Johnson, and the motor ran pretty well. I had a new water pump installed as well as new spark plugs. Running lights were not required on small boats at that time, only a white stern light that could be seen from all directions. We rigged a stern light for our new "duck special" using a two-cell flashlight taped to a wooden broomstick, with a white pill bottle affixed to the lens-end of the flashlight. It was attached to the boat's transom using screws and radiator hose clamps the size of the broom handle. As long as the batteries were good, the make-up light could be seen a long way.

The boat did leak some around some loose rivets, but my friend, Dick Powell, happened to have some metal washers with rubber coating on one side. We drilled out the old rivets and used the washers with short bolts and nuts to seal the previous holes. This would last a season, but eventually the leak would start again. It's a good thing the boat had a drain plug, as it was needed frequently. Tie-down straps were too expensive then, so we used rope.

On Saturdays, before the duck season began, Robert and I would do our exploring and tentatively plan where we might hunt in the multiple creeks of Hutchinson Island. We decided that there were four pretty good spots: one in Long Ashepoo, another in Two Sisters, and another where Two Sisters and Long Ashepoo joined. But our best and most frequently hunted spot was Bank Creek.

One Saturday during the season, we were set up in Long Ashepoo and doing right well with the ducks, but we kept seeing flocks of mallards going down farther over and across the marsh. So, leaving that day, we decided to see just what was going on over there. To get into that area, some big-water boating was necessary, and we always respected the wind and waves. It required going out the mouth of the Ashepoo River far enough to find sufficiently deep water in the sound away from the many oyster bars. The right tide was always a help. We noticed in the sound a small island up close to the marsh grass line, and just beyond it was the entrance to a sizeable creek. In fact, after getting into the creek, we found it to be quite large and deep. Venturing on into the creek, we found that it made an abrupt right turn and continued on through the marsh. On that right-turn bend must have been three hundred mallards, just sitting there. Of course they got up when we rounded the corner. They got our attention pretty quickly though, and we began to look for a place to build a blind. Directly across from the bend was a small creek about twenty-five feet wide, which flowed on behind the corner of the creek's entrance. We liked the spot instantly. We could build a small blind on the corner and cover it with palmetto fans, leave the boat behind in the little creek's marsh grass, and walk across the hard marsh back to the blind.

There appeared to be an eddy pocket of water right on the corner. Our decoys would look good there and would be protected from the fast-moving tide. We had found Bank Creek, a spot we would hunt countless times and enjoy some of the best duck hunting we ever experienced. The problem with hunting that spot was the sometimes treacherous water that had to be navigated in the darkness. Actually, there were two ways to get to Bank Creek, and both could be very dangerous for our boat and our safety. The wind direction and the level of the tide dictated which way we went. If we came down the Ashepoo River, we had to come out far enough to have adequate water to cross the flat going toward the little island that marked the entrance to the creek. Eventually, we used a red can channel marker that prompted us to make our right turn out of the river. Using my compass, I would follow a line to the island. We learned that Bank Creek had cut a very narrow channel from its mouth all the way to the Ashepoo River. Sometimes we could follow it when the tide was lower than we had figured. On occasion, we have gotten out of the boat and pulled it along in the little washed-out channel. I remember having sizeable fish bumping my hip boots as we progressed in the dark. Robert and I have braved all kinds of conditions while hunting together, but none so hazardous as getting in and out of Bank Creek. I remember very well just how risky it really was.

Coming in the opposite way led us out to Rock River, which also could be rough. If the marsh was at least half full, we could ride the edge of it to the mouth of Two Sisters Creek. The tricky part here was making it across the three-hundred-yard-wide area at Two Sisters. A mistake would mean that instead of motoring to the other side and following the marsh edge to Bank Creek, we might let the wind or tide take us into the mouth of Two Sisters and then in the wrong direction. Directions can surely get mixed up in the dark, especially when you're unnerved about where you're going to begin with.

Getting to Bank Creek in the dark is one thing, and coming home is another, even when daylight is on your side. On occasion, we have had to wait for the tide changes and wind changes to help make possible the trip back to Bennett's Point. Each would dictate just how we would make the trip. We even worked out a way to jump the marsh on flood tides in order to get from Bank Creek over to Long Ashepoo and on out to Two Sisters. This was a way to keep from having to go across St. Helena Sound on white water, and we did this more than once, as Bank Creek wound within a couple of hundred yards of Long Ashepoo.

Almost at the very end of Bank Creek was a widened little pothole, and a blind had been erected there. It was always ready to be used and had plenty of palmetto fans covering it. I do remember a hunter from Orangeburg hunting it several times. He had a black Lab named Bubba. I can still hear him screaming at his "Bubba" when the dog misbehaved.

We learned that the blind had been built and maintained by a hunter named Fontaine, who lived at Edisto Beach, South Carolina. I believe his name was Teddy Fontaine. We also learned that he maintained other blinds in the nearby Fish Creek area. He may have had a duck-hunting business. We took note that he only hunted the little blind on incoming tides, as he came from Edisto Beach by boat. His boat was huge, about a twenty-five footer, behind which he towed a smaller boat. Usually he would anchor the big white boat down the creek from us and take the little one on to his blind farther down Bank Creek. Robert and I were always complaining about where he parked the big boat since it had a tendency to scare off our ducks.

Early one Saturday morning, while still dark, we had a close call with Fontaine and his big boat. We had gotten to the creek and were riding in the middle, going to our blind. I happened to look back of us and was scared half to death to see Fontaine's big boat not more than fifty or sixty yards away and closing fast. I turned my little boat toward the bank instantly and the wake from Fontaine's boat nearly washed us up on the bank. Water poured over the side, but at least we didn't get hit. Fontaine evidently didn't see us and passed at a high rate of speed. That morning he didn't park in the usual spot, but proceeded far into the creek. I don't think he ever saw us, but had I not looked when I did, he would have certainly hit us that morning.

There were occasions, when both of us were hunting Bank Creek, that Fontaine would, on his way out, slow down while passing our blind, and compliment us on our good calling. Many Saturdays we were able to call the ducks that were headed his way; but, then again, there were days he could return the trick! Fontaine's duck calling reminded me of an old call used way back, called the "Paducah." It sounded like "per-duke-a-duke-a-duke-a." But it worked for him.

Our blind in Bank Creek progressed from just palmettos stuck up in the mud to a framed blind with seats. We worked on it nearly every trip and always added extra palmetto fans. We also kept some extra fans in the marsh behind the blind to cover the boat with. We never had any trouble with other hunters. However, in succeeding years it became a well-known hot spot. Robert and I maintained that blind and one other in Two Sisters from 1963 to 1974. One friend from Orangeburg kept saying, "Jay, when you decide to give up that Bank Creek blind, I want it." He was Bobby Hutto, an avid duck man who hunted mostly on the Edisto River, a few miles upstream from Hutchinson Island. Between hunting the big saltwater marsh and the Santee Cooper swamps and lakes, I had two great places to hunt my ducks. Even though the marsh was great hunting, I visited the Santee every year.

Just to say the marsh was great hunting, however, wouldn't be enough, as we had many memorable times there. We used a maximum of seventeen decoys. They were beat-up, used-up, with poor paint jobs. But seventeen seemed to be the magic number. In fact, they were all we had! We've called in birds that seemed to be in the stratosphere, and they came in readily to those aging imposters. The ducks loved them and so did the porpoises. On several occasions, porpoises swam through the decoys, but never took any with them.

Most of our hunts were productive. It was just a matter of getting there and having some wind to keep the ducks from rafting up on the sound. When the plantations were shooting, and we knew that was on Wednesdays and Saturdays, the ducks would be plentiful in the marsh. Robert and I used a system for shooting the decoying flocks. He always shot the ducks on his side, and I would shoot the ones on mine. We took many mallards and black ducks from the Bank Creek blind. We would put them in a burlap bag to keep them clean, and then place them in the boat or on top of some marsh grass. On one trip, we had put a sack of ducks in the grass and upon leaving that morning we found that some animal had ripped open the bottom of the bag and had eaten the breasts from several of our mallards. We could only assume it was a saltwater mink or raccoon that lived nearby.

Here's an example of some good shooting one windy morning. I had about retired my Sweet 16, and had wrangled a 12-gauge Remington 1100. The gun was a hit with me from the very first day, as it seemed to fit me perfectly. It was as if it was always looking at the target. Seven big mallards decided to look us over and, after a circle or two, put their feet down. They were spread out just right, and Robert took his side, as usual. We shot our three shells apiece, and six ducks hit the water and marsh. The seventh mallard, a greenhead, was now skying with the wind pushing him to Robert's side of the blind. I reached for a shell and dropped it into the open breech of the Remington. While keeping my eyes on the skying mallard and Robert, and closing the breech at the same time, I shouldered the gun and fired. The big greenhead folded, and we had seven. We were "big shots" that day!

Our duck harvests during 1963 and 1964 were so consistent that we hardly knew what to do with our many birds. So we began to give a lot of mallards to friends who grew accustomed to our supplying ducks for "occasions." They would say, "I'm gonna need about six ducks for next weekend. Are you going to hunt before then?" Then they would tell us, "Go by the hardware, as they have some shells for you. By the way, what kind do you shoot and what size shot?" The hardware store in Walterboro knew we were coming and always had a bag for us. So we spent our shotgun shell money on gasoline for the car and boat. Gas was about thirty-five or forty cents per gallon then, and a trip to Bennett's Point probably cost us about four dollars including gas for the boat!

Each season for several years, I took vacation time during the last two weeks of duck season. After moving to Orangeburg in 1965, another Liberty Life promotion to a bigger office, I still hunted with Robert. I would go down to Walterboro and stay with him. We hunted every morning and would stay in the blind until 11:00 A.M. Then, hopefully, we would be able to get out of Bank Creek and back to the landing safely. We always had good lunches with us, our wives saw to that. Robert's wife, Marilyn, could cook the best fried chicken, and Carolyn fixed delicious olive sandwiches. Carolyn kept up the old lunch special, olive sandwiches, that my mother concocted when I was a youngster. I still enjoy them to this day. Every morning at our hurried breakfasts, Robert would say, "'Tis the morning of the first day," then, "'Tis the morning of the second day," and so it went for two weeks. We always said the third day was the hardest. It was good going after the third day. Those were great times I'll never forget.

I am amused when I remember eating those lunches in the blind and having to spit out some of our good food because I needed to blow my duck call. I did most of the calling then and do today. If only I could have called as I do now, and had the great calls that are available today. Goodness knows how many ducks would have worked our seventeen decoys back then!

The Bank Creek blind holds many fond memories, one of which is my son's first duck hunt. It was a very cold day. He was seven or eight years old and had seen many ducks I had bagged. I wanted to show him the big marsh, the decoys, and the blind; hopefully, he might have the opportunity to shoot a mallard. I had borrowed my brother's .410-gauge single-shot for Jay that day. It had an exposed hammer that had to be cocked in order to fire the little gun. The ducks flew well that morning, and we decoyed several pairs close enough for us to get a mess. But we needed to get some to come in and sit in the decoys so Jay could try one on the water. Before the morning's hunt was over, I did get a big greenhead to light in front of the blind. Jay was sitting between Robert and me and I pointed to where the mallard had settled down. But the morning cold had taken its toll on Jay's little hands and he could not cock and aim the .410 before the mallard figured out that he was in the wrong company. It was the only chance he had that morning; I remember it quite well.

Dick Powell, whose hometown was also Sumter, moved to Walterboro about the time I did, and lived not far from me. I had gone to school with his sister, but had never gotten to know him well. Walterboro being a small town, I saw him in several places from time to time and, eventually, we became acquainted. He had a small boat about the size of mine with a 7½-horsepower Johnson on it. Dick was another fisherman and hunter, a few years older than I. He heard about the good local duck hunting and wanted to go. So we made plans for me to take him to Bank Creek. I wasn't particularly enthusiastic about the hunting that week because the moon was full and my experience had not been good under such conditions. But, of course, the best time to go hunting is whenever you can, just like fishing. So regardless, we put in at Bennett's Point in the bright moonlight, using my boat. It was a very clear night, and we hardly needed a light going out and down the Ashepoo River. Looking behind me as we motored along, I noticed something I had never seen before. I had a habit of watching for large boats on the river and cuts, since they were part of the inland waterway system. Several times Robert and I had had to run to the side of the river to be able to handle the huge wave or wake that large yachts made. I have seen wakes coming from yachts that seemed to be five feet high. And that is scary, even in the daytime.

I didn't see anything coming behind us that morning, but what I did see was a silver glow in my boat's wake as we proceeded down the rather calm river. The moonlight was illuminating the water behind the boat for several yards. It was a beautiful sight that I had never seen in my many early morning trips in the river. Dick said it was the phosphorus glowing in the salt water.

We arrived in plenty of time to make ready the decoys and hide the boat. I had put Dick out in front of the blind and proceeded to put out our decoys. With just a few out, I heard him hollering at me something about hurrying up, the ducks were coming. I couldn't really understand him very well, since the outboard was idling, and needed to be when setting the decoys. Anyway, I finished right soon and drove the boat around back as always, got my gun from its case, and walked the fifty yards across the hard marsh to our blind. Dick had already loaded his gun and was pointing skyward. What he was trying to tell me was that ducks were hovering all over the decoys and me, and in the moonlight, yet! The sun hadn't begun to come up, and legal shooting time was thirty or forty minutes away. But the mallards wanted in. This was a new experience for me, shooting ducks in the moonlight. I gave a few lonesome hen quacks and here they came! We let some light in the decoy spread to pull in others. By the time we pulled the triggers, there must have been twenty or so on the water, and more putting their feet down around our decoys. We only needed the one barrage to take a limit of mallards. We had ducks falling everywhere. Dick jumped in the boat with me and we picked up the ones floating down the creek. Then he had a couple more spotted on the bank.

I don't know how many we lost in the dark marsh grass, but I do know we had our limits or more and were picking up the decoys before the first rays of sunlight. As usual, we hadn't seen or heard any other boats. In all my years of duck hunting, moonlight shooting never happened again.

———————

Dick could be quite amusing at times, and used to keep Robert and me laughing when the three of us got together. I remember one Saturday morning that our fourth partner had to cancel out on Friday night, which left Dick to hunt a blind by himself. So Robert and I said, "Heck, you may as well join us in the Bank Creek blind. Three can shoot from it, and we can really work on those big flocks of mallards that the plantation hunters are going to run our way in the morning." Robert and I carried our usual seventeen decoys in my boat, and Dick brought his boat along, as three were too many in the Arkansas Traveler.

The wind was calm on the way out that morning as we made our way down the Ashepoo River, meeting the gentle swells of an incoming tide. The light wind made the trip easier, but I began questioning whether we had the conditions needed for a good hunt.

After setting our well-worn decoys, we settled down and waited impatiently for some action. And wait we did, as every flock of mallards, pintails, and blacks passed us by on the way out to the slick waters of St. Helena Sound. There they rafted up by the thousands, as Robert and I had seen before. But Dick said he hadn't and wasn't going to put up with that situation long. The three of us sat for an hour or so, enduring our frustration at seeing so many ducks ignore our favorite hunting-blind site, when Dick suddenly said, "Enough is enough." The next thing we knew, Dick was climbing into his little flat-bottom boat and was starting the motor. As he passed us, still standing in our blind, he hollered, "I'll be back in a few minutes." Robert and I watched from the blind as Dick rode out the mouth of Bank Creek and headed straight toward the huge raft of ducks covering the sound. I said to Robert, "Dick's gonna run 'em up." And that he did, only problem being Dick's effort just moved the cloud of ducks farther out into the sound.

Disgustedly, Dick rejoined us in the blind and exclaimed, "There must be a blue million ducks out there!" I asked, "Well, Dick, how did you know it was that many?" He chuckled and said, "It's easy. I counted the feet and divided by two." If anybody had been in the marsh that morning, they surely would have heard us laughing until our sides hurt.

The morning continued to be slow, as the light wind never freshened. The three of us hadn't fired our guns all morning and we could smell a skunky kind of hunt in the making. We had eaten our lunches and were close to calling it a day, when I spied a lone duck coming off the sound and heading our way. A short highball from my call turned him toward our motionless decoys, and it looked as if we might not get skunked after all. With wings backpedaling and orange feet down, the duck skidded to a stop on the outside of our decoys. Then he began to swim toward our setup. Dick slowly reached for his gun and readied it for the shot, as the big green-head swam steadily our way. I said, "Dick, you know you're not gonna shoot that duck swimmin' on the water." Dick replied, "Of course not; I'm gonna wait 'til he stops." And he did!

The salt marsh has many hazards, not only from the big, rough water and the great number of shell banks, but the marsh itself can be a real problem. Learning to walk here and not there is something I learned over time. Using the marsh grass to increase firmness as I walked helped me to wander across acres of open marsh in search of downed and crippled ducks. I would, with my feet, push the grass over to aid my maneuvering. The tide in varying water levels exposed mud banks and bars on the edges of creeks. My hunting partners and I very seldom hunted on dead low tide. We liked at least a half tide, or preferably, a rising tide. Trying to walk into or across a creek that the tide had left with no water could leave you stranded or pull your hip boots off.

We learned, also, that a crippled black duck that fell in the marsh was impossible to catch. Black ducks could run across a marsh and be gone "somewhere" before we could get to them. You would think that by spotting them down and then walking straight to them that they would be there. They seemed to disappear magically.

———

After moving to Orangeburg in 1965, I invited Dr. Eugene Gehry to hunt my blind. Doc was a very tall and strong man and an excellent shotgunner, whether at doves or ducks. Hearing me talk about the marsh and all the waterfowl there, he was after me to take him. He was probably ten years my senior. He had fine shotguns and equipment, and big guns were his favorite when duck hunting. We were shooting lead shot then, and Doc would shoot 1⅞ ounces of number four at big ducks. He was deadly with his three-inch magnum Browning semiautomatic.

We chose a day in the latter part of the season to visit my blind in Bank Creek, as after New Year's Day was mallard time in South Carolina. The blind had been shot heavily during the Christmas holidays, but Doc said he'd take a chance anyway. The tide would be right our day, so we left Orangeburg quite early. Most mornings, we arrived at Bennett's Point about 5:30 A.M. It took about forty-five minutes to make the trip to the blind.

We had no difficulty with the water on the way out and arrived on time. I put Doc in the blind with his gun and our lunch, set the decoys, and hid the boat as usual. Duck activity was slow at first, and we waited quite a while before getting any shooting. I hoped we would have a big day, because I knew Doc would only have that day to hunt before the season ran out. I think we had a duck or two picked up when a nice flock looked us over and was listening to my calls. They came in on Doc's side and he didn't give them much chance of getting away.

Ducks began hitting the water as we unloaded the two semiautomatics. A couple of greenheads along with a hen lay among the decoys, and one hen had hit directly in front of the blind, but very near the water's edge. The tide had fallen since our arrival that morning and had exposed the mud bar below us. As I left the blind and headed toward the boat, I turned to tell Doc that I would use the boat to retrieve his mallard. He was quite excited and had already taken several steps off the edge of the marsh grass and onto the mud bar. I had warned him that morning to stay on the grassy areas at all times, but in his excitement, he had not remembered my warning. Before I reached the boat, he was calling my name. He was already past his knees in mud and couldn't pull a foot out. In fact, he had already lost his balance and the Browning magnum was in the mud too.

When I got to him, he was fussing and wallowing in the mud. He had on waders and I had hip boots. I walked down a little ways, caught his hand and pulled. Doc had tried to pull his feet out of the mud, but his waders remained firmly stuck about two feet deep. I went to the boat and got my stoutest paddle in hopes of loosening a foot. I felt it would be easier to get his feet out if the waders were still on him. So Doc wiggled back into his waders and was shouting some choice words about this "confounded marsh." I said to him, "Doc, I'm gonna save your life, but in return I want free medical care for the rest of my life." He said, emphatically, "You got it. Just help me get the heck out of here! Here, take my gun. At least, we can save it!"

It was a struggle to free Doc from the sucking mud, but the paddle helped, until it broke. There was nothing else I could think of except to try pulling his feet out with my hands. He had completely exhausted himself with the struggle and was accepting any ideas I had left. So, after picking up as much marsh grass as I could find and piling it alongside his knees, I eased down beside him. Together we pulled and pulled until one foot was free, and then the other. I was up to my elbows in the muck. We looked like we had been mud wrestling. I don't think Doc had ever been in such a fix.

Back at the landing, we used the little pump to wash ourselves, as had been Robert's and my habit. Doc looked at the ducks we had brought in and asked, "How in the hell did they stay so clean? Why in the hell do they like this messy place so much?"

---

Cliff Gardner, my wife's brother, lives in Barnwell, South Carolina, and was in the car business a long time. He owned and operated Cliff's Used Cars, and had some good salespeople working with him. His schedule was somewhat flexible, and he could take off a day when he had the urge to do something special. I always called him "Big Brother" for several reasons. When I married his sister, he was bigger and heavier than I was at that time. Also, he was always like a brother to me, and could and did solve our car problems over the years. He would do me a favor for the asking, and on our hunting trips, I would tell him that I would rather go off with him than to go with Richard Nixon, or whoever was president at the time.

We met in Walterboro at McDonald's one Saturday morning at the start of my two-week duck-hunting vacation. We loaded up and traveled on down to Bennett's Point. Dick Powell and Son Smoak were going to tag along in Dick's boat and hunt one of our nearby blinds.

Arriving at the landing, we immediately realized we had a duck day with wind, but the wind was on the increase, for sure. It hadn't been really strong when we left Walterboro, but now it was blowing harder. I knew we would have to be very careful taking on the rough water with our small boats. Dick was hesitant even at first, especially when we rode out of the protected waters of Mosquito Creek and into the Ashepoo, where the wind was blowing straight down the river. The river was rough, and I mean whitecapping rough. A little ways out into the river, I saw Dick turn around and hastily make his way back into the sheltered waters toward the landing. I did the same thing. Dick's boat was a little smaller than mine and the sides were not nearly as high. His motor was smaller, too. He and Son said they were afraid the water was too much for their rig and were not going out. I certainly didn't argue with them about their decision.

I studied the wind direction carefully and told Cliff that if we could safely cross the Ashepoo, we could go in the back of Two Sisters safely. My "crowd" had a small blind in the left fork of Two Sisters that we didn't hunt that often, but it was in protected water.

We bade farewell to Dick and Son and said we would see just how bad the Ashepoo was. I hugged the left side of the river with spray flying everywhere. The waves and wind were to our side, and we were getting soaked for a short distance. Motoring slowly and carefully down the water, I knew we had to cross the river to get into the government cut that connects the Ashepoo with Rock River, another large body of water. At that point, I decided to ride and quarter the whitecaps at an angle and ride the troughs at the right speed. It was scary, but we got across okay. The government cut was somewhat sheltered, and we progressed, looking for a very small cut through the grass that I knew existed. It was only a few feet wide, and only had water on high tide or flood tide. If I could find this, and it had water enough to go through, we could enter Two Sisters Creek from the back end and never confront any more rough water. The little cut was hard to find, as few even knew it existed or where it went. Luckily, we did find it with a little water left from the outgoing tide. I pulled the boat over the oyster-covered bottom about twenty-five feet and out into the open water. We had done it—safe water, at last. About a five-minute run with the 10-horse, and the creek leading to the blind would be on the right. Cliff was running the light and pointed as we neared the entrance. The water seemed lower in the creek than I expected, but plenty for decoys in front of the blind.

While hiding the boat down the creek with some extra palmetto fans, and heading back to the blind to see if all was okay, the wind continued to howl. With the wind this strong and in an open marsh, I knew that the only ducks I could call would be downwind. Both of us were concerned with the boiling clouds and a wind that seemed to be twenty-five to thirty miles per hour. But ducks were on the move, and I knew they wouldn't care to sit out on the sound this day, and they must have known it too. Any mallard that could see our decoys or hear my calling would come right on in. Cliff had no experience shooting in the wind, but a big target like a mallard flying in against such a strong wind made an easy target. We wasted few shells that day, and in less than an hour had collected our limit of mallards and blacks.

We didn't waste any time picking up the decoys and the last couple of ducks that fell across the creek. I told Cliff we needed to get out of this weather fast. The sky was dark and threatening; I had been in bad weather out there before, but never anything this bad. Despite the good hunting we had that morning, I now wished we had not left Bennett's Point. I knew that going back the way we had come was not possible, as the back end of Two Sisters almost dries up on low water, and the little gut we came through would be dry. By blowing this hard the wind was helping the tide to fall faster than usual, and I knew the only way out was to go around the front side of Hutchinson Island. That meant going out the mouth of Two Sisters and turning upstream in Rock River. That also meant we would be going directly into the strong wind and the accompanying whitecaps. The only alternative was to wait out the storm for a while or stay for six or so hours until the tide changed. And that would be a long day in weather like that.

I told Cliff that we should try the Rock River route in hopes we might be able to ride the edge of the rough water. The problem with that turned out to be there was no edge with water deep enough to run the motor. We had to move farther out into deeper water, which put us going directly into the wind in waves about two feet high. The Arkansas Traveler had a flat bottom, which is the worst type of bottom for rough water. We were taking one of the worst beatings I had ever encountered in a flat-bottom boat. The pounding was taking its toll.

The first problem that confronted us was that the motor started losing power, something we, certainly, didn't need in such conditions. In those days, a '59-model Johnson had a pressurized gas tank and fuel system and no fuel pump. The pressure from the tank pushed the fuel to the carburetor, but somehow the pummeling that the boat was taking seemed to cause the motor to lose power. I couldn't keep the boat's bow up as high when the motor started dying, and waves began breaking over it.. The only solution I could think of was to quickly move the six-gallon tank from behind me and put it under my legs, in front of the back bench seat. This way, I could pump the pressure button to see if that would help the motor rev up again. While Cliff used the paddle to stabilize the boat as best he could, I pumped the tank, the motor came to life, and we turned into the wind once more. The situation was quite unnerving, and had I not been able to get the motor running, we would have been pushed out into the sound. The terrible hammering continued, and we had a long way to go, still keeping the bow high enough, which meant hitting the oncoming waves that much harder.

The Arkansas Traveler had only two bench seats. The front bench was farther back from the bow than most three-seated boats that size. This left a lot of floor space in front of that seat, and the lack of a third seat lessened the bottom strength. The bottom was flexing to its maximum with the pounding, as were the braces in the floor. The stress was too much for the boat's construction, and one of the braces in front of the seat Cliff was sitting on broke in half. The bottom began to tear, and water was gushing through. I slowed a bit, and Cliff quickly put the life cushion on the floor over the broken brace and sat down on it. We had no idea what would be next. I was fighting to keep the motor running by pumping the tank with one hand and holding tight to the tiller with the other. Cliff was sitting on the floor trying to keep the bottom from tearing any more. Also, I had to open the drain plug to let the rushing water coming in under Cliff flow on out the back. We were in a difficult situation, to say the least, and there was much rough water ahead.

The intersection of Rock River and the government cut was very wide. But here I could run sideways to the wind and not directly into the waves. The boat could be speeded up a little in order to run between some waves and quarter others. What a relief if we could keep afloat that far. We were wet to the bone from the spray and waves coming over the bow. But being wet was of little concern at that point. The intersection was getting closer and closer as we fought to keep the rig up on top. A little calmer water lay ahead as we buffeted the waves and held on.

I made the right turn and crossed toward the government cut, running between the waves and calling on all my knowledge of handling rough water as we went. The bottom, with Cliff sitting on it, did not tear any further; but water continued to come in and was drained out through the drain hole in the transom. The Johnson had continued to run while I pumped the tank's pressure button. The government cut was sheltered, but the next crossing would be rough. We had to cross the Ashepoo and head into Mosquito Creek and the landing. I felt sure the wind was a healthy thirty miles per hour, as sometimes it had pushed the boat down and into the quartering waves as we made our turns.

Cliff and I were completely fatigued by this time and unnerved to the core. Coming out the government cut and into the Ashepoo, we were able to get a little help from the riverbank due to the tide being low. We hugged this calm side of the river and made our turn to cross toward the landing in Mosquito Creek. It was the last rough spot, and I eased the boat through the waves and ran the troughs. The landing was once again a welcome sight.

I had never seen Cliff so cold. He could not even talk, but backed the trailer down to load our leaky and disabled craft. It had brought us through the toughest conditions I had seen at Bennett's Point. We just sat in the car with the heater doing its best for quite a while.

The next week, while on vacation, I heard that the commander of the Beaufort Marine Air Station had drowned while duck hunting that same Saturday. His party had been hunting the Beaufort, South Carolina, side of St. Helena Sound.

That second week of vacation started out about on par for Mr. T. and me. On Monday we had a good shoot in the marsh. There were plenty of ducks to call, and we were excited about the prospects of a good week of duck hunting. But we had noticed several helicopters working the marsh near where the Combahee River entered St. Helena Sound, which was on the other side of the sound. On the way out on Monday, the helicopters were closer to Hutchinson Island. It wasn't until we were back in Walterboro that we heard about the drowning.

Tuesday morning, ducks were scarce in the salt marsh, and helicopters were hovering over our area. They were military and we figured they must be searching for the drowned hunters. At times, they would almost light in the marsh, and had covered our general area over and over. There was very little activity in the Bank Creek area, other than noisy helicopters. They proceeded to scare off every duck that week. We hunted the rest of the week and never fired another shot in any creeks on Hutchinson Island. Quite a change from Monday.

I have always had mixed emotions as each duck season closes. I'm usually worn out from lack of sleep and all the exertion, but ready to go again in a day or two. The last day of the season is usually a sad one, knowing it'll be ten months before opening day comes again.

The last day of the 1966 season was something to remember. My brother-in-law, Cliff, was to hunt with me, and Robert was to hunt with my neighbor, Jimmy Gamble. The day looked to be a good duck day weather-wise, and we planned to hunt at Bennett's Point.

We all figured the plantations would be shooting near Bear Island, too. Lots of ducks should be moving, and we wanted to get in a good hunt that last day. Ducks had been plentiful that season, and the report around Walterboro was that the plantations' duck ponds and old rice fields held many big ducks.

Cliff and I were headed to our blind in Bank Creek, and Mr. T. and Jimmy were going across the marsh to Long Ashepoo Creek. We started toward our respective routes about 5:30 A.M. and arrived on schedule with no trouble en route. We added a few palmetto fans to the blind, and after setting the decoys a little upwind, settled in to spend the last day of the season in my favorite marsh blind.

Sometimes, when the wind was just right, shooting could be heard inland. That's what we heard that morning, and very early, too. Our experience when hunting the Hutchinson Island creeks was that the island seemed to be directly under the ducks' flight path as they were leaving the inland plantations. And this morning was going to be the best example of that we had ever seen. As the sunlight peeked over St. Helena Sound, we saw flight after flight of big ducks winging out and over our position. They were really on the move toward the sound, and conditions were right for them to raft up out there. It might be a while before they filtered back inland. Sometimes they would decoy on their way out, and other days every bird wanted to sit on the sound. But one thing was sure, many ducks were coming out that morning. We were sure to decoy some before the morning was over. And we felt sure Mr. T. and Jimmy would have a good hunt in Long Ashepoo. The first hour passed and we hadn't fired the gun. What we thought was a lot of ducks early was nothing compared to what we saw coming across the marsh for the next hour. Many thousands of big ducks, in a steady stream, had left their inland waters and were coming to the saltwater and marsh creeks. They were lighting all across the marsh, and now some were close enough to call. Cliff was getting excited at the sight of more ducks than he had ever seen, and I was delighted that it looked like we were going to get some shooting. That we did! I've always said when few ducks fly, few will decoy; and when many are on the move, the hunt will be a good one.

Cliff was shooting his Remington semiautomatic and soon my Remington joined in as the mallards worked our decoys. There were so many ducks flying in big and small flocks that we didn't know which ones to call to. And it appeared nearly all the ones close by were listening. Decoying as they did, we could pick easy shots for clean kills. Since there were so many coming in, we picked as many drakes as we could, and in minutes we had taken our fill. Cliff said he had never seen anything like it, and I agreed days like that don't happen every day of the season. There must have been a hundred thousand ducks that flew the marsh that day. I wished I had brought my movie camera instead of my gun!

On the way back to the landing, we saw Mr. T. and Jimmy coming up the Ashepoo slowly, as if they might be having a motor problem. So we pulled over on the grassy bank and waited. They recognized my boat and came over for a chat. We knew we had had a good hunt and hoped they had, too. We really hadn't heard them shooting much, but maybe it was because of the wind direction. I knew Long Ashepoo was a great spot when the ducks were moving and, of course, Bank Creek too. But what I saw I couldn't believe. They had put their ducks in a burlap bag, and only the Lord knew how many were in there. They definitely had more than we did. I never asked just how many were in that bag. All I can say is I'm glad Cliff and I didn't have to go to the landing with that many ducks and risk getting checked. We had never worried about things like that, but the wardens seemed to keep tabs on where the ducks were. And, sure enough, as we were going up the Ashepoo en route to the landing at Bennett's Point, we spied the warden coming down the river on the other side. We just waved as he went by. He kept on going down the river, and to this day we have always wondered why he never turned around to check us.

Besides the duck hunting in the big Santee Swamp, I would have to rate our hunting in the salt marsh at Bennett's Point as some of the best I ever had in South Carolina, even though I had some close calls in dangerous conditions that I don't care to repeat. At my age now, I have no desire ever to hunt there again. But I do have fond memories of our many hunts, some successful and some not so successful. For a long time, it was just a matter of getting out there. The difficulties that went along with hunting the salt marsh were all neutralized by my youth and desire. I shared the great hunting with my friends and relatives until 1974. I was forty-one years old by then, and now many years later I tell the young hunters about the place. I guess the old parking lot with the little pump has been enlarged, and the hunters have increased there like everywhere else. But at one time it seemed so wild and unrushed.

Today it's part of what is called the ACE Basin, consisting of land and marsh around the Ashepoo, the Combahee, and the Edisto Rivers. Most of the ACE Basin is preserved lands under our South Carolina Department of Natural Resources, but some of it is still huntable.

# 15

# A Call from
# Murphysboro

I first met Jim Gibbs in 1959 when we both were employed by Liberty Life Insurance in Sumter, South Carolina. Jim was being discharged from the United States Air Force and was hired by Liberty's local office to be trained. I liked him from the beginning, as he always had a positive outlook on everything, a trait that followed him all through his very successful business years and won him many friends. I soon learned that a friend of his was a friend for life. Even though we live in different worlds today, we still touch base nearly every year. Our friendship has stretched over a forty-year period.

Jim didn't get to stay in South Carolina but a year or two, as he was called back to his home in Illinois. Jim's father had become ill and he was needed by the family to help maintain the family farm.

But during his time in South Carolina, we not only worked together, we did a lot of fishing on the Santee lakes. Jim loved the Santee as I did, and got hooked on catching Santee's famous landlocked striped bass. Every chance he got, he fished for the big rockfish that were growing larger and stronger each year. These fish had appeared in our lakes a few years earlier, and had become the talk of the fishing world in the southeast.

Jim's home was Murphysboro, Illinois, a town very close to the Mississippi River bottoms. He had told me about the duck and goose hunting near his home, and of his exciting hunts on his family's bottomland near the river. Of course, my eyes always widened with the prospect of joining him when he did, especially when he would call each year with the question, "Are you coming up this fall?"

Until 1964, I could never seem to make it up that way, but when Jim called that fall, I said, "What would you think if I said yes?" Jim replied,

"Come on, you can stay with me." So plans were made for a friend of mine to make the trip with me. Neither one of us had any money to speak of, so my friend got in a poker game the night before we left, and luckily won a pot or two with our money.

We drove a Volkswagen that had no heater on that trip, and our feet nearly froze most of the way. But we were going goose hunting with Jim! Cold feet didn't matter!

That trip in '64 was the beginning of several trips to the Illinois goose and duck hunting grounds. Jim always had things lined up with the best clubs and friends. We hunted with well-known clubs near the Mississippi River, such as Runnin' Lake Club. It bordered the river and was near a refuge, too. The club was something else! It had small water holes scattered through the huge cornfields. Blinds were built near the water, but in standing corn. Each blind had a small charcoal heater, and it was from one of these blinds that I pulled the trigger on my first goose. It was skying right above me and crumpled as the load of number two's found their mark. I was so accustomed to shooting smaller waterfowl that the huge Canada goose looked like an airplane over my gun barrel.

Other clubs we hunted were Honker's Corner and Jack Bowman's Goose Club. I believe these two were near Crab Orchard Lake. We had fine hunts at these clubs, as well as one near Horseshoe Lake. Jim knew everybody around those parts and he would get us in to hunt the best spots.

I remember one particular shoot at Jack Bowman's Club when I bagged a huge goose that had a seventy-two-inch wingspan. When Jim and I brought it in to have it tagged as usual, other hunters said the big goose was a greater Canada. I remember its head was as big as the driver in my golf bag.

When my son, Jay, graduated from high school, I took him to Jim's place in Murphysboro as a graduation gift. Jim not only owned a marine dealership but had built a marina on a new lake near all the area's great waterfowling. The marina was really doing well for Jim and was a great treat for area sportsmen. Jim set us up on a nice houseboat and we stayed there hunting several days at the goose clubs. Hunting always seemed to be good when visiting Illinois.

One of Jim's friends, whose name was Glenn Campbell, led us all into a spot in Oakwood Bottoms early one morning. We were mallard hunting that day in a  flooded state-owned green-tree reservoir. It was a beautiful place and very similar to the Arkansas Wildlife Management areas.

On down through the years and on my trips to see him, Jim took care of me like I was his brother. His being in the marine business afforded me many favors from him. He kept me in new MotorGuide electric motors for years. My boats always had a Jim Gibbs gift or two on them. I remember in 1976 he swapped motors with me, giving me a new 9.8-horsepower Mercury for my older model Evinrude. And several years later he worked a trade with his banker who needed a smaller outboard. I ended up with an almost new 20-horsepower Mercury in the swap. Jim was always helping me as a friend, as he did with all his friends.

Jim surprised me in 1978 when he and his family drove down to Stuttgart, Arkansas, to be with me when I participated in the World Duck Calling Contest. I had won the South Carolina championship, which qualified me to represent our state in the world contest held each November in Stuttgart. Jim brought his wife and two boys, and they certainly made my first visit to Arkansas more pleasant. I certainly didn't know anybody in Arkansas except Mrs. Chick Major, and only by telephone. Having Jim's support helped calm my nerves on contest day, and I managed to get all the notes out my call while performing on the contest stage.

Afterwards, he invited me to his home in Murphysboro for a few days of goose hunting. I always enjoyed going north to Murphysboro to hunt, and when we weren't hunting, we tended to Jim's business. We were here and there doing what needed to be done to keep up with his ever-increasing marine business. I came to know Jim's family quite well, and my feet were under their table quite often.

Another hunting opportunity came in the eighties as Jim moved farther north. He settled in the farming community of Farmer's City, Illinois, and developed another marina and lake nearby. Not far away is the Illinois River, a top spot for duck hunting. In 1986 Jim invited me to join him on some fine duck hunting there. He had met a longtime hunter who had spent his life on the Illinois River, near Bath, and Havana, Illinois. Jim's new friend was Dale Hamm, who at one time made a living for his family as a market hunter. Dale knew the area better than anyone, and knowing where the ducks were was a normality with him.

When I arrived at Jim's marina in October of 1986, he had already packed his Winnebago motor home with the food and hunting supplies we would need for our stay near Bath. He had already pulled a boat and motor the eighty miles to the river's backwaters and had checked them out. The Winnebago would be our headquarters while hunting some historic areas of the Illinois.

Dale Hamm turned out to be such a likeable old duck hunter that I could not spend enough time with him. He reminded me somewhat of my Uncle Johnnie Zeigler, another memorable duck hunter. But, in Dale's day, he had been a breaker of the state's game laws. He always said he followed in his father's footsteps and learned market hunting as a youngster. Just listening to his tall tales mystified me. Jim and I were always eager to hear how Dale managed to do the things he did and stay out of jail. And later, I believe federal wardens finally compiled enough evidence against him, resulting in some jail time.

But that was many years before I met him. Dale was now in his seventies, but still enjoying his duck seasons on the river. During our days with Dale we hunted just about where we needed to, as long as Jim and I were with him. The floodwaters bordering the Illinois wintered many ducks, mostly mallards and wood ducks. Dale would say, "Let's go here; I've got permission to hunt this," or, "They won't mind." Jim teased him about having a "floating forty acres that he owned." Jim said the forty was anywhere Dale wanted it to be!

We had great duck hunting with Dale Hamm. It was enjoyable in so many ways. He was always telling Jim and me a tale or two while sitting over our decoys. For a man to be in his seventies and completely outshoot both of us was nothing short of amazing; but he could do that every day. He seemed to have a knack for knowing just when a duck was going to settle or come in from any direction. The quickness he possessed for mounting his shotgun and getting off an accurate shot was that of a twenty-year-old. Dale's old semiautomatic had certainly reduced all the duck populations that came his way.

In getting to know a little about Dale Hamm, I came to realize that he was almost a legend around the Illinois River. His biography was a most interesting one, due to his controversial lifestyle. At times, he took waterfowl out of season, never regarding limits, and became the most notorious poacher on the river. He poached waterfowl in great numbers so they could be sold to feed his family, a way of life he had learned from his father and chose to continue for years.

After the market-hunting era died out, Dale's love of waterfowl hunting continued, but only as a sport. His knowledge was unparalleled, and he enjoyed talking about it to those interested in listening to one of the last market hunters. His story is now in publication and is titled *The Last of the Market Hunters.*

The winter of 1986 was the last time Jim and I hunted together. Both of us have more aches and pains than we used to, and we do things a little differently now. We won't go to quite as much trouble to shoot a bird these days, but as long as ducks and geese migrate our way, we'll continue to plan and to remember our good times together and enjoy the friendship that has lasted all these years.

# 16

## ORANGEBURG

## AND STUMP HOLE

The two years I spent in Walterboro were among my most enjoyable duck-hunting years. There were so many places to hunt and fish, and there were so many folks in Walterboro who loved the outdoors like I did. But my office with Liberty Life Insurance was one of the smaller ones, and my family was growing and needed a bigger home.

The opportunity arose for another promotion to a bigger office with more agents. I was offered the manager's position in Liberty's office in Orangeburg, South Carolina. The day the offer came, I went home to Carolyn and our two children and said, "It's time to get our bags packed," something I had said three times before; and Carolyn knew exactly what I meant.

So, off we went to Orangeburg in May of 1965. Carolyn, Jay, my daugher Liz, and our little black Dachshund named Weenee were eager to make the move and be back closer to our parents in Sumter. And, of course, being only twenty-five miles from the Santee Swamp had a lot to do with my quick decision to accept the promotion.

We were lucky to find a nice house that was larger than ours in Walterboro, and one that we could afford. It was recently built, outside the Orangeburg city limits. The lot was large and had plenty of space for Jay and Liz to play with new friends and Weenee.

Soon we were enjoying the Santee lakes again, swimming and boating and fishing our side of the water. Carolyn and I had grown up on the other side and had not learned much about the Orangeburg and Calhoun County side. One of our favorite places became Rocks Pond Campground, and we spent many weekends there. Camping became something we loved, and soon we had a little trailer that was perfect for hauling our new Sears ten-by-twenty-foot tent, picnic canopy, bedding, lights, tables, Coleman cooking stove, and about everything we needed for enjoying the Santee outdoors. My brother-in-law, Cliff, gave us the nice little trailer around 1966. We treasured it for years, and it now continues to go camping with our daughter, Liz, and her husband, Kevin, along with their sons, Jason and Jeffrey. We camped at Rocks Pond many times during the springs and summers of our children's childhoods. Also, we spent some weekends at the Santee State Park near Elloree, South Carolina. Fishing was fantastic in those days, and Jay and I soon got into bass fishing with both feet. One weekend at Rocks Pond when Jay was nine years old, he caught a nine-pound, five-ounce largemouth which stood as the family record for years, until he caught a ten-pound, seven-ounce brute at Santee State Park. I never topped that one, as my biggest one came later on at ten pounds, three ounces.

During the next twenty years we improved our boats, from the flat-bottom aluminum with 10-horsepower Johnson, to several bass boats, including such brands as Terry Bass, Ranger, Hydra-Sports, and Dyna-Trak. All of them we enjoyed, and during those years, the bass fishing was tops.

When we got to Orangeburg, I still had the old Arkansas Traveler rig, but after several years, I sold it to a friend who needed an old boat. He paid me $125 for it in 1969.

Needing a boat right soon, I shopped around and decided on a fourteen-foot Delcraft flat-bottom and an 18-horsepower Evinrude motor. The Delcraft was braced stoutly in the bottom and was made of .64-gauge aluminum. I thought it would be great for my swamp hunting and fishing. The Evinrude would move it nicely with a load. So one afternoon a friend, Ralph Thompson, who spent many days fishing with me, and I brought the boat and motor back from Columbia, South Carolina. It came from Columbia Sport Shop, and I remember Gene Argoe was managing the place at that time. Gene had priced the boat at $225 and the motor at $375. At that time, the $618 including the 3 percent sales tax seemed like a major purchase.

In the next couple of years, I believe it was 1971, Johnson made a 25-horsepower motor that was the same size and weight as their 20-horsepower and 18-horsepower before that. So, I began to trade motors quite often, and kept a new 25-horsepower Johnson almost all the time. Even though I caught the bass boat fever in the early seventies, I kept the flat-bottom rig for duck hunting in the Santee.

Two of my insurance agents whom I worked with a lot lived in Elloree, quite close to the Santee. One of them, Lawrence Griffith, who I called Lou, was an avid bream fisherman. The first landing I became acquainted with was Stump Hole. It was fairly undeveloped at that time, but very suitable for small boat launching and close to where the Santee River enters Lake Marion. A very large body of beautiful, flooded cypress trees was and still is living across from Stump Hole. They offered some excellent bream and bass fishing, and Lou and I spent many Saturdays enjoying that area together. I had fished hardly any of it prior to that time, as I had cut my fishing teeth on the other side of Lake Marion. Lou familiarized me with places he called Baughnight Ridge, Chesterfield Ridge, and Liquor Still Ridge. These areas were once hardwood ridges running all through the huge cypress trees. The Griffith family had once owned a sizeable tract of land bordering the lake, some of which is now covered by its waters. Lawrence had mentioned that his grandmother had sold to the Public Service Authority about one thousand acres for a sum of five dollars per acre. Of course, that was about the time I was born and land was being acquired for the Santee Cooper project. Lou always kidded me that we were fishing in "Griffith waters."

One of the most productive areas we found for bream was Liquor Still Ridge. Sometimes Lou called it Bootleg Ridge. Before the lake was made, I imagine that there was a lot of varied activity going on in those woods. The Elloree people could always be seen fishing along with us. There was a game warden who was a native of the area, and I believe his name was Parler. We saw him many times in the Stump Hole woods, and as he passed he would holler, "You boys from Elloree?" Lou would always reply, "It's Lawrence Griffith, Mr. Parler." They knew each other's families, and he never interrupted us when we were fishing or checked our fish.

Lou and I were constantly looking for bream beds with the huge blue male bream. Liquor Still held several bedding spots, particularly around the grass. There were sizeable areas of alligator grass in that region, and as we eased around, we could always hear the big bream "smacking or popping" under the grass. What a beautiful place to fish!

It was protected from the wind and had clear water and shade for the fish and the fisherman. Many times after locating a big bream bed, I would bring the family back to fish. Carolyn loved to pull the big bream, and I remember so well how Jay and Liz would have to hold their canes with both hands to land those big blues with their copper-colored heads. Normally, the bream would bed on the ridges that appeared to have a hard bottom. Five feet of water seemed to be the magic depth.

On occasion, I would call my wife's brother, Cliff, to join me. Once we located a rather large bream bed in eight feet of water on Liquor Still Ridge. Fishing had been slow that Saturday, and boats were slowly riding around the ridges looking for activity. Our deep-bedding bream were right out in the open water and directly in a pathway for boats moving up and down the ridge. But those fishermen never saw us pull any bream. Even though our lines were still in the water, we always took the crickets off our hooks when someone was headed our way. And sometimes we just sat there, not fishing, but drinking a cool Coke. Over the years Cliff laughed about our trick many times. And how our lines would sing when a big one would bite. In the clear, blackish water, the big buck bream in their colorful mating dress were a prize indeed. In addition to their deep blue scales with their copper-colored foreheads, some would have an orange chest just behind their chin. My daddy always called them government bream and said, "The government put 'em in here, Son." If bream grew much bigger, they would be hard to hold with a light bamboo cane.

When I was really into bream fishing, and at the start of each season, I would test out every ten-foot bamboo cane in town. I loved the feel of a certain shaped handle, and a certain flex. The taper had to be just right for the cane to have that feel. I always selected two just in case I might break one, and I always kept my eye open for that special bream cane. This was long before the fiberglass "bream buster" came on the market.

I remember when Lou and I had one spectacular Saturday, after a very slow start. We had fished our arms off in all our familiar bedding spots, and these had produced only a couple of small yellow hen bream. We just could not seem to get anything going that day. The wind was up and the clouds were building. We sought a sheltered area on the back side of the Santee River channel that I had named Alligator Corner. Some giant gators used the area, and we had even seen several baby gators sunning on logs in weeks past. The battery for my little electric motor was getting weak, as we had fought the wind most of the morning. We were slowly drifting down a grass line, and we could hear the boats running out on the river. Both of us were about in the same shape as my battery, and I said to Lou,

"See that log yonder? Let's fish down to it and if nothing changes by then, we'll call it a bad day. And I think the weather is getting terrible."

In a matter of minutes, the wind had moved us almost to the log. I pulled on my paddle to slow the boat, and turned to toss my cricket toward the log whose end was extending into the gator grass. I didn't expect anything to happen, but the strong pull on my line changed my mind.

It was a line-singer that had my cricket. I fought to keep the boat away from the log with my paddle while holding on to the strong fish I had not yet seen. Lou helped with the other paddle. The fish finally surrendered and turned up on its side. It was a dandy bream, about a pound in weight. What had we found? Lou flipped his long cane across the boat toward the log and his little red cork never settled as it took off under the log. Talk about luck; we had stumbled upon a huge bed!

The wind and weather were terrible and getting worse as a little rain began to fall. Neither of us had a rain suit that day, but leaving because of rain was not even considered an option at that point. We wanted to see just what we had found. Out came my anchor, and we managed to position the boat within reach of the log. Every time we whipped our crickets that way, it was "hold on tight." The big buck bream were not allowing anything near their bed and were very aggressive with our crickets. They bit like they hadn't eaten in days, and every cast netted a fish. The rain came in a hurry with drops hitting the water so hard that our little red and yellow corks were almost invisible. We sat in the downpour and just held on to our canes.

Sensing a tight line at every bite, we didn't pull until they pulled. In a quick hour the cooler filled, and the crickets we had bought that morning were almost gone. We always started out with a hundred in each cage. I asked Lou what in the world were we going to do with all these bream, and he said one thing was for sure, we weren't going to clean them, but he knew some folks who would. He was well ahead of me on that.

We struck out for the hill with a lot of fish, for sure. Luckily, the rain had about put everybody toward their homes, and only a couple of cars were at the landing. We loaded everything and headed to some of Lou's policyholders (he called them members) and left the fish with them. It was about one o'clock by then, and the folks said they would clean them up fast if they could have a mess or two. That was fine with us.

Lou pointed the way to the bait shop and hurried in for some more crickets. He came out with our refilled cages and some ice, and we headed back toward Stump Hole. I said, "Lou, your arms aren't tired and sore?" He replied, "You bet, but we got to get 'em while they're there. Remember, we got that office fish fry next weekend, and they might not bite when we need them to. You know, we're the only decent fishermen in that crowd."

The rain was still coming down as we slipped the boat in and headed across to the woods. We wondered if anybody had seen us in our spot and had moved in. But no one was there except more line-singing buck bream. The number of huge blue bream we took from that one spot beat anything I've ever seen. We never counted them, but Lou's members who cleaned them said they must have cleaned a refrigerator full, though I doubted that. What a day of fishing at Alligator Corner!

The Stump Hole woods and another body of water behind the Lake Marion dam were my favorites for bream. The water behind the dam was referred to as the "Bar Pit," short for borrow pit. This great fishing spot was created when the seven-mile-long dam was being built back in 1939–41. Much dirt was removed to make the sixty-year-old dam, and the by-product of this removal was the four-mile-long Bar Pit. I would guess that over the many years of fishing it, my family fed thousands of crickets to the beautiful bream there.

Most of the bream lived on the edges of the pit, and around the many willow trees that were overhanging the banks. Also, many vines had grown onto the willows and down near the water. The bream loved this cover and shade. So did the many snakes that inhabited the Bar Pit. They would sun themselves out on the limbs, and we had to be very careful when approaching the leafy willows. I would always look for that wide, flat, sinister-looking head belonging to the cottonmouth moccasins, as we wanted nothing to do with them. Their color was similar to the abundant but harmless water snake, but their head was a dead giveaway.

During the bedding period each month, April through August, we fished a spot in the very middle of the Bar Pit. The area was probably seven or eight feet deep, and there were several old posts below the water level. To find the exact spot, we would use a rod and reel with a weighted treble hook. Casting it across the spot, we would hook a post, then line it up with trees on the bank. On many trips we caught limits of big, blue, bedding bream from this spot. They seemed to love the bottom around those posts.

I first learned about the spot from my longtime friend, Joe Drose, who lived on the lake. I had seen him late on Saturday afternoons, anchored there by himself and pulling those big bream. Joe was quite a character, and I loved to listen to him tell stories of fishing and hunting the Santee. We shared the same outdoor loves. Seeing Joe with one leg propped up on the side of his boat, his bamboo cane arching toward the water, I knew he was having a ball. I can hear him now drawling out his description of the fish. When a line-singer tightened, he always said, "That's a *nice* one." The Bar Pit was one great bream fishing hole!

# 17

# LOW FALLS AND
# THE BIG SWAMP

I stood in front of a small bait and tackle shop at the top of the hill overlooking a semi-primitive landing as W. E. Shuler from Elloree pointed and said, "The river's right there." I could see the yellowish water flowing into the cut that fed the backwaters of the Santee River. W. E. said, "I wanted to show you this unusual place since you're new to our side of the lake."

W. E. and I were working his insurance route together that Wednesday, and we had taken a break to come this way. "Everybody calls it Low Falls and they tell me it's a great place to fish. As you know, I'm not a fisherman, but the folks around here frequent this place. They get their crickets and worms right here, and if you're hungry, there's a little lunch counter in there that serves good hamburgers. And the folks running this place are friendly, for sure."

Later on, I came to know the owners, Fran and Ted Gray, and we became friends. Ted was known as the "Fisherman's Friend." I ate many of Fran's hamburgers on my trips to Low Falls. Their hilltop store overlooked the river's backwaters, and from its front door one could see downhill the Santee River and the Rimini trestle.

For many years the landing had only one paved ramp, and it was right where the paved road to Low Falls ended. The single boat ramp had a little sandbar running out from its left side. We would launch the boats and then park them on the sandbar created from the river's current and from the big motorboats being driven up on trailers. The rest of the landing was dirt and about an acre in size. This area was for parking, and some folks would launch small boats there. About a dozen houseboats dotted the backwaters adjacent to the dirt parking area. They were the brainstorms and handiwork of locals who spent their weekends fishing and camping at this entrance to the big Santee Swamp. The floating houses and shelters were mostly built on fifty-gallon metal drums and were all sizes. I was always amused at their owners' creativity.

I soon became a Low Falls fixture, as my fishing and hunting buddies and I were there several times a month. During duck season we were there several times a week. Low Falls was located close to the Rimini trestle, a railway that crossed the upper part of Lake Marion. From the trestle northward, to the forks of the Wateree and Congaree Rivers, lay the big swamp.

On opening day of duck season, and if the hunting was good for several days afterwards, the small landing would overflow with cars and trucks with boat trailers. The landing was so popular that vehicles with their trailers would park out on the paved road for half a mile or so. And, of course, business was good for Fran and Ted since they had the only gasoline for sale in that neck of the lake.

Today the landing is changed from many years ago, as our Department of Natural Resources has spent many dollars on making Low Falls a modern facility. An enlarged parking lot completely paved, with four paved ramps for launching all sizes of boats, is now enjoyed by many. At the end of the ramps are convenient docks for entering and leaving one's boat. But in the sixties, seventies, and eighties, Low Falls was unique and somewhat primitive.

I made the run under the trestle and up the river many times to my favorite hunting spots. The run up the river took me by the camping sites used by the "rough-it" hunters and fishermen. These were numerous and, usually, all were located on the highest sections of riverbank. Sometimes there would be five or six boats at one campsite. In those days, I used powerful spotlights connected to the boat's 12-volt battery. They were a great help compared to the small battery-powered lights I had used years before in the swamp and the salt marsh out of Bennett's Point.

Some hunters would speed up the river in the darkness as if they cared little for their lives. Going fast was dangerous and much colder. I always proceeded at a moderate speed and ran the safe sides I had learned from my countless trips. Being careless has resulted in disasters for many on the big river. Even after being in the swamp itself, some had no respect for their equipment or themselves. Once, on his way out of the swamp, my son came upon a hunter standing in the middle of the creek leading out of

Moe's Lake. He was by himself standing on a stump—his boat nowhere to be seen. He evidently had knocked a hole in its bottom, and it lay at his feet on the creek floor under six feet of water. My son rescued him and carried him all the way to Pack's Landing down below.

The one thing that I could never conquer was fog. A bad fog in the darkness is, by far, the most confusing condition to cope with. Making a trip up or down the river in dense fog was almost impossible. I remember several occasions when idling the motorboat along the riverbank and straining to see the willows or anything that would help me to stay on course, that I would find myself going in the wrong direction. Not knowing, I would have crossed the river and come to the bank on the opposite side or be headed downstream instead of upstream. No matter how powerful the spotlight was, it was no match for fog.

The first creek entering the big swamp above the train trestle was Catfish Creek. It entered right near the trestle and ran in a northerly direction up through the swamp timber and flats for several miles. I never used it much and only hunted it a few times. However, the area itself and the swamp area just east of it featured the largest duck roost in the Santee Swamp. One could spot many ducks going to roost there most any winter afternoon. I used to watch from the Pack's Landing area at the eastern end of the train trestle. The roost was widely known, and in years past many shotgun shells were fired in that section of the big swamp.

On up the Santee, the swamp was mostly on the right side of the river. In fact, the swamp extended five miles wide in places. One small creek leaving the river had a little waterfall effect just as it entered Moe's Lake. It became a place I used often when hunting the lower swamp areas such as McGirt's Lake and Otter Flat. The creek was handy if I didn't want to go very far into the swamp. But most of my hunts were farther up the swamp, and I entered the deep swamp using Riser's Gut and Broadwater Creek. Both were easy to find in the dark, and boaters entering these creeks kept them open with their chain saws. When the water was high, motoring through was easy, and I never broke anything on my motors when using common sense; I learned where the logs were and slowed my boat accordingly.

Riser's Gut flowed directly east and away from the river into Riser's Old River, which was a sizeable dead lake. I was told that years before my time it was part of the Santee River channel. It was the largest body of open water in the Santee Swamp. Once as I was leaving the area on a foggy afternoon, I observed flocks of mallards winging their way down the swamp and directly over, as if they used the big lake as a navigational checkpoint. Also, Riser's Old River offered some good fishing when the water level was stable.

At the mouth of Riser's Old River and to the right were two creeks flowing down the swamp. The first one made its way through some excellent duck-hunting territory and entered the top end of McGirt's Lake to the south. There was a large flat on the right side of the creek that the ducks liked when the water was high. My younger brother, John, and brother-in-law, Lanny, and I spent several mornings shooting the upcoming flight there. We waded out into the flat and stood in the shallow water behind the larger trees. Mostly mallards used the flat and, as I remember, we took many limits that week. Both John and Lanny were good shots on passing ducks. I remember I killed a mallard hen that week that was wearing a Jack Miner bird band. It was the week's highlight for me. Jack Miner was a prominent bander in Kingsville, Ontario, Canada. The band was numbered sixty-nine. I still have the band on a duck call lanyard, which also holds a special Chick Major call, along with my lifetime collection of duck bands. Those bands now number about twenty-five, some so old and worn smooth that when I removed them from the ducks they could hardly be read. Whenever I took youngsters hunting, I often transferred several bands to ducks' legs before presenting the young duck hunter with his first bird. They were always thrilled that their duck was banded.

On low water, this creek was connected to a cypress pond which I hunted many times. Wood ducks loved it, and I felt it was one of my two best low-water spots in the whole swamp. Cypress trees surrounded it, and it always had some water. Deer must have loved it too, as the abundance of tracks revealed. The second creek flowed down toward Otter Flat, but only on very high water did they connect. It did, finally, flow into McGirt's Creek a mile or so downstream.

Riser's Old River had a very old tram road crossing it and on low water it was visible. Its many posts were under water most of the time, and a boater had to be careful crossing it. A logging operation in that section of the swamp had built the road many years before. I always slowed my boat and held to the right side when crossing. Just beyond the tram road a creek led out to the right and entered Otter Flat, a main body of the swamp that ran north to Broadwater Creek and south to Mill Creek and Sparkleberry Lake.

From the Santee River through Riser's Gut, into Riser's Old River, and out the creek to Otter Flat was a main route for hunters and fishermen who wanted to get to the middle of the Santee Swamp. Up until September of 1989 when Hurricane Hugo came through, I went this way hundreds of times over a twenty-four-year period, mostly hunting ducks in areas accessible through and out of the Otter Flat swamp. After the hurricane's powerful winds pushed over nearly all of the swamp's shallow-rooted oaks, both large and small, Riser's Gut became impassable, as many oaks fell across the gut, and this entrance into Riser's Old River was no longer useable. The water still came through, but boats could not.

After the hurricane, my first trip into the swamp was in November of 1989. The swamp's oak ridges and the beautiful trees on them were felled and laid down like hair on a dog's back. Everything that could be blown over was. The beauty of the huge oaks, some probably over a hundred years old, was gone. I was never again to walk beneath them on my hunting excursions. The great oaks, a lifetime old, had created a canopy over the ridges and very little undergrowth was present. Therefore, hunting on foot and sneaking around looking for ducks and squirrels would not be possible again in my lifetime. I was completely heartbroken by what I saw. I enjoyed the seclusion the trees were able to provide. There were so many things to see by walking and hunting, and unlocking some of nature's secrets was a part of exploring the ridges. I always felt that nature divulged some of her secrets easily, but she always kept some safely locked away.

Hunters and fishermen before me had built cabins of various descriptions throughout the swamp. Some even had shallow wells with simple hand pumps. I remember seeing the first pump well on Otter Flat, and another right by a large cabin just off the flat. This particular one, whose porch I used several times on rainy days, was quite elaborate. I thought it was the "swamp mansion" until I found one much bigger just off Hog House Creek. Both of these cabins were on ridges of great size, and evidence of their use was always noticeable. I remember their owners would tack up squirrel tails around the cabins' porches. Over the years, I located cabins near other locations such as Pine Island Creek, Hog House Gut, and Fuller's Earth Creek. They were built on big posts, high off the swamp floor, to escape the frequent high water levels. Eventually, the South Carolina

Public Service Authority declared them undesirable, and after adequate notice to the owners, burned the ones they could find. Those structures that weren't burned, ultimately were destroyed by the hurricane.

There was a ridge where the creek from Riser's entered Otter Flat Creek. It was popular as a campsite, and many times when I motored by tents were present. One camper always pitched a sizeable green canopy for extra shelter; it was the cooking and eating spot for his hungry crowd. The green canopy reminded me of the tents used by funeral homes around the Orangeburg area. I quipped several times that it looked as if there was a funeral going on there, so before too long, I named the ridge Dukes-Harley, after a funeral home in Orangeburg. The name stuck among my swamp-hunting friends and we often used it as a reference point.

Early each season, I made it a point to sit near Dukes-Harley in order to check the duck population as they flew to roost just before dark. There was always a good flight of wood ducks in November, and I observed it many times from this vantage point.

My early season hunting was mostly for wood ducks. I have seen some unusually large flights, numbering in the thousands, over the great swamp, and it was always a sign that our early season would be good. Dukes-Harley was almost in the center of the swamp and seemed to be a major crossing point for the woodies.

A few hundred yards past Riser's Gut is Broadwater Creek, which leaves the awesome Santee in a northerly direction, and flows a very long way into some of the most beautiful swamp anywhere. Broadwater is also the largest creek in the area, and on high water boaters could plane their boats up the swamp for miles. Broadwater Lake was a popular fishing spot, and its floodwaters were popular for duck hunting. On through Broadwater and past Broughton's Mound to Indigo Flats, Gar Lake, Tavern Creek, and Fuller's Earth Creek, all of which carried me deeper into the great Santee Swamp. They all hold fond memories of duck and squirrel hunts on the huge oak ridges bordering them.

———————

From 1965 to 1980 I enjoyed hunting an area that was located almost in the middle of the swamp, but not far from Otter Flat. There were so many good spots that ducks were using that I just rotated hunting here and there. I loved to explore and hunted many times by myself.

When leaving Dukes-Harley and turning downstream on Otter Flat for several hundred yards, I found some floodwater that carried me to a few oak ridges on the west side of Pine Island Creek. The tall oaks on the first ridge or two could be seen from Otter Flat, and they prompted my curiosity to check them out. Most oak ridges run parallel to the cypress flats between them. Many of the ridges in the Santee Swamp run north to south in this area. I eventually named the ridge I usually hid my boat on Squirrel Ridge. Squirrels were attracted there because they loved to eat not only the small acorns from the giant oaks, but also early in the season they fed on the large white-oak acorns. There were more large white oaks on this ridge than most, and they drew the gray squirrels early in the year. It has been said that over a hundred different species of wildlife feed on acorns of different sizes. Deer and wild turkeys depend on acorns for a large percentage of their diets, as do squirrels and ducks. My uncle used to say, "When water is under those oaks, the ducks gonna come up." He meant they would travel up the swamp from the duck refuge near Jack's Creek. Over years of hunting on foot and on the flooded oak ridges, I found this to be true. It was as if the mallards preferred the little acorns over their hand-fed corn in the refuges.

The Squirrel Ridge was bordered by two cypress flats that I hunted on foot many times. Wood ducks loved the area, and I shot the early morning and late afternoon flights from several good openings on both sides. Wood ducks seemed to use the same flight paths over and over. I learned these paths in several different areas of the swamp. I enjoyed arriving at these crossings ahead of time and getting set up and concealed, mostly behind or beside a strategic tree or stump; sometimes I stood on land, other times in shallow water.

At the northern end of Squirrel Ridge was a natural pothole of open water. It was there that several oak ridges ended, and these oak ridges nearly surrounded the pothole. With the oaks dropping their acorns here it became one of my best spots for decoying ducks, and I enjoyed good shoots there for years, particularly after Christmas. The mallards were usually in the swamp in good numbers by then, and I always looked forward to hunting the big pothole at the end of Squirrel Ridge, a spot I kept quiet about for years. But I weakened once and carried a duck hunter from Orangeburg with me one morning. We had an excellent hunt on mallards coming to my decoys. I had an agreement with this hunter that he would not try to go back to my spot without me. But, as is usual with some duck hunters, he didn't honor my request. I saw him later on and he made the comment, "You know, I could never find that spot I hunted with you over in the swamp." I said, "You weren't supposed to. Remember, it wasn't your spot to find." We never hunted together again.

When the area's water level was high enough to be on the ridges and under the oaks, hundreds of mallards and woodies would feed on the small acorns. This area reminded me of areas in the Wateree Swamp, where I had hunted with my uncle years before he died. He loved to sneak the ridges, and I became fond of doing the same. Squirrel Ridge had several other larger ridges nearby that I never named, but hunted regularly. Eventually, I had created a regular trail that I followed. I had learned the ducks' preferred spots and would sneak along very quietly from one to the next. The beautiful part of hunting this area was that for years I never saw another person or another footprint. I had the whole place to myself.

In crossing the cypress flats at the same spots over and over, I almost established a "milk run." When I got a shot at ducks feeding on the water, usually I would get a shot or two at the flock when they got up. Carrying strong cord in my coat pocket, I would hang the ducks up as high as I could get, and on the way back to the boat, I would collect what I had killed. Hunting all the ridges would take all day, and I always had some lunch and canned Cokes in my hunting coat. Canned sausages, square cheese Nabs, and my boyhood favorite, olive sandwiches were always with me; I had candy bars for quick energy, too. All my friends have teased me over time about my olive sandwiches, a family snack my mother started me on when I was young, and my wife continues. I ate many such lunches in the Santee Swamp. That was part of the hunt.

I had seen my uncle make some great shots at ducks on the water. Some hunters I knew frowned on this, but I didn't. Maybe they disapproved because they didn't have the skill to get close enough and didn't know just how to shoot a swimming duck.

The phrase "like a sitting duck" has circulated for many years and means "an easy target" to most. But I assure you, making a clean water kill on ducks is not easy. Before I learned to make the shot effectively, I crippled many ducks. I'm sure most died from wounds and broken wings from my poor shots. Learning to shoot effectively at feeding ducks started many years ago when I hunted with Uncle Johnnie. On hunts in the flooded flats of the Wateree Swamp, I saw him make unbelievable shots with his old single-barrel Stevens 12-gauge. The gun had a killing pattern out to about forty to forty-five yards. Bubba, as the family called him, always shot number six lead shot at sitting ducks. His idea was to have plenty of shot in the shot pattern so that the duck's head and neck areas would be hit. He would always say, "Shoot below the duck's body so the number sixes will rake the water." "Ricochet" was a word I never heard him use, but that is what we both thought was happening when aiming only slightly below the duck. It worked for him in my presence, and I perfected this technique early in my hunting. I raked the water many times at groups of ducks, and usually tried to roll at least two with my first pull of the trigger.

Most deer hunters in South Carolina now sit in various types of tree stands and wait for the deer to come out to their piles of corn. In my opinion, the only skill in this is the deer hunter's ability to make a killing shot with his scoped, high-powered rifle resting on the bracing of his tree stand. The hunter does not move to the deer, the deer comes to him. I don't see much skill in this.

Getting close enough to shoot a duck on the water takes both patience and skill. Ducks are constantly looking for danger, and any strange sounds or movements in the woods will flush them in an instant. Getting within forty yards can be difficult, and one must pay the price to do so. While hunting the oak ridges I developed a technique that worked consistently. Rising water, usually caused by local rains and rains occurring in the watershed above the Santee Swamp, was the key to good sneak hunting. The swamp floor would be wet, and the leaves would not be crackling under my feet. The new water on the oak ridges would offer new food availability by covering the acorns that had fallen from the huge oaks. Wood ducks and mallards loved these conditions, and the Jack's Creek refuge would empty daily as the ducks flew up the swamp to meet the rising water.

In those days, my hearing had not deteriorated, and detecting the contented quacks and whistles was usually the first clue that ducks were present in good numbers. Very seldom would a mallard hen sound off without having a lot of company with her; the exception being if she happened to be looking for the company of other ducks in the area. Yet a large group of mallards would sometimes be completely silent as they went about feeding on the little acorns in the shallow swamp.

Listening was just one tool I used in finding the feeding mallards. Tell-tale ripples in the flat or on its edge were a sure sign ducks were there. I never walked the water's edge, but stayed out on the ridge about thirty yards away. My pattern of movement was, first of all, very slow. A hunter must spot his quarry first, and to do that, caution is the answer. It might take me an hour to go a couple of hundred yards down a ridge, being careful not to break limbs or pull vines as I went. I would walk in a looping pattern, never walking the water's edge, but occasionally coming to the bank to listen and look for ripples, then back out into the wooded cover; I would walk down fifty or so yards and then loop back toward the water. Once ripples or ducks themselves were seen, the job of getting close enough for my first shot might take an hour. My uncle always said, "Never flush a duck. He'll warn every other duck around." I was always disgusted with myself when I goofed up and didn't see them first. I hadn't hunted slowly enough.

The Santee swamp attracted mostly mallards and wood ducks. But thirty years ago a fair number of black ducks used the swamp, too. The blacks preferred a little different territory than their other feathered friends. I have seen them sitting in small water holes by themselves, almost as if they were loners. The blacks were extremely cautious, and getting close enough for a shot was more difficult. I've heard other veteran duck hunters say, "If you can call to your decoys a flock of four blacks or more, then consider yourself a duck caller." I bagged the big blacks only in a few special spots, and usually there would be only three or four there. The swamp's dark-water flats camouflaged the blacks well, and recognizing them in those surroundings was not easy. A black, dark duck in dark water was very hard to see.

I remember a day in 1958 or 1959 when I eased up on a trio of blacks sitting in an almost dry cypress flat. The water left wouldn't have filled a backyard swimming pool, but these ducks were busy harvesting the small insects and minnows left in the little pond, something I learned other swamp ducks did not do. The fact that the swamp's water level was very low must have prompted the blacks to take what they could find. My 16-gauge took care of all three with one shot.

When I returned to my brother-in-law, Frank, who had already reached our boat, he almost became indignant when he saw my trophy birds. He said, "I haven't seen a duck since we parted. Where did you find those beautiful blacks?" I replied, "They were just sittin' in a little puddle I happened to stumble upon."

The wood duck drake is the most colorful and majestic duck in the Santee Swamp, but his mate is almost totally gray. Her color is practical, as she blends with her nesting habitat, insuring the safe arrival of her brood each spring. I enjoyed watching them in their contrasting colors from behind logs on the swamp floor. Making my way to the cover, I always envied the contentment I witnessed. They loved to sit on the logs and stumps out in the flats while preening and oiling their feathers. They seemed to always enjoy each other's company, and many times I have seen them come to the water's edge to retrieve acorns from under the great oaks. They sometimes would waddle out onto the dry ground for an acorn. Woodies were the only ducks I ever saw do this, and they always returned to the water for its help in swallowing the acorns. They were year-round dwellers in the Santee, and they nested in tree cavities near the flats and ridges.

Despite the beauty of the wood duck, mallards were always my favorite. They came to visit each fall and stayed until the full moon in March. Being the most abundant duck in the swamp, they filled the woods with glossy green heads atop chestnut and gray bodies. Like the wood duck, their dress was to be admired. The brown mallard hens that followed their handsome mates were not so vivid, but their vocal ability was second to none. They sounded their call frequently when visiting the Santee, and as it would ring through the shallow flats, the greenheads would answer in their casual, softer quacks.

When the water came, the mallards came too, and serious duck hunting commenced. Making my way close enough was, most of the time, a difficult task. It nearly always included some crawling. In those younger days, my energy level was almost inexhaustible, and crawling across the swamp floor was never a task. I would slow down after locating a flock of mallards or woodies. As long as the ridges had exposed or dry swamp, sneaking was a lot of fun. If the water level ever covered an area though, sneaking was out. Approaching ducks while wading was almost impossible, except when I got lucky and had them swimming toward me. And, on occasion, that did happen.

I recall one such incident on Squirrel Ridge where timing was everything. Hunting almost the full length of the ridge that morning, I had neared the big pothole on the north end, and after standing a few minutes, I heard some mallards in the distance. Due to so much quacking, I determined that the ducks were in the flat next to a huge ridge that extended all the way over to and bordered Pine Island Creek. I usually hunted that ridge by coming in from the other direction. As I continued to listen, I heard another flock quacking in a different spot, and as their quacks seemed to be getting closer, I suspected these mallards were coming to join the flock out in front of me and farther across the flat. I thought, just maybe, I could ambush them if I could position myself out in the flat before they made too much progress. Easing into the water and watching for any movement from the direction I felt they were coming, I made my way out near the thickest part of the cypress flat. The water was waist deep where the largest cypress trees were.

Stopping there, I listened and looked again for any signs of movement in the distance. The ducks in the flat were still talking once in a while, and I figured I had made it as far as I could without a stray duck spotting me. There was a large stump that had once been a huge tree, but was now only a memory to the others nearby, and I decided it would provide a blind for me and a rest for my gun. It was there I would wait in hopes my ambush would take place.

I had retired the Browning Sweet 16 and was toting my Remington 1100 12-gauge. The gun had proven itself, and I was confident I could make shots out to forty-five or fifty yards with it. And since I had gotten into reloading my own shotgun shells, I had developed a load that was a sure thing on swimming ducks. Reloading shells was not only economical but also strategic, as by matching various loads to a particular barrel, shot patterns could be improved. I had tested the new load on paper, and it was clearly special. My Remington had a 2¾-inch chamber and a 28-inch modified choked barrel. The shell I loaded for sneak hunting had 1½ ounces of number six lead shot over Winchester 540 ball powder. The wad I used was a plastic one-piece wad made by Alcan. They called the wads Flite Max. This plastic wad featured additional felt cushion wad on the inside, and I believed it helped the gun to shoot such consistent, even patterns.

My concealment behind the old stump afforded me a view of what I thought might be the path that these mallards would follow. Sometimes experience is a great teacher, and I was counting on it this time. Remaining motionless and patient, and watching for the slightest ripple down the flat, rewarded me with a shot I'll never forget.

I had no idea just how many mallards were in the flat, but I knew that with all that quacking, there must be several flocks close by. I'd surely take what I could get a shot at. The 12-gauge with my homemade loads was ready and resting on the stump, when I spied movement in the cypress out front and downstream. I could see several green heads on top of light gray bodies, one behind the other, and wasting no time in coming upstream in my direction. They were, evidently, intent on joining others farther over. All knew the acorns were waiting on the big ridge not far away. The iridescent green heads shone brightly as several drakes crossed a small opening in the cypress trees and disappeared behind them. I was beginning to get a shake in my bones in anticipation of what may come shortly. The mallards I had first seen were not visible, but following their same path up through the cover was company. Another group of greenheads and their camouflaged mates were hurrying to join up. Hoping all would continue to follow each other in my direction, I moved not even an eyelash. And follow each other they did. I figured they would pop out into a small clearing about thirty-five yards from the tip of my barrel, and I was beginning to think greedily. If they were lined up just right I might get a limit right here and be headed home sooner than expected. They played follow-the-leader as I had hoped, and with four greenheads and a hen leading the whole group of maybe a dozen, they appeared in the opening I had expected. My gloved fingers gripped the Remington ever so slowly, and my aim was slightly below several lead greenheads. The load of number sixes awakened the swamp and the big mallards, but for the lead bunch it was too late to fly, as all I could see were ducks flopping on their backs with their red feet kicking skyward. The pattern of number sixes had covered the whole bunch of lead ducks, and as I made my way eagerly toward them, I counted one hen and four greenheads, all on their backs. What a shot— a limit of mallards with one shell! The water was almost too deep for my waders, but I managed to gather all five without getting wet. Every day in the swamp is a good day; some are just a little bit better than others!

One of the creeks flowing south out of Riser's Old River possessed a favorite spot or two for black ducks and mallards. A longtime friend, Joe Drose, showed me the spot when we roamed the Otter Flat area several seasons before. The ducks liked the area due to a few scattered, but productive, medium-sized oaks that grew on the edge of the creek. Joining the big ducks on occasion, were a half-dozen or so wood ducks. The little spot the woodies liked was a shallow body of floodwaters and, of course, it had plenty of acorns in the fall. We used to take care of woodies easily and often, as they seemed to be local visitors to the area. The bigger ducks were normally present after Christmas each season. My usual method of hunting these ducks was on foot. I liked outsmarting the visitors, and did so many times.

On one particular hunt, I could not locate any ducks in their usual spots. I had searched the area thoroughly and thought maybe I had overhunted the little creek area. On the way back to my boat on Otter Flat, I saw a couple of mallards showing interest in the swamp on the far side of the creek, and watched them finally go down not far from where I was. I knew the area well, as I had been to it by boat when coming in from Riser's Old River. The creek was ten or twelve feet deep in places, and no place for my hip boots that day. I had taken note several times of a particular tree that had fallen a number of years before, but had never attempted to use it in crossing the creek. I hadn't gotten a shot that day, so I decided to investigate crossing on that tree. It looked plenty strong, but was not as big as I would have liked. Its diameter was close to eighteen inches at its base. The hip boots I was wearing were my favorite in the Santee Swamp, even though I used waders many times, but the boots were better for this adventure.

I decided to cross the deep creek by way of the log. Using a homemade sling, I could shoulder the 12-gauge and allow both hands to be free for the crossing. As I remember, this was the only time I tried this. Crawling out on the log, I straddled it and moved out and across a little at a time. To move forward, I would have one hand ahead of me and one behind, so that I could shimmy along on the log. I was able to keep my balance using this sit-down method. I will never forget how nervous I was getting across on that log. Halfway across, I wondered whether I had made a bad decision, but there was no turning around at that point. Successfully across, I turned my attention to finding those mallards, and it didn't take long. They had joined several others on a bend in the creek and were busy feeding along the edge as I made my sneak. Crawling close to them, I made my first shot count and rolled two mallards. The others started out through the trees, and several came out toward my ambush point. I made a couple more shots at the fleeting big ducks and bagged a big greenhead to go with the pair on the water. Many times the startled ducks don't seem to know from which direction a shotgun blast originates, and in their confusion will fly out over a hunter, affording him an easy shot.

The creek's current moved the ducks close enough for my retrieve, and now I was confronted with crossing the creek again. I threw the ducks across, one at a time, to give myself as little baggage as possible. I was even more shook up as I eased across the log on the return trip. I had a successful hunt and learned one thing, for sure—no more crossing deep creeks twenty-five feet wide on logs! Even at my young age, I decided that was not the way to go.

———————

I always enjoyed shooting the wood ducks late in the afternoon, during the first part of the season, and always chose spots where finding the downed birds would be easy. During my years of hunting the area, I had found many crossings, one of the best being a small island at the entrance to Pine Island Creek. The dry island bordered Otter Flat and an adjoining body of water known as Water Oak Neck. Some pretty ridges connected there, and I had never taken the time to check them out. New territory fascinated me, as every step could be a new adventure.

In December of 1961 or 1962, I had the urge to hunt the Water Oak Neck area following a very cold period in our state. We had several freezing nights that caused a lot of the shallow flats to have ice. The ducks would be in the deeper water that hadn't frozen, and most of my frequented spots would be iced over. So new territory was my plan that day, and a lot of walking, too. I had put on my hip boots for easier movement. I was still hunting with the Browning Sweet 16, and walking the woods and swamps with it under my arm was my favorite pastime. I walked a lot with my hands in my coat pockets while cradling the shotgun under my right arm, as my Uncle Johnnie did all his years. I can see him now, walking without a sound with his old single-barrel neatly positioned under his right arm.

I had hoped to find some open water that morning and had hunted down the side of a large open flat. Most of the area had some ice, but near the end, the swamp floor had thawed and the sun was warming the leaves as I crossed to the other side. Coming up out of the muddy bottomland

and not particularly watching where I was stepping, I was suddenly aware of something white in color and a shape that triggered my instant response to jump. How I don't remember—whether up, to the side, or where! I was about to put my foot down on a huge cottonmouth moccasin and the white of his wide-open mouth had caught my eye. After gathering my senses, I thought what in the world is that snake doing out of hibernation, with all this ice around the last few days? It was December, and snakes are not much of a consideration in the swamps that time of year. I had seen many cottonmouths and certainly killed my share in Pocotaligo Swamp, near Sumter. The pure white color of the snake's mouth had stood out from his muddy, dark body and the rest of the swamp floor.

At first, I could not figure why, after being so close, that I had not been struck by the big snake. As I stood some distance away, his mouth closed but he never moved. He, evidently, had come out from somewhere to sun himself on the warm, dry leaves where he lay. After my heart slowed its pounding, I looked around for a lengthy stick to use in disposing of this resident of the Santee Swamp. The one I found was half-rotten, and broke when I swatted the snake's head. I didn't want to use the shotgun and betray my presence, and the stick breaking did nothing to make me feel any better. Even though grateful, I was still puzzled as to why the snake had not struck, but then I realized it had to be the weather. He was just too cold to make the strike. A large log lay close by, and with his slight headache, he moved ever so slowly under it and, perhaps, back to some more winter sleep. He had warned me not to step on him. Luckily I had not, and we arrived at a mutual understanding that going our respective ways was best for both of us. He would let me run my boat in the creeks and waters of his swamp, that I might continue hunting ducks; and I would let him spend the rest of the winter under his log, so that he might continue to lord up and down his favorite flat where I had found him.

# *18*

# PINE ISLAND CREEK

Ducks flying any swamp seem to have a prime flight path, and the Santee Swamp offered a great one. It was Pine Island Creek, located in the approximate center of the five-mile-wide swamp. In my years of duck hunting the swamp from one end to the other, I learned that more ducks flew over and up this creek than any other. They were mostly leaving the refuge down below at Summerton, South Carolina. We called the refuge "The Bluff," and most mornings, particularly when the water was rising in the swamp above, the ducks would make the long flight to feed on the many ridges. Oh, there might be a day or two a season when Otter Flat might be hot, or Hog House Creek; but, generally, Pine Island had the most ducks. In 1959 I saw several thousand mallards light all over the Otter Flat area at daylight, but only once. In certain areas of Pine Island Creek, I have several times seen many thousands congregate in acorn flats. It just seemed that the huge acorn ridges bordering this creek pulled the most ducks.

Leaving Otter Flat, Pine Island Creek ran north for miles and made a circle around the top end of Pine Island itself. The huge ridges on the right included Big Backwater Slough, a dandy spot for decoying the mallards headed northward. Farther over were several creeks such as Hog House (called Snake Creek by some hunters), Briar Log, Fifty Fools, and the last one close to Sumter County was Mill Creek.

On the left side of Pine Island Creek was where I spent many of my years roaming the countless flats and ridges. On the left were several size-able oak ridges that were some of my favorites, including what I referred to as Squirrel Ridge. Many times I roamed these from the Pine Island Creek side instead of the Otter Flat side. Eventually, they all became home to my activities. This area had many good openings that bordered the acorn ridges and were good for decoying mallards. One such spot we named the

Big Flat. It was, perhaps, a quarter mile above Squirrel Ridge, and it was one of the top spots for pulling in ducks on their way up Pine Island Creek. A good decoy spread ambushed many flocks there over the years. The period I hunted this area was from 1965 to 1985. Getting into the Big Flat was easy from Pine Island Creek, except on low water when the whole area was just mud puddles. I also knew how to enter from below by Squirrel Ridge, or come in from the Otter Flat side through a beautiful pothole I referred to as the Roost Hole. A very old, rotted blind indicated this may have been someone else's favorite spot long before I came upon it. Shooting over decoys in the Roost Hole proved to be another one of my favorite spots for calling mallards.

I explored the Big Flat area thoroughly, on foot and with my sneak boat, and learned it well. I don't think there was a good spot that I hadn't visited or hunted several times.

My son, Jay, was a teenager when he began to hunt the swamp with other young duck hunters, and his love for swamp hunting started in Pine Island Creek. I took him to Squirrel Ridge and other ridges close by many times. He learned to get around and to locate the good spots I had told him about. The Roost Hole became one of his favorites, and he hunted it successfully for several years.

About 1985 was the time this area began to be overrun with what my son and I called "slob hunters" and "rednecks," referring to duck hunters who have no consideration at all for others. With their arrival, the best hunting in the Santee Swamp began to disappear. Baiting ducks with corn was common with these undesirables. They would attempt to close off an area, gaining cooperation from other hunters. They used loudmouth tactics and profanity. These bullies became commonplace. Shotguns were fired in the dark at unsuspecting hunters as they tried to enter. They would burn gas lanterns all night long and try to monopolize an area.

One morning I attempted to hunt Squirrel Ridge, and upon arriving, saw lanterns glowing all the way down to the big pothole at the end of the ridge. What a disappointment—slob hunters had taken over. Another incident occurred one morning at the entrance to the Big Flat just above. I was coming in from the Pine Island side, when two boats suddenly appeared and blocked my way. These hunters were from Florence, South Carolina, and said they and a dozen other hunters had been there for a week before the season opened and that they had the area covered.

Spending the night in their boats in order to claim a spot became common in the Santee Swamp. And even that didn't keep the strong-arm tactics from contributing further to the decline of courtesy in the swamp. Jay and his chocolate Lab, Cajun, resorted to spending the night in their boat near Moe's Lake in hopes of hunting an area I called Big Roost Flat. Braving cold all night and even having his decoys out were not enough, as two boatloads of rednecks came in and said, "You're not hunting here, we are." They jumped out of their boats and immediately picked up my son's decoys and threw them into his boat.

Before the inconsiderate slob hunters were numerous, Pine Island Creek was tops. The left side above the Big Flat is known as the Great Ridge. This ridge extended all the way westward to the upper end of Otter Flat, to Little Creek and Broadwater Creek, and ended at Indigo Flat. I hunted the Great Ridge many times for squirrels, as they were abundant among the huge oaks. Many ducks fed on the edges of Pine Island Creek, that far up. I walked its edges countless times and saw few people that deep in the swamp. From that point, a boater was a good two hours away from getting out of the big swamp. Boat or motor trouble was something a hunter didn't want, way up there. I always ran Johnson outboards because they were reliable and durable, and always teased someone running a Mercury that he was mighty brave coming that far with a motor like that. Mercurys were always fast, but not so reliable in years past. The Santee Swamp took its toll on boats and motors. The stumps and logs a rig had to run over bent many aluminum boat bottoms and propellers. It was my habit to keep a new 25-horsepower Johnson on my boats, as Carolyn was always expecting to see me arrive in the backyard an hour or so after dark. We had a standing rule that if I wasn't home by ten o'clock at night she was to send someone after me. I was close to the deadline a few times, and I knew she was about to stand on her head! But I always assured her that I knew the swamp well and respected its dangers on every trip.

About a mile from the top end of Pine Island Creek was a flat off to the right that fed floodwater into some giant oaks on several ridges. When the water was not high these were ridges I hunted, mainly for squirrels; but they would attract thousands of mallards when the water was higher. I used hip boots when squirrel hunting, and I could cross most of the flats between the ridges with them.

There was quite a crop of squirrels that year, and in planning a trip to hunt them, I invited my brother, John, my son, Jay, and two friends: John Jackson and his pastor, the Reverend Lynn Corbett. We would take two boats and carry cooking equipment in hopes of having a squirrel stew on Pine Island Creek. Conditions for squirrel hunting appeared to be good. Not much wind, and sunny weather should have the squirrels moving.

We left Low Falls shortly after daybreak and hurried up the river, on into Riser's Old River and down Otter Flat to where Pine Island Creek entered. Then we jumped stumps all the way up to the flat on the right and parked our boats there. I sent my four guests in the direction of easy walking, but good squirrel-hunting, territory, and I took off in the opposite direction. Wearing hip boots, I crossed the little washed-out gut that fed water to the ridges beyond. As I reached the ridge across the little gut and entered a cane break on higher ground, I heard ducks chattering ahead. Slowing down and staying in the canes, I eased to the edge of the cover and peered out. When I did, mallards by the hundreds ran off the edge of the nearby flat and joined hundreds more in the water.

I retreated ever so slowly, as the ducks had not seen what they had heard. What a sight! I knew nobody would believe me without seeing it for themselves. Backtracking as quickly as I could, I found my guests not far from the boats. I told them, excitedly, about coming upon the multitudes of ducks and they said, almost in unison, "Let's get a look at that many ducks!" They followed me as quietly as possible, and soon we were all crawling through the canes on our hands and knees. As we approached the edge of the canes, hundreds of mallards again ran off the edge of the oak ridge like chickens running to be fed. They joined thousands crowding the shallow flat. They had been disturbed and began to take flight. The air was so full of ducks it seemed as if they would touch wings as they beat skyward. Not only was the near flat full of ducks, but the next one over, also. We all agreed it beat anything we had ever seen in such a small area. We estimated their numbers to be around ten thousand. Had they spent the night up there, or had that many come in since daylight that morning? I wish my Sony camcorder had been with me way back then!

The mallards milled around all morning, and quite a few returned to feed on their swamp acorns. The four of us went on squirrel hunting, but wished the duck season had not ended the week before.

My squirrel rifle at that time was a Browning lever action BL-22 rim-fire with a 4X telescopic sight. It was very light and had a fairly light trigger pull for accurate shooting. I loved to squirrel hunt because I got the chance to walk again beneath the beauty of Santee's huge oaks. There were so many animals of the swamp that depended on oaks for their food, but none more than the squirrels. My eyesight has always been good, and with the help of the scope on my little rifle, I could find the cagey squirrels hiding high in the big trees. I loved to find a feed tree, betrayed by all the cuttings beneath it, and just sit off a ways and wait for the hungry squirrels to make their way through the branches early and late each day. But, when the temperature was low, activity didn't start until the midmorning's warmth.

By noon, everyone was back at the boats and reporting in. We had squirrels aplenty for our stew. John Jackson was the best field cook I'd ever seen, and he took over from there. I had told him I would provide the squirrels if he would fix us a "sho-nuff" squirrel stew. John cleaned several squirrels in the creek and then finished washing them with jugs of water he had brought along. Several of us had never eaten squirrel before, and we hadn't brought much else to eat. Watching the squirrels being prepared for cooking kind of turned my brother off. He said to all of us sitting around watching the process, "I ain't eatin' none of that rat stew. Those things look just like large rats." And indeed he didn't eat any. We all laughed when John Jackson stirred the pot and served us each a plate of Santee Swamp squirrel stew. It certainly wasn't as good as John's duck "purlow," but we ate some anyway.

Another friend of mine loved to hunt squirrels, and I took him with me several times. We had a good place to hunt near Rowesville, South Carolina, but we loved the trip into the Santee. Ralph Thompson owned a hardware and sporting goods store in Orangeburg. We became friends when shooting skeet together, and Ralph was my dealer for squirrel guns. I had purchased the BL-22 from him in 1969, and used it one season. It now resides in my closet in its original box. I thought perhaps the BL-22 would become a collector's item over time, but Browning still makes it today. When it was introduced in '69, it was considered to be a copy of the lever action rifles of the old West. Ralph was using a Browning T-Bolt 22 with a Weaver 4X scope. The trigger for a rifle must be crisp and sure, and the T-Bolt's was both. Ralph agreed to order a T-Bolt for me, and I selected the grade two with a 24-inch barrel. We also ordered a pair of Redfield variable-powered scopes for our squirrel specials. The magnification was adjustable from two to seven power; they were ideal for our squirrel hunting. This rifle was the very best for the tall-timber hunting. We shot long rifle cartridges, and the seven power setting was great for searching the tree trunks and leafy limbs high up.

One fall morning, I carried Ralph to the Squirrel Ridge, one of my favorites. We had just gotten out of my boat when he spotted a hole on the side of a big oak. He showed it to me, and we agreed the edges of the hole were freshly worn. It was a good sign squirrels were using it. Ralph wouldn't leave that spot and sat down against a neighboring oak. I left him there and eased on down a piece to get out of his way. During the next hour or so, I heard him shoot six times, and when I returned to him he was right where I'd left him, only now he had five squirrels piled up beside him. I started to tease him because I'd heard him shoot six times. I asked him, "What's the matter with your rifle, doesn't it shoot straight?" He replied, "Of course!" Then he pointed to the water's edge. There lay a sizeable cottonmouth moccasin as dead as he could be—with half his head shot off.

Ralph was twenty years my senior, and our last trip for squirrels was way up Fuller's Earth Creek. His eyesight for the woods was failing then, and his hearing, too; but not his desire to hunt. We cooked hamburgers in the swamp that day, and he again thanked me for taking care of him and continuing to carry him to the Santee. The trees were his friends, too. We even named some of them. One big white oak the squirrels loved, we named "Hardees." Ralph had only one child, a son who was a doctor living and practicing in Denver, Colorado. They were together only a couple of times each year, and I believe that's why he and I became such special friends. Ralph passed away in 1994 and my wife and I miss him so much. Carolyn always described him as a real southern gentleman, a breed that is disappearing all too rapidly.

———

Every hunter wants to be successful as often as conditions allow, and I had many successful hunts in the Santee Swamp. Yet there were some miscues, too. I recall a hunt with my son, Jay, who at that time was a young teenager, when I was beginning to show him the swamp. He was old enough for us to travel in separate directions in search of ducks on the ridges. He loved the big swamp and a chance to shoot the mallards in Pine Island Creek.

A small oak ridge bordered Pine Island Creek where I frequently parked my boat and proceeded to hunt. Adjacent to it was a very large ridge bordering the big flat and extending all the way to the squirrel ridge pothole. A shallow slough separated the two ridges and could normally be crossed with hip boots or waders. Jay had started using my Sweet 16 and I was carrying the Remington 1100. I was sending Jay across the little slough and on down the big ridge, which had been very productive. Many mallards and woodies used the big flat and the ridges around it. I would walk down the little ridge and cross the flat down a ways from where Jay was to cross. So we split up and I was already out of sight when I heard him fire the 16-gauge one time. I was surprised that he had taken a shot so soon. I wouldn't know what had happened until I returned later.

Headed on farther away, I was about ready to cross the little slough as planned, when I spied a dozen or so mallards tipping up and feeding on the very end of the little ridge. They were very busy and were underneath a rather large gum tree, which had stood there for many years. I had actually stood beside the gum years before and shot woodies going up the swamp in the early light. The old tree was a spot the ducks flew over and on up the swamp, following Pine Island Creek.

Sizing up the situation and how I might get close enough for a shot, I concluded that cover would run out about sixty yards from the feeding ducks. But I had good sneaking cover for a ways yet. I thought to perhaps crawl the last twenty yards or so and end up behind a large log which I figured would be as close as I could get. Everything went as planned, and I reached the log without any noise. The ducks were still under the gum and probably hunting the little seeds that fall from the gum balls. My Uncle Johnnie had passed that bit of hunting savvy on to me when hunting the Wateree Swamp many seasons before.

Making sure the 12-gauge had three shells in it, I raised up slowly to take my first shot from behind the log; but peering across the top of the partially decayed log, I realized the distance between us was just too far. The sun was making those greenheads shine, but they still looked too far away. They weren't coming any closer, so if I wanted a crack at them, the only thing left was to close that distance as fast as I could by running. I knew the mallards would get up, but I might be close enough to bring down a couple when they jumped. Getting to my knees, I stepped over the log and began to run. I must have gained ten yards on those ducks before they took off. I stopped and fired into the midst of the fleeing flock. Ducks hit the water, and all were cripples, swimming away and out the little slough. I began to run again in hopes of getting closer for some more shooting, but I was in for a surprise! The hard swamp floor gave way to soft Santee Swamp mud. My wader boots were promptly pulled from my feet as I ran, and down I went. The Remington hit the soft mud just as I did, and I went sprawling. Its barrel gathered six or eight inches of clogging mud, and mud covered the front of my waders from the waist down. What a disgusting predicament—a clogged barrel, mud all over me, and ducks rapidly getting away. As I watched from my knees, the cripples disappeared, and I could see their ripples no more.

I managed to get my feet back into my waders and retrieved my gun. Not only was mud in the barrel, but in the receiver also. I washed some of the mud off me and the Remington, and headed back to Jay, or where I had left him. He was nowhere to be seen, so I cut one or two canes and pulled the barrel off my gun. I was standing in the shallow slough poking a cane into the clogged barrel when I saw Jay coming. He had crossed the slough and had hunted, with no finds this day. He saw me with the barrel off my gun and asked, "Where did all that mud come from?" I told him that the end of this little ridge had plenty, and that I had had some close contact, but the Remington had gotten the worst of it.

The shot I had heard from him was at an unexpected greenhead that had swum in from the big flat. Jay had hunted slowly and had gotten a shot at the big duck and hit him, but he had been outsmarted by the mallard, which disappeared into the little flat. Jay said the duck had gone under water and had never come up. So this day was not the best for the Reynoldses, but the good part was we only shot two shells!

I spent some time around the top of Pine Island Creek where it makes a loop around Pine Island. Through the huge oak ridges were flowing creeks teeming with wildlife. I had some good hunting in one of them with my sneak boat, but I never followed them all the way down to their entrances into the lower Otter Flat area.

Just as Pine Island Creek began to turn northeastward, there was a sizeable flat on the left that flowed back into Indigo Flat. The edge of this flat had an old roadbed on it, which ultimately became a path that led through some of the swamp's biggest oak timber. It followed behind Indigo Flat's many primitive campsites and on around to Broadwater Creek and to a high mound of dirt called Broughton's Mound. It was a long walk, but a beautiful one to take through the woods. It was beyond my imagination how a road could come from the Sumter County hillside and go all the way to the mound, but this is what old maps showed. To cross the many creeks on the way seemed to me to be almost impossible way back then. It was said that the Broughton family used to run hogs in the swamp, and the mound was built for the hogs to retreat to when high water came.

The mound was very close to Broadwater Creek, and I passed it many times. It was an unusual landmark most hunters and fishermen had heard about. It became a popular campsite, even though few folks actually camped on the mound itself.

Thinking of Pine Island Creek brings forth so many memories of exciting, adventuresome times spent there. I remember the first ducks of each morning, normally the woodies, whose whistling wings passed at speeds too swift for a shot. I remember the magnificent oaks—so tall, so plentiful, but not stout enough to withstand the fierce winds of Hurricane Hugo. They once were so dominant on the island that they created a world of their own. I remember the carpet of acorns underneath them that fed the swamp's wildlife abundantly for so long. Some years the earth was dry underneath their leafy arms, and other times I've seen the waters come, and it was as if they stood majestically in a shallow-water world. I remember a few times when their ground became covered with the snows of the late season, signaling the coming of season's end.

Simply put, the big duck with the green head and blue-barred gray wings no longer swims there as before. But, just maybe, another era will come when the trees will stand tall again and drop their acorns in preparation for the big greenheads' return.

# 19

## POCOTALIGO SWAMP
## AND THE HONEY HOLE

It was Tuesday of that special last week of the season in the mid-1960s, and above the small opening in the timber were thirty to forty mallards setting their wings and making their final approach to our decoys. My brother, John, and I had hunted the same spot the day before, and he had also hunted it the previous Saturday. The water level in Pocotaligo swamp was high due to good rains in recent weeks, and the ducks from the Santee Refuge were flying up our way in numbers we had never seen. John had discovered the many mallards on that Saturday and called me about his terrific shoot that day. I had made plans to be on vacation those last days of the season and had come from Orangeburg to hunt the spot with John. Our Monday hunt was productive, like we were shooting in a duck sanctuary. Flock after flock flew up the swamp, and it seemed nearly all of them knew about the hole in the timber.

I had introduced my brother to this section of the swamp in 1964 on Thanksgiving Day. We had been given permission to hunt the swamp, and permission to go through the land bordering the swamp. And now, John with his eight-foot aluminum boat had found this opening in the trees, which was on the far side of a main and deep creek he had crossed with his boat. The area looked like a natural opening in the flooded timber, with cattails growing in most of the area. John had started the clearing of it days before I pitched in. Each trip we would clear a little more, and soon our "Honey Hole" was born.

We erected a blind on one side of the hole, using brown cotton sheets and moss. There was plenty of natural cover to use that would provide a frame for the sheets and moss we had gathered. The blind was large enough for three hunters but, so far, only two of us had used it.

Our hunts that week were memorable, to say the least. I can truthfully say more ducks came to our Honey Hole that week than any other one spot I had ever hunted. Flock after flock decoyed to our setup. And we only used, perhaps, as few as two dozen decoys. Both John and I were pretty good callers, but the mallards' desire to visit the hole in the timber made us feel like we were world champions. We would start our calling to several ducks, then several more would join, then another flock, until at times forty mallards would be backpedaling to settle with others already on the water.

Shooting was so easy that we only shot the big drakes. Shooting the big greenheads at such close ranges, a 20-gauge shotgun would have been all we needed, but we both had 12-gauge Remingtons. With ducks on the water, some coming down, and some leaving, we had our pick of shots, and the shooting was beyond description. There were plenty of vines clinging to the cypress and gum trees that surrounded the opening, and I do remember some of the mallards became lodged in vines as they folded and fell.

On Monday and Tuesday we heard another party shooting some distance from us, but not close enough to cause us any significant problems, at first. But they must have been close enough to see the mallards working our area; and they were using an illegal electronic call with a loudspeaker. We knew the call could be heard a long way, but that didn't seem to be a concern to them. By Tuesday, these hunters had moved closer, and they were clearly a concern to John and me. Little did we know what was in store for Wednesday morning.

We had invited two friends from Walterboro to join us in the Honey Hole on Wednesday. One was an attorney and one was an optometrist. Both had hunted with me in St. Helena Sound when I lived in Walterboro. They had a small boat just right for our hunt and brought it in the back of their station wagon.

We were probably a half hour late in launching our two little paddle boats that morning, and much to our dismay, two guns began shooting as we were leaving the swamp's edge. At first, John and I were not sure of their exact location; but as we paddled farther out into the swamp, we were convinced they were shooting over our decoys. We pulled on the paddles as hard as we could, but before we could cover the distance to our hole, the hunters must have fired two boxes of shells. The daylight couldn't have been fifteen minutes old, but that was all it took for those hunters to do their damage.

Since our guests were following us, John and I were the first to enter our spot and to see two Labrador retrievers running and ripping through our decoys. Mallards lay in every corner, and helping the dogs pick them up were two hunters, probably the ones with the electronic call. Shooting over someone else's decoys is poor duck-hunting etiquette, but that didn't seem to worry these guys. I immediately did some screaming at them to get out of our hole and take those "so and so" Labs with them. They gave me the usual backtalk as we paddled over to our blind. They said they would not leave, and I said, "We'll see about that. Just stay where you are, I'm coming." As I jumped from our boat and was wading out toward the middle to put this fellow down in the water, or have him put me under, his partner said, "Aw, come on, we got enough ducks." These fellows knew John and I meant business and that they were wrong. As I fought the waist-deep, weedy swamp toward them, they turned away with both hands full of mallards they had killed in short order. I surely would have gotten wet that morning!

After those slob hunters left our spot, we straightened up the mess that their Labs made of our decoys, and John and our two very nervous guests waded to our cotton-sheet blind. I headed over about twenty yards to a large hollowed-out, partially rotten stump. It was just large enough for me to hide in. By that time, it was nearing eight o'clock. Conditions had settled down, thankfully; and luckily, I was dry. It wasn't long before a flock was circling and listening to our calls. With heads low and no movement, we watched the cautious mallards look over the opening in the trees, and check out the "fakes" on the water. The wind was gentle and in a direction from my back. The first ones broke their pattern around the treetops and settled down, only to be followed by others confident that all was okay. One mallard with landing gear down came so close to me as I crouched in the stump that I could have reached out and touched him. I'm confident that if I had had a fishing net, I could have caught him. Our volley from the heavy duck loads was loud and brisk as mallards fell to four shotguns. Our guests congratulated each other on picking out the glossy greenheads as they scampered skyward. We had crumpled the majority of the flock with some good shooting.

The morning flew by as we landed a couple more flocks, and our shooters scored several more times. I knew we must be getting close to our limits, so I waded to our hidden boat and retrieved a burlap bag. John had gathered the ducks and separated them into limits. We would put sixteen mallards in the bag and head out, satisfied that we had an excellent day despite the morning skirmish. It was the fourth consecutive day that our Honey Hole had produced a limit shoot.

Thursday and Friday were carbon copies of our first three days. In V-formation they came, on cupped wings they sailed, backpedaling down to our decoys. They challenged us with their matchless ability to come and go so quickly. Once over the decoys, the wiser ones, realizing their mistake, could put limbs and trees between us in an instant. Their wings could claw the air so furiously that they escaped time and time again. Many times we just let them come and go, enjoying the sight, as the drab hens followed the vivid gray bodies and gleaming green heads of their male counterparts. Some say the wood duck is the king of color in the duck world, but in the sunlight of the early morning, it's the mallard drake that gets my vote.

I have sometimes questioned the taking from their wild world the waterfowl that I have. In the infancy of my hunting experiences, I would crawl on hands and knees to get a shot. In the years of seeming abundance, I have taken over a hundred of these beautiful creatures in a season without the first inkling that this might be wrong. When fewer ducks flew my way during later lean years, I hesitated to take the shot, and when I did, an apology to the downed bird seemed appropiate.

The five days I spent with my brother in the Honey Hole, I realized that our taking so many may have been wrong. But plentiful as they were, it didn't seem so at the time.

On Friday of that week, a most unusual incident happened that prompted me to unload the gun for the rest of the season and reawakened my misgivings about taking too many waterfowl. John and I had not picked up our downed birds yet, but we had plenty on the water and others not far from the decoys. We had been shooting from the burlap blind. John had left to retrieve the birds he had spotted, and when leaving the blind, he left the burlap flap up on the entrance side. The water depth in the blind was, perhaps, eighteen inches, and we had our foldaway stools standing in the water. The bottoms of the cloth seats were almost getting wet.

Out of nowhere a mallard hen came sailing in. She was a surprise, for sure, and I struggled and fumbled to get the gun pointed in her direction.

As she reversed her decision and beat the air frantically to leave, my shot was a poor one, as only one pellet must have found the mark. She tumbled to the water, almost directly in front of our blind. She righted herself, and with her head slightly to one side, paddled, not knowing where she was headed. But her paddling took her around to the open end of the blind. In she came, through the shallow water, right on past my waders, until she bumped into my almost sunken stool. There she laid her head on my stool where she took her last breath. Things like that still make me wonder, and that was many years ago.

# 20

## Guns I Could Shoot

Hunters, especially duck hunters, can be a strange but dedicated bunch. Some, like me, do nothing during duck season but hunt ducks, and doing something else is almost unheard of and borders on the realm of the ridiculous. Then there are those who hunt only on occasion, and they may take a trip somewhere to try their luck only once a year. They own a shotgun that was perhaps bought years ago and gets two boxes of shells run through it each year. It stays in that remote corner of the closet, safely tucked away in an expensive, leather gun case. It sees very little daylight and, chances are, will be the only shotgun this hunter will ever own. That shotgun will last him a lifetime.

But some of us are constantly looking for that special shotgun that feels just right and comes to our shoulder with our eyes in perfect alignment down its ventilated barrel. My first such shotgun was the Browning Sweet 16 semiautomatic that my wife helped me buy while we still lived in Kansas. Browning guns were not discounted in those days; they were sold for retail price only, and were highly priced. The balance of the gun with its 28-inch barrel seemed just right, and the light weight of the 16-gauge appealed to me. I've always thought the Sweet 16's bigger brother, the Light 12, had too large a hump on its receiver. And, being slightly built since childhood, I didn't want the recoil of a 12-gauge. I had shot a 16-gauge Ithaca pump gun previously and felt somewhat loyal to the 16-gauge family.

The Sweet 16 took its toll on the ducks at Cheyenne Bottoms that last winter in Kansas. And after returning to South Carolina in 1958, I shot many cases of shells with it at doves and ducks. In the early sixties, Winchester introduced their Mark V shell, which features a plastic collar around the shot column, and it was this shell that made the 16-gauge an outstanding shotgun. I remember one particular dove shoot when I was really "on," and every dove that came my way fell to the Mark V shells and the

Sweet 16. A hunter behind me remarked, "We may as well leave; that fellow is not gonna miss this day."

I carried the Sweet 16 for seven years, and it accounted for hundreds of doves and ducks. From Kansas to the salt marshes of South Carolina, and particularly places like the Combahee River marsh, the St. Helena Sound marsh, and, of course, the Santee Swamp, the little gun was my favorite. Today, it honors my gun cabinet and stands there in proud remembrance of our days together.

After coming to Orangeburg in 1965, I met Al Fischer, who introduced me to his hobby of reloading shotgun shells. Al loaded 12-gauge and 20-gauge shells, but his favorite was 20-gauge. We hunted some together, and through him I became interested in reloading, mainly due to the economy of it. But 16-gauge empty shell cases were not readily available. Most of the "empties" came from gun clubs around the state which featured skeet shooting in 12- and 20-gauges There were no 16-gauge guns being used in skeet.

Just before the 1965 duck season, I bought my second special shotgun, a Remington model 1100 12-gauge, with 28-inch modified barrel with ventilated rib. The gun fit me to a T, and I knew that if the barrel would shoot where I was looking, it should be very productive. I remember the first shell I fired in the 1100; a wood duck drake fell from above the trees of Pocotaligo Swamp. I knew this was a good omen.

The Sweet 16 was my first gun with a vent rib, and that spoiled me from then on. Remington had introduced the gas-operated Model 1100 in 1963. It had followed other gas-operated Models 58 and 878. The gas operation reduced the recoil considerably, enough for me to feel comfortable about having a bigger gun and the availability of using reloaded shells. Another bonus to reloading was being able to match the load to a particular gun's barrel characteristics. By using different components and different propellants (gunpowder )in reloading, a particular combination would pattern better than others.

I worked with the 1100 for months and shot many of my reloads at pattern sheets on a door of an old barn near my home. During that time, I was shooting doves and ducks constantly. The 1100 with my reloads was working. The 1⅛-ounce load of number eights was terrific on doves out to fifty yards; and the 1¼-ounce load of number fives took many ducks from the Santee Swamp and from the salt marsh in St. Helena Sound. Not only was I shooting well, but my reloaded shells functioned well in the gun. Eventually, I created a 1½-ounce load for the Remington. It would be the heaviest load for a 2¾-inch chambered 12-gauge. The big load was extremely effective for my sneak hunting in the swamps. I used number six shot for the on-the-water ducks, and made some unbelievable shots, bagging several ducks at a time with just one of the big shells.

In 1967, I helped organize a gun club here in Orangeburg. It would become a skeet-shooting club, and started out with a few avid shooters and manual target traps. But it grew to over a hundred members and participation on weekends was high. After leasing a location or two for several years, the club prospered to the point that we bought some property for a permanent home. Mid-Carolina Gun Club became a prominent club in our state, and competition among members was fierce.

I really enjoyed skeet shooting, as it continued to improve my hunting skills with the shotgun. Remington guns were very popular with skeet shooters, and since I shot my field gun well, I bought a 12-gauge SB grade Remington 1100 and then a 20-gauge SA grade Remington 1100. Great skeet-shooting champions like D. Lee Braun and Alex Kerr used Remington skeet guns, and I think those two had some influence on my gun selections. Also, fine shooters I came to know casually, such as Al Morrison and Ken Wilson, who were on a Marine skeet-shooting team, did well with Remingtons. The SB-grade skeet model had a higher grade of wood in the stock and forearm, and were beautiful guns. With these two guns, I won the Mid-Carolina Gun Club championship three consecutive years, in 1969, 1970, and 1971. I was very proud of this accomplishment, because as I looked back on my shotgun shooting early on, I struggled to learn wing shooting. Those two Remingtons were fine target guns, and I considered them special on the skeet fields, but skeet-choked barrels were not much for hunting.

My son, Jay, was coming along with his hunting, and had been using the Sweet 16 on occasion; being a tall youngster, he took a liking to my Remington 1100 hunting gun. He knew its reputation and had heard me talk about the remarkable 12-gauge patterns the gun produced. He would take it on hunts, and eventually I gave it up to his use.

I bought a 28-inch modified barrel for the 12-gauge skeet gun in hopes of duplicating the effectiveness and patterning of my now older and almost worn-out hunting gun. I remember one day as I disassembled the old 1100 for cleaning that a couple of parts just fell out of its receiver. Many heavy duck loads had been run through it, and thousands of dove reloads, too; they had about shaken the gun apart. So we sent it to Remington for a rebuilding job, and my son used it for several years while I struggled to find another gun I could shoot. The new barrel for my skeet gun was nowhere near the great barrel I had hoped for. I shot it poorly on hunts even though it was my championship skeet gun.

A couple of years of poor shooting prompted another gun purchase. I had always wished that Browning would market a 12-gauge gas-operated model and, finally, they did. Just maybe this would be my next special gun! I bought a Browning model 2000 semiautomatic with two barrels, a 28-inch modified and a 26-inch improved-cylinder. The gun was quality all through, but on the heavy side. I immediately took the gun and both barrels to the pattern board. Neither barrel did well. I was really disappointed, but tried to overlook the poor patterns, and shot it two or three seasons with poor success. The 2000 functioned well and held up, but it was never exactly what I had hoped for.

My hunting partners had begun questioning my shooting, so I tried a new model Browning B-80 semiautomatic. It was lighter and was a fair gun. I even bought a beautiful Browning Superposed 12-gauge over-and-under made in Belgium with barrels choked, improved cylinder, and modified. I shot the over-and-under quite well, but the recoil was terrible. It cost a bundle, and I hated to mar it while hunting ducks. So I sold the Superposed and made a few dollars on the sale. Next, I ran into a Remington 1100 with 30-inch full-choked barrel with 3-inch chamber. It was the biggest gun I had ever owned. Since I had hunted with friends who had the 3-inch chambered guns, just maybe one might be what I was searching for. But, in the end, it was just another heavy, slow gun that shot big shells. I still had the Browning B-80 12-gauge so I sold the 3-inch magnum Remington.

I continued to shoot the B-80 for a couple of seasons, while acquiring a 20-gauge Browning over-and-under with 26-inch barrels. Unfortunately, the gun was too light on the front end and swung badly due to poor balance.

Guns were getting quite expensive by now, and I still hadn't found another really special 12-gauge to use in the duck blind. A sale came along for the 20-gauge Browning over-and-under, so I let it go without regret. I had enjoyed the 20-gauge in dove fields, and the smaller 1-ounce load shells made for less weight to carry. I was attracted to the smaller and more slender barrels on 20-gauge guns, and on the skeet field I shot the smaller gun about as well as the bigger guns. I really felt the 20-gauge was sporty in dove fields. The recoil was less, and carrying the light gun was a joy. Age can change your mind, and I wasn't a youngster any more.

I checked around for a 28-inch Browning Citori 20-gauge. This over-and-under, made in Japan for Browning, was balanced much better than the 26-inch model I had sold. I could never run up on one that was priced right. But my brother-in-law in North Augusta knew a dealer who would order what I wanted at a discount. I checked with him several times about a 28-inch Citori over-and-under, but his distributor never could deliver the gun. This dealer offered me a good price on a Ruger 20-gauge over-and-under, and the gun had screw-in chokes included. This was a feature that would save money in the long run. I remember Browning was the first manufacturer I had heard of with this feature, but now most all the big gun companies were offering it.

I asked this dealer to order a Ruger Red Label 20-gauge with 28-inch barrels. The gun came in a couple of weeks, and my brother-in-law picked it up for me. I bought it sight unseen and on reputation only. The Red Label had a silver stainless steel receiver and was an attractive gun, but I quickly sensed it was heavy. I took the gun to the grocery store and had it weighed. Much to my surprise, the new 20-gauge weighed almost eight pounds. Gosh, what would a 12-gauge weigh?

I immediately put it to use in dove fields and found the heavy gun shot quite well. The extra weight helped with follow-through on the fast-moving doves, and this 20-gauge was far superior to others I had owned. Performance was excellent, and the choice of the over-and-under's two chokes was something to play with in the field! I had several excellent shoots with it.

The duck-hunting scene was converting to steel (nontoxic) shot, a change nobody welcomed. The steel shotshells were expensive, and nobody knew exactly what their performance would be. All my 12-gauge guns were 2¾-inch chambered. Steel loads that size were said to be poor performers in the duck blind and almost useless in pass-shooting over the treetops. Choke for choke, steel shot loads patterned tighter than lead loads. The word was to use open chokes for steel, and I just happened to have the Browning 2000 with two barrels, one of them bored-improved cylinder, and the Browning B-80 with screw-in chokes, one of which was improved cylinder. I got good results at short ranges with the 2000 and B-80 using the improved cylinder barrel and the improved cylinder screw-in choke. They would take ducks out to about thirty yards. I don't think the ammunition companies had figured out how to load steel shot effectively in the early going. I was never pleased with the apparent lack of range with steel shot. There were a lot of favorable comments being written about the new 3-inch loads in 3-inch chambered guns.

Since steel shot was here to stay, I decided I'd make the change to a 3-inch-chambered 12-gauge. My duck-hunting reloads had become illegal. My son had bought a 12-gauge Beretta with 3-inch chamber, and I liked the feel of it. Jay's Beretta was a Model 303 semiautomatic and was to be discontinued shortly in favor of the new Model 390 semiautomatic. The 303 was not a heavy 12-gauge, but with the longer chamber would give me more firepower and, hopefully, a little more range.

I shopped around, but the 303s were scarce since the introduction of Beretta's 390. The Model 390s that I tried were heavy, but said to have an improved gas-metering system for a greater variety of loads. I had left word with a gun dealer in Columbia, South Carolina, regarding my desire to have a Beretta 303 semiautomatic in the 3-inch chamber with screw-in chokes. Finally, I received a call from him saying he had two coming in, and wanted to know if I was still interested. I was, and he phoned me a few days later. I carried my Browning B-80 with me and drove over to look at the guns. Both were very nice and had different barrel lengths. I chose the 28-inch barrel, as it balanced out nicely. The trade was favorable, and I came home with the Beretta 303 and left my Browning B-80. A few days later, I sold the Browning 2000.

Beretta shotguns were featuring a method of changing stock-drop, cast-on and cast-off. Their owner's manual gave instructions on how to do this, and very soon I had the new 303's stock dimensions just like I wanted. I had learned to prefer a little more drop at comb and heel than other shooters, mainly because I have a tendency of not keeping my head down on the stock when shooting. Other gun companies copied Beretta and featured a similar stock-change system, such as Benelli and, recently, Browning also.

During the nineties, I had much success with the 303 on ducks around the Santee. Diving ducks had migrated to the lakes, and shooting the rapid-moving divers over decoys became my favorite duck hunting. Lakes Marion and Moultrie held a good concentration of ringnecks, canvasbacks, and redhead ducks due to the grass infestation that covered much acreage in sections of the lakes' shallow water. The Beretta 303's improved cylinder screw-in choke, along with number three steel shot, was consistently effective out to about thirty-five yards. But, farther than that, the steel seemed to be nothing but a crippler. Beretta, in the late nineties, made some attractive changes to their Model 390 and lightened these models considerably. These changes brought the weight of the 390 to about the same weight of the discontinued Model 303.

I learned of a gun shop in Augusta, Georgia, that had received five of the new, lighter-weight 390s. They were designated AL 390s and were made in Silver Mallard, their field-grade gun, and Gold Mallard, their deluxe model with a much higher grade of wood in stock and forearm, with gold inlay on their receiver. Seeing five Gold Mallard Berettas at one time was too much for me. All five were simply a sight to see, and the gun dealer said, "Take your pick." It took quite a while to choose one, but the most beautiful shotgun I've ever owned now stands in my gun cabinet. With the screw-in chokes and stock adjustments they feature, Beretta is very high on my list. Their quality is tops and they are extremely reliable. The Gold Mallard 12-gauge is my backup gun for the 303 and goes on special hunts, both dove and duck. It shoots like a champ with most factory loads, which I now use exclusively, as reloading shells has become cost prohibitive. As of this date, the 303 and the AL 390 are both killers. With improved cylinder chokes in the barrels and ducks over my decoys, I feel as confident as I ever have that putting ducks on their backs will be almost a sure thing. In 1998, I bought from this same dealer a 20-gauge Gold Mallard Beretta, and it too has provided some good shooting in dove fields. It seems to pattern number 8 and 7½ shot equally well. When I can pick up a limit of twelve doves using seventeen or eighteen shells, I figure that's good shooting; and I seem to be able to do that with any of my three Berettas.

Before the '99 duck season started, I was, as usual, thumbing through a hunting-supply catalog and noticed something I was not aware was even made. There was an ad by Briley Mobil Chokes listing a light modified choke for steel shot for most major brands of shotguns. I thought I had heard of most chokes, but never a light modified, so I called Briley. And, as I thought, the choke was slightly tighter than improved cylinder but less than modified. Now, that just might be exactly what it would take to make my Berettas special guns. So I ordered one for the 12-gauge and one for the 20-gauge.

Just prior to the opening of duck season, I screwed out the Beretta improved-cylinder choke and screwed in the Briley light modified. Steel shot shells are so expensive that I gave up pattern testing several years before. But, as they say, "The proof's in the puddin'," and so it was with the 303 and light modified choke.

My son, Jay, and I began the '99 duck season with a trip to Arkansas. Jay had leased a flooded soybean field of about sixty-five acres located in a major flyway on the banks of the Cache River. It was his first year of the lease, and we didn't know just how good it would be. Two pits were located in the field, and we chose the one farthest from the river because more water was around it.

Arriving the afternoon before our first hunt, we found thirty-five to forty ducks sitting around the pit, feeding on the soybeans. They promptly left and circled several times before flying to who knows where. Jay and I cut bamboo canes from nearby and camouflaged the pit and little island of field dirt pushed up by our lessor. There had been some rain, which had put about two inches of water in the metal pit. We began to bail out the water and found a dozen or so small frogs that had taken up residence in our new pit. They were relieved to get back outside. The blind wasn't covered too well, but was suitable for our opening morning. It would also be Jay's young Lab's first duck hunt. Drake had made the trip with us and was eager to be a part of his daddy's hunt the next morning.

We arrived in good time to make the walk out across the flooded beans and to put out about three dozen decoys. Drake ran ahead in the darkness and checked out the shallow ten-inch deep water around the pit. Jay would place the decoys like he wanted, and Drake would pick them up and try to deliver them to his master's hand—puppy play, for sure. Finally every decoy was out, and we had coaxed Drake down into the pit, which he immediately showed a dislike for. I had brought along the Beretta 303 with the new light modified choke. As the choke was an extended model it reached past the gun's barrel, probably a half-inch. I had not yet fired the gun with this choke. Also, my Sony camcorder was in my carry bag to record Drake's first hunt.

The first rays of sunlight appeared from across the Cache River swamp. We hoped the ducks would be early, as we had done just a light afternoon camouflage job the day before. Jay had put me on the river end of the pit, and I was tending my post by straining to see any movement from the river swamp. The Beretta was stuffed with number two steel loads, and Jay was using his big Benelli 3½-inch magnum 12-gauge and number one steel loads. We really didn't know what our action would be, but in the very early light three dark shapes appeared, coming from the river toward the decoys on my side of the pit. I alerted Jay that ducks were on the move. The sun had just peeped through the river's timber; and as I watched the shapes coming from the sun's blinding light, I could not make out just what was coming, but I knew they were sizeable ducks. They never circled, but backpedaled to slow their landing. I stood without any hesitation, took the first bird on the right, and it folded. Then the Beretta swung to the left and covered the next dark bird as he put his feet down. The "twos" were sent his way and he folded. The third bird, in his startled state, changed his mind and veered to his right, only to be met by another load of steel. Much to my surprise, I had made a triple on the first ducks of the season. The three weren't wiggling, they weren't going to swim away. Jay got Drake up and out of the pit, and I retrieved my camcorder. Drake had never picked up a duck, but he eagerly went where Jay directed. His first retrieves were for his granddaddy's triple on still-unidentified ducks. Drake went to the first one and picked it up gingerly, and then dropped it. He did this repeatedly while Jay coaxed him to bring it to hand, and the Sony whirred away, recording the comical retrieve. Jay walked out to where the first duck was being mouthed and hollered back my way, "Mallard!" His young yellow Lab was sent to the second duck lying still on his back. Drake mouthed this one too, and demonstrated his method of partial retrieval. Jay again called "Mallard!" Then Jay sent Drake, with feathers still in his mouth, toward the third downed duck. He was learning fast, and as Jay clapped his hands for Drake to "Bring it here," we were rewarded on film with the young dog's first full retrieve. The duck was a drake ringneck. It was hard to figure just why a ringneck was flying with a pair of mallards. What a beginning for me and for Drake!

I felt good about the new choke, and as the season progressed, I made shots at ranges previously not possible. I had found and put together a combination of shot size, choke constriction, and gun that would prove itself throughout the 1999 season. And, even though coming quite late in my hunting years, I could indeed designate this Beretta 303 as another special gun I could shoot.

I have yet to try the new choke in my Gold Mallard AL 390, but I will this coming season. Even without the new choke, it shoots like a champ in flooded timber. This gun is beautifully balanced and comes to my face and shoulder like all my other specials. I have a good feeling about my backup Beretta. The two always accompany me on trips to the duck blinds.

During the early part of 1999, my left shoulder suffered an injury known as a torn rotator cuff. The constant pain in it ran through my left arm and down to my elbow. I really didn't know what was wrong, but that fall a shoulder specialist in Charleston, South Carolina, diagnosed it and we considered an operation at that time. But, since hunting season was approaching and trips were in the making, I begged him to get me through hunting season with medication, and we would consider the operation the first part of the coming year.

Through most of the '99 season, my shoulder bothered me when mounting the shotgun. It ached most all the time, but as the season progressed it gradually hurt less and less. By the end of the shooting season, I only had occasional pain. I could again do things and make moves that previously hurt. It still cracks and feels odd, but I'm getting by.

Just recently, I added to my gun cabinet a new, very light 20-gauge. It is a Benelli Montefeltro Super 90 and weighs 5½ pounds. I hope this little semiautomatic will be a joy to carry and shoot in the dove fields. And down the road, I may try it on ducks. Who knows, my shoulders may not be able to handle the heavy 12-gauge loads. And, just maybe, the little 20 can pull me through a bit longer.

My search for guns I could shoot has brought me much enjoyment, and as I reminisce about the good ones and the not so good ones, I remember each for what it contributed to my cherished experiences in the fields, marshes, and swamps of South Carolina.

# *21*

# JOHN JACKSON AND
# THE HOUSEBOAT HUNTS

I met John Jackson in 1967 when I was actively shooting skeet with the Mid-Carolina Gun Club in Orangeburg. We both were trying to break a hundred targets without a miss, commonly called "a hundred straight" in the skeet world. John was a great natural shotgunner. He shot from his left shoulder, as he had lost the sight of his right eye as a child. He was a true competitor and very tough to top. We did get our hundred straight the same week. As I recall, that was June 1968. I saved the target scorecard.

We became hunting and fishing friends after that, and I managed to get John interested in hunting ducks. He had always been an avid deer hunter, and spent most of his hunting season listening to his pack of dogs on deer drives all over the state. Managing to break him loose from that was no easy task, but after the first season of shooting decoying mallards, his interest picked up. He soon spent a couple of weeks during December and January working on his duck hunting.

Not too long into duck hunting, John and two friends bought a factory-made houseboat, complete with 55-horsepower Evinrude motor, gas furnace for heat, gas stove for cooking, and plenty of space to sleep two or three hunters. It was truly a "home away from home," and we referred to it in that fashion from then on. They painted it an olive drab color and covered all the windows with plywood, cutting the glare and shine from the glass windowpanes. Then, a very comfortable blind from which we could shoot was erected on the top, as well as seats, door, and gun racks. Steve Eagar, one of the three owners, did a great job making the blind. And J. L. Pinckney, the third owner, provided the camoflauge netting to cover the sides, front, and back. We also used natural cover such as moss, cypress limbs, and bamboo canes.

My early years of houseboat hunting were done around the Jack's Creek area which is located on the Summerton, South Carolina, side of Lake Marion and very close to the Santee National Waterfowl Refuge. South Carolina had many ducks in those days, and this refuge regularly wintered 100,000-plus mallards, and many wigeon, pintails, gadwalls, teal, and wood ducks. The refuge contained prime duck habitat, and its fields were planted in various grains to attract and hold the many ducks that were regular visitors to the Santee lakes area. At times, the refuge was home to as many as 25,000 Canada geese.

Some of the best hunting from the houseboat occurred when the boat was located on what was known as the Line. And it was about then that I began to enjoy shooting with John and J. L. The Line was actually the refuge boundary line that ran through an area known to the duck hunters as Line Island. This area was well liked by both the ducks and the hunters; it consisted of low cypress trees, ironwood bushes, and several nice-sized potholes of shallow water. It was not an area for feeding, but rather a resting area. The ducks were back and forth in flocks, pairs, and singles, and they afforded us many opportunities to fool them to our decoys. Our little pothole on the Line held about three dozen large mallard decoys in a natural setting, just right for attracting the refuge waterfowl.

To experience the sunrises and the view from atop the houseboat was worth the trip itself. From it, we could see across the slough separating our location from the refuge bluff where the cornfields and small rest ponds held thousands of puddle ducks and geese. Several times each day, large flocks of geese would take to the sky and, lucky for us, they would sometimes come over our setup on the Line. Bagging a couple of Canadas would top off a good duck hunt. We learned that the key to decoying the ducks was getting their attention quickly with loud and long calling. Our duck calls possessed great volume, and with two of us calling loudly, we got our share of the Line Island ducks.

We were able to hunt Line Island only a couple of seasons, as the refuge boundary was extended to include all the good hunting around Jack's Creek. Needless to say, we were extremely disappointed about that.

Following the refuge expansion, we moved the houseboat up the open lake about two miles. For years, we knew the ducks left the refuge each morning to fly up the lake to what we called "the swamp." This swampy area of Lake Marion consisted of about twelve thousand acres of prime duck habitat. The cypress flats that mingled among the huge oak tree ridges attracted mostly mallards and wood ducks. Especially when the water level was high enough to overflow the flats and flood the great oaks, the ducks made daily trips from the refuge to the swamp. Also, above the Santee Swamp, the Congaree and Wateree Swamps drew the acorn-hungry mallards like a magnet. I remember Uncle Johnnie telling me how much an acorn meant to a duck in the Wateree.

The new houseboat location developed into the most enjoyable spot we ever hunted. It seemed to be just right not only for calling mallards to our oversized decoys, but also for encountering the many wigeon also using the area. The lake had begun to grow several varieties of grass in that section, and the wigeon loved frolicking in the grass. Our location was on the edge and open water side of several large cypress trees that formed a sort of island. The boat covered up easily, and hiding our fourteen-foot jon-boats beside the houseboat was also facilitated by the cypress tree growth at our spot. We even designated certain cypress trees as range markers. A decoying duck inside our range trees meant a clean kill. The flight from the refuge each morning was indeed a picture for a duck man's eyes. The middle of the lake was the primary flight line, but good calling and a large decoy spread swung many birds our way. The beautiful sunrises from atop the houseboat I shall always remember. The anticipation of a good day kindled my desire to be atop the houseboat before sunrise. We knew that the ducks were already on the move at the crack of dawn. John and I would begin our calling using the single quacks of a lonesome hen. We had many early mallards come to those calls after making only one pass over the decoys. John was a great "quacker." He could fool the early ducks and often give us a head start at our limit. An early duck was always looking for company.

John, J. L., and I often hunted together, but on the days when John and I were the only two atop the houseboat, we seldom let a good opportunity go by. We had a system for shooting the decoying ducks. First of all, we never let a duck light on the water, always taking our first shots when the ducks had committed to landing among the decoys and just before they got their feet wet. John always took the duck on his side and worked on getting that one, then moved toward the middle if it was a decoying flock. I would shoot the duck on my side and also work toward the middle. If only a pair came in from his side, he would let the first duck go by for me to shoot, and the same for me. If three of us were shooting, the shooter in the middle shot the middle duck or ducks. We teased each other for years about the ducks switching sides, which frequently caused us to make a mess of a flock of greenheads that were hovering, then scrambling to leave our setup.

One of our great enjoyments was having J. L. Pinckney with us when the birds were really moving. He was a character in so many ways. We called him "our Daddy" because he was always doing something for us and the houseboat. We finally ended up calling him "Pappy," even though he was younger than John and me. He could not use a duck call very well, but he felt confident of a good shoot when John and I did the calling. He referred to us as his guides and callers. Having him on board contributed to some of the most enjoyable days on the houseboat. On occasion, while in the blind and during a lull, he would casually mention that he was going to take a short nap. We all had stools up top, and Pappy could sit on his, and while leaning back and putting his head down on his chest, in a matter of two or three minutes, would be snoring away. He could do this anytime he wanted. I used to ask him how in the world he could go to sleep so fast. He would reply that he never had a trouble in the world, and he had a clear conscience. Nothing worried him, even though he experienced frequent business reversals during our years together.

We usually stayed atop until about 9:00 A.M. Then John would go down via the ladder on the back end of the houseboat and cook a breakfast we considered a great treat.

The houseboat had a gas stove, and the boat was well stocked for John's cooking. We always ate well, whether the ducks flew or not. I remember vividly the aroma from John's bacon, sausage, eggs, and frying-pan toast. The ones of us up top in the blind seldom lingered when all those good smells made their way up from "John's kitchen" below. John would always blow a feed call on his duck call when everything was ready.

In those days, hunting was allowed all day. There was never any real hurry to limit out, as we enjoyed going back up on top after breakfast. Spending the night on board and getting out of the rain and bad weather were houseboat luxuries that spoiled us. It was hard to go anywhere else to hunt! And getting to the houseboat from Low Falls Landing took just a matter of minutes. Down the Santee River to Tutti's Cut and idling back up the lake for about five minutes brought us to our home away from home.

I guess the houseboat must be twenty to twenty-five years old now, and over the years we've moved it several times. Presently, it's a little farther up the lake in another group of cypress trees where it's made its home for six or eight years. A new top and a new blind were added a few years ago. John is the only original owner who occasionally hunts on it. I go with him some; but the duck population is not what it once was on Lake Marion, or anywhere else in South Carolina. Fewer ducks fly over the boat than in the seventies and early eighties. Her pontoons are partially filled with water and she sits a little lower in the lake, but she's always ready to accommodate us when a new season fills us with great expectations. This year is no exception. John has plans to do some repairs that will restore her as our favorite spot to set out our decoys and blow our calls, and we'll shoot once again from atop our home away from home.

# 22

## Saving the Swamp

In 1971, the sportsmen of South Carolina stood against a proposal to sell the beautiful timber in the Santee Swamp. The Public Service Authority, the Santee lakes' governing body, had agreed to sell it to a logging operation that was poised at the swamp's edge. This proposal was not well known for a while and almost passed unnoticed until sportsmen got wind of it.

I happened to be a lessee for a section of Pocotaligo Swamp between Sumter and Manning, South Carolina. In reviewing my hunting lease that year, the lumber company lessor I was dealing with just casually mentioned the Santee Swamp cutting. As I remember, this lumber company would be a beneficiary from the cutting. I was floored, to say the least, about even the possibility of the swamp being logged. Then, a short time later, a local newspaper employee further verified that the Public Service Authority planned to do this. Next, I heard that the contract involving it all had already been signed.

Our local newspaper gave me their permission to write a long article to inform the public and the sportsmen of our area of the proposal. The article, considered a letter to the editor, initiated public protest against ruining the swamp as we knew it. I had contacts from sportsmen all over our state, who were going to lose some of their favorite hunting and fishing opportunities. Public hunting was going to take a turn for the worse if the sale occurred. I decided to take a firm stand against the destruction of not only many sportsmen's favorite place to hunt, but mine, too. I was willing to do whatever I could to save the swamp.

Several public hearings took place around South Carolina, and I attended them all. I made statements at these meetings; and I returned to the auditorium's stage of the high school in Sumter for the first time since my graduation. As I stood on that stage, I took special note of the various individuals who were seated on the front rows. They were representatives of the involved companies whose contracts might be changed or even with-drawn. But I spoke my views against cutting down the very old and beau-tiful timber on the many ridges I and others had roamed. I definitely had a selfish point of view because I would be losing my hunting home, but the logging companies were selfish too. Money was their motivational factor and, in my opinion, they were very greedy. I could envision nothing but clogged creek beds, impassable ridges, and loss of wildlife habitat that could not be replaced in my lifetime. I did not want to lose what I had, and I wanted my son to enjoy the great swamp as I did.

Eventually, the swamp issue rolled into our statehouse in Columbia. A representative in the legislature took up the crusade against the cutting of the swamp. I and several others led a tour through the swamp's many creeks and boated officials of our legislature to view the huge oak ridges that had stood even before they were born. They viewed the homes of the swamp animals that called the twelve thousand acres their home. We traveled in flat-bottom boats from the Rimini trestle up to Sparkleberry Lake, and on up Mill Creek and through the flooded swamp to Otter Flat. Out of Otter Flat, we took Pine Island Creek through the very heart of the great swamp. The huge old oak ridges bordering Pine Island Creek would be lost if the cutting should occur, and our visitors got to see the extent of the loss first hand. At the top of Pine Island, we motored through to Tavern Creek, and turned downstream to Gar Lake and Indigo Flat. Our legislators saw the numerous campsites on Indigo Flat and on Broadwater Creek as we made our big circle through the Santee swamp. Out to the Santee River channel, and we sped downstream the seven or eight miles back to Pack's Landing. On the way, campsites could be seen on the river's bank, beneath the shade trees that might be lost. Trips like this one helped others to realize that the Santee was indeed a treasure to be saved.

In the end, the companies involved withdrew their contracts. The people and the sportsmen of South Carolina saved the swamp from the logger's saw. I had done my best to save it, along with the many others who can proudly say, "Public opinion saved the Santee Swamp."

# 23

# THE SANTEE GUN CLUB

It was very early that Saturday morning as I left Orangeburg and drove up Highway 301 North en route to Eutawville, a sleepy little South Carolina country town nestled very near Lake Marion, the larger of the two Santee lakes. Behind my car on its trailer was my almost new orange and white bass boat. Earlier that morning, I had filled the Hydra-Sports gas tank in preparation for the day's fishing, and I expected its big Johnson outboard would greedily empty the twenty-four gallon tank as I searched for the shallow-water largemouth bass that were beginning their annual spring-time spawning ritual. The Saturday before had been good fishing, and the lake's water level was just right for a productive day on the Santee.

I had agreed to help guide a party of eager fishermen, who had come to sample our kind of bass fishing, and would meet the other guides at Bell's Marina, a landmark on the edge of Eutaw Creek, one of the large coves off Lake Marion. Danny and Maureen Bell had fashioned their business to accommodate the sportsmen who annually would come great distances to try their luck. Bell's Marina offered its guests overnight lodging right on the water, a restaurant with southern cuisine, a tackle shop featuring the area's "hot lures," and guide services to put fishermen on the trail of San-tee's brute largemouth bass. My trips as a guide helped me to pay for my many boats during those years, as the fifty bucks plus tips added up nicely during the season.

The morning had seemed clear with little wind, but that changed as I ran into patchy fog just outside of Orangeburg. The closer I got to the lake, the thicker the fog became. I wondered whether I could arrive by 5:00 A.M. and join everybody for breakfast. I got there just in time, as Danny and Maureen were pairing the guests with their guides for the day. Over my years of guiding fishermen, I have fished some real characters who knew nothing about fishing and cared little about respecting my boat or my efforts that day. But this day would be very different, and to say "I stubbed my lucky toe" would be an understatement.

My guest for the day would be Eldridge Johnson from Ardmore, Pennsylvania; and, much to my liking, he would be the only fisherman in my boat. Usually Maureen would pair two guests with each guide. I soon learned that this group of fishermen represented Club Limited, a club whose membership was composed of very wealthy sportsmen from all over the United States. The stop on our Santee was one of several outings the club planned for that year.

Meeting Eldridge and knowing I would have only one "unknown" that day really perked up my outlook, despite the fog problem. Of course, Eldridge was concerned that we would not go out in those conditions, but I cheered him up by explaining my plan for the day. He was agreeable and I felt I had met a very understanding gentleman.

After picking up our box lunches for the day and a bag of ice for the cooler, we headed for Angel's Landing, about ten miles away. Angel's was located on Lake Moultrie, one of my favorite fishing holes for years. The shallow coves, points, and structure around Angel's were my favorites. I knew nearly every inch of the territory, and it was my first choice that day, with the conditions as they were.

The stubborn fog was still with us as we approached Angel's Landing. I had hoped the lower lake, Lake Moultrie, would have less foggy conditions, but it was just as bad! My clean boat was as wet as if it had been rained on all the way from Orangeburg, and I told Eldridge to put on his rain pants to start with.

With the boat launched and the car and trailer parked down the road, Eldridge was surprised when I didn't start the boat's engine right away, but, instead, put the electric trolling motor down and eased away from the launching ramp toward some barely visible saw grass patches. What Eldridge didn't know was that we had launched the boat right where I'd planned to start fishing. I figured we could stay close to the launching ramp until the fog lifted, and if it didn't, I would still know my way around by staying close to the saw grass shoreline and small islands in Angel's Cove.

Right away I learned that my guest for the day knew how to handle a casting reel and rod. Usually I let my guests take a few practice casts before hitting the prime spots we planned to fish. Eldridge proved he could present the lure quite well. The cover we were fishing dictated the use of spinner-bait lures. The color of Lake Moultrie's water was a little dingy, so I chose yellow-skirted, quarter-ounce spinnerbaits. Water depth was from two to four feet near the saw grass and button bushes.

We had not progressed very far from the Angel's ramp when our first bass, about a two-pounder, hit my lure. The Santee bass was healthy and strong, and had jumped on my lure aggressively. It was the start toward our limit, and I laughed when Eldridge said, "Swap rods with me." Even though our equipment was identical, I did just that. Over my years as a guide, I have many times, after catching a nice fish, transferred my lure to my guest's rod. It seemed to please them, and they gained confidence that the next bite would be on that lure. We cast our spinnerbaits into the small pockets around the grass, and every few minutes we would boat another keeper. Even though the sun had not penetrated the fog, the hungry large-mouths were holding tight to cover. Strikes were coming only from precise casts to the ambushing bass. I soon put down my rod and watched my guest load the boat's livewell with the scrappy male bass. A big sow had not taken our lures yet, and perhaps only the smaller males were holding real shallow.

There was a small lily pad pond connecting the shallow flat we were fishing, and soon we were casting to the pads dotting its surface, when Eldridge leaned heavily on his rod. I knew instantly he had hooked a lunker and was having a time moving the fish toward open water. The big sow broke the water, and I reached for my net this time and told Eldridge not to let her go under the boat. He skillfully guided her into my half-submerged net. I said to him, "You've done this before, haven't you?" He just smiled and said, "A couple of times, and I always release the big ones." And he did. I responded, "Can you think of anything more exciting than seeing a six- or seven-pound bass jump and almost throw your lure?" Eldridge said the only thing that thrilled him more was a flock of greenhead mallards backpedaling over his decoys. I thought, "My gosh, who have I met today?" For the remainder of that morning, and while not opening the boat's livewell, we talked duck hunting, my favorite subject.

It didn't take me long to ask Eldridge just where he did his duck hunting, and, of course, I expected him to name famous and faraway places, such as the Mississippi Flyway. So, was I ever surprised when he asked if I had heard of the Santee Gun Club near McClellanville, South Carolina.

"Goodness, yes," I answered. "Well," he said, "I'm the president of the club, would you like to hunt with me sometime?" I was flabbergasted! Here in my boat was the head man of one of the most famous duck hunting clubs on the Atlantic Flyway, and I was being invited to hunt there.

Eldridge explained that the club was owned by a group of wealthy sportsmen since way back, but in just a few years it would become the property of the State of South Carolina, and that he usually came down from Pennsylvania to hunt a few days after Christmas. He would let me know ahead of time, and just maybe I could join him.

What a day on the lake and what luck! Eldridge had enjoyed the limit catch and exchanging our duck-hunting tales. It was a pleasure getting to know him, and I hoped he would remember me later on during the holidays.

———

Just before the South Carolina duck season ended in January, 1977, I received a much-welcomed phone call from the manager of the Santee Gun Club. I believe his name was Tommy Strange. He asked if I knew Eldridge Johnson and I said, "Yes, indeed." He told me Eldridge had called and informed him that due to a conflict he would not be coming to hunt the club as he had thought. But, Eldridge was inviting me to come down and hunt on special invitation; and, could I come on Thursday of next week? Of course, I was somewhat disappointed, but happy that I would still get to experience a hunt at such an exclusive club. I accepted the Thursday date with my thanks and made plans to be away from my office. At the time, I was district manager for Liberty Life Insurance Company's Orangeburg office.

The days couldn't go by fast enough, but finally I was turning off Highway 17 near McClellanville and following Tommy Strange's instructions on how to find the clubhouse. The improved dirt road led through some South Carolina lowland timber, and once I glimpsed wild turkeys feeding under some very old and picturesque oaks. The gate designating the club property had been left open, and I proceeded to a split drive leading through a huge grove of live oaks, whose limbs laid down a welcome to newcomers before reaching skyward again. The view of the huge two-story clubhouse through the storied lowcountry oaks caused me to pause and savor a way of life gone by many years before my time. As I remember, the very large clubhouse was mostly black in color, with a large porch across its front, and very near was the bank of the mighty Santee River. The several rocking chairs being used faced the live oaks in front. I could almost envision the wildlife that would come late on the fall afternoons to share the acorns they cherished.

As I slowed my Oldsmobile at the entrance to the great house, I was met by a gracious attendant who welcomed me and opened my car's door. He was dressed in a red tailcoat atop his shiny black boots, and looked like he was ready for an old-style fox hunt. But his first words to me set the tone for the care and service I would enjoy while a guest. He said, "My name is Booker T," and asked, "May I take your bag and hunting clothes to your room? I'll come back and take care of your car."

Booker T led me through the large rooms downstairs and on up to my room, and suggested, "You might want to freshen up before supper, which is served at six o'clock. Our other guests are downstairs in the gun room, and they would like to meet you before supper. After supper, the huntmaster will assign your hunting location for in the morning."

Before returning downstairs, I looked around a bit. Booker T had indicated the bathroom was at the end of the hall. There must have been several on the second floor, as there were twenty-four bedrooms up there, each with its own fireplace.

Entering the huge gun room, I was pleasantly surprised to immediately recognize a long-time acquaintance, Francis Hipp. Mr. Hipp was CEO of Liberty Corporation, the company I had been working for since 1958. He and the other guests were giving their guns a little attention before the morning hunt. We exchanged pleasantries, and he asked me how I happened to meet Eldridge Johnson, and said that they had missed seeing him this season. Thursday was a work day, and there I was taking a whole day off to go hunting—but, this was a special hunt, for sure. Mr. Hipp just said, "I see your office is having a pretty good year." I nodded in agreement, and then he introduced me to other club members. I had no idea that Mr. Hipp was a member, but I knew he loved to hunt ducks. His stature in our state as a business leader was well known, and Liberty Corporation was the largest financial institution in South Carolina.

The call to supper was heard shortly, and all were served a coastal treat, seafood. The huge table in this dining area would seat many hungry sportsmen, and I'm sure thousands of dishes from it had been served to many South Carolina "blue bloods." All the attending servers were dressed in antebellum dresses and stood on one side of the room as we were seated.

Their manners and courtesy certainly matched their attire of yesteryear. I had never been exposed to such attentiveness, and it reminded me again of a period in South Carolina long since passed. I soon learned that the employees at Santee Gun Club were descendants of others who had served the club. Positions such as cooks, waitresses, groundskeepers, and club maintenance personnel were passed on to younger family members as the club aged.

After supper, we drew for blinds. I was told each of us would have a paddler who would be our guide the next morning, and that we would be hunting Murphy Island that Thursday. The huge island was just a part of the club's 24,000 acres of prime "duckdom." An explanation of the club's management policies was most interesting to me. I listened intently as the members explained how they had undertaken to keep the club from being over-gunned, as too much hunting pressure would move their duck population. So, many seasons ago, the club, after building dikes and planting the shallow marshes with duck-attracting foods, divided the 24,000 acres into three hunting sections. Each area covered approximately eight thousand acres, which were hunted only two days each week. Only nine guns were allowed each day. Sunday would be a rest day, not only for the sportsmen, but their ducks, too. Six days of hunting with only two days in each area each week, and only nine hunters taking limits each day, almost guaranteed success every hunt. All hunting was done only in the morning. I understood from my paddler that the afternoon of the season's last day was open to them. They looked forward to harvesting all big ducks that late in the season.

Outboard motors were not allowed in the marshes, nor anywhere inside the diked waters. Paddling and poling small boats continued, so as to prevent disturbing the waterfowl as little as possible. The blind I was assigned to was maintained by a paddler of many years' experience. His name was Theodore, and the club members assured me that he would take good care of me.

It was early to bed, in hopes of getting a little sleep before being awakened before 5:00 A.M.; but I knew the excitement of it all would allow me very little sleep that night. And so it was, I awoke very early from my shallow sleep to see Booker T starting a small fire in my own bedroom's fireplace. It was just enough to chase the chill from my room and to warm my cool hunting clothes. Booker T said breakfast would be served at five o'clock and all guests should come down about then.

What a breakfast it was—biscuits as big as Krispy Creme doughnuts! Our servers were again dressed for breakfast as if they were headed to a ballroom dance, with full skirts that reminded me of the famous "Aunt Jemima." Herlene, who seemed to be the head cook, stopped me on the way out of the dining room, and requested I shoot some coots for the kitchen folk that morning. I assured her I would, if I got the okay from Theodore. She indicated that sometimes coots were brought in along with the ducks, and that the cooks were always asking for them.

I joined the rest of the half-asleep, but eager hunters on the front porch as three station wagons were brought around for our short ride to the boat dock just behind the clubhouse. Two twenty-foot boats with canvas tops were waiting, motors running, all checked out, and ready to take us down the awesome Santee River and on to Murphy Island. Theodore and I sat together as he passed on bits of his knowledge about the area and about reaching the inland waterway. It would take us on to the club's docks on Murphy Island where we would then make our way to his blind.

The big Glassmaster boats sped from dock to dock letting off other hunters and paddlers. When we arrived at our dock, Theodore made sure I didn't make a bad step when leaving the big boat. The coastal sunrise was just showing as we crossed the massive dike that separated the waterway from some of the most beautiful marshland that God ever created. I could barely see two small flat-bottom boats pulled up on the bank.

There appeared to be some saw grass scattered around on the boat's floor, not just for camouflage, but to keep things a little cleaner. The little boats were about twelve or thirteen feet long and only thirty-six inches wide in the bottom. A simple single-board seat spanned the middle, with another nearer the front. The last half of the stern end had no seat, but this space of flat floor was perfect for Theodore to stand while poling and paddling the small craft. A lightweight reclining seat was attached to the middle board, which added to my comfort.

With my gun, ammo, and camera aboard, Theodore pushed us off and began using the long pole that had been stored in the other boat. I did notice a small, muddy burlap bag in the back with him. He said it held a half-dozen or so well-used decoys.

As we began to move away, only the stars could see down the narrow canal; but, soon the sun began chasing away the darkness, and we began chasing away the many ducks that had roosted in the marshy areas near the deep canal. Ducks were flushing everywhere, and the slight breeze was freshening. It looked like a terrific duck day to me, and Theodore agreed with a big smile. He flashed a big white-toothed smile every time a flock would rise from the shallow, weedy marsh. He was happy, too!

About thirty minutes down the canal, we turned off into a narrow entrance to a pond nestled among thick marsh grasses. On the far end, I could make out several decoys scattered around, and what appeared to be a small natural grass blind. Checking the wind that was now putting a slight ripple on our pond, we straightened up the few decoys and placed six or seven more just upwind of the blind. They danced just enough to look like real foolers, for sure. I had no idea where we were going to hide our boat, but Theodore had that figured out, too. I stood in the shallows while he pulled the light craft into the blind, which had been built around a small tussock of dry marsh. We would stand in the boat and shoot from it. The paddlers were not allowed to shoot, so it was up to me and my Browning 2000 semiautomatic. The early flocks of teal, which love the marsh, were constantly buzzing Theodore's little pond, so I mentioned to him that the spot should be named Teal Hole. He said the area already had a name, and it was referred to as Hoyt Stand. I never did ask him why, as ducks were really getting active about then.

The first big duck that came our way headed straight in, and it turned out to be a mallard hen. I promptly splashed her among the decoys. The morning was young, and I certainly wasn't in any hurry to shoot five very quickly. But then a large, dark-colored duck came over rather high, and Theodore said, "That's a big black, shoot that one." I shouldered the 12-gauge, pulled out to a good lead, and fired. Theodore almost caught the falling black, which broke down some of our marsh grass blind. One on the water, one beside the blind, and only three to go. I asked Theodore what time the Glassmasters were due to pick us up, and he replied, "We need to be back at the dock before eleven o'clock." I kidded him, "Looks like we'll have to pass up some ducks, or do some poor shootin'."

I soon found out that Hoyt Stand was not a favorite of the Santee mallard population. Why, I never figured out. But teal and gadwalls poured in for the next two hours. I decided to shoot only the biggest gadwalls that offered me a shot, while enjoying the passing high flocks moving with the coastal breeze. Once in a while, a coot would come in, and I started filling Herlene's request. By nine o'clock, I had bagged three big gadwalls to go with the mallard and the black duck. So we pulled the boat out and poled around the pond picking up our birds. Theodore was proud of his pond and his effort for me that day. I told him it couldn't have been better. A real ducky spot, liked by many choice ducks. He then told me his daddy had discovered the little pond and later showed it to him.

We had heard some shooting just a little ways down the canal, but didn't know who had been ahead or behind us before daybreak. After reaching the canal, I recognized Francis Hipp being paddled our way. He had gotten his limit and was headed back in. We chatted a minute, and then Theodore poled me out into some floodwater to shoot a few more coots for the kitchen cooks. We ended up with seven or eight of the "black water chickens" by the time we arrived to be picked up.

What a treat the day had been, in so many ways. To hunt at the slow pace we did, not being concerned about others "sky-busting" (the habit of some irresponsible hunters of shooting at random from too far a distance) or setting out their decoys in view of our blind. To have so much to see, and to experience a hunt still patterned after yesteryear, was a treat I'll remember all my life. To turn back the clock and travel through hundreds of acres using just a pole and paddle helped me realize how the hunting life once was.

Thank you, Theodore, and my sincere appreciation to Eldridge Johnson of Ardmore, Pennsylvania, for making it all such a special occasion for this South Carolina duck hunter.

## 24

# THE SNEAK BOAT HUNTS

Calling ducks to decoys is probably the most fun in duck hunting. Greeting a flock of interested mallards and fooling them with my duck calls and decoys has been the highlight of my duck-hunting years. I began calling ducks while in high school, when hunting with my school chums on the Santee and in Pocotaligo Swamp. I didn't really become proficient with a duck call until I began hunting the big salt marsh in 1963. I was using a Mallardtone call at that time, but after moving to Orangeburg, my brother introduced me to the Chick Major calls made in Arkansas. To blow the new style of calls, I had to learn a new system of air support and tongue placement. It took several seasons to conquer the new technique and to discard my old habits, but it was worth the effort.

Nearly all the states have duck-calling contests, which are judged by previous contest winners, duck call makers, and hunters. The South Carolina contest was held each October for years, and I entered for the first time in 1974. Although I did not do well that year, my second try in 1978 was rewarding. I won our state championship over forty other participants and took home first prize. I will never forget pulling the little trailer into our yard and sitting on the horn as I drove in, a signal to my wife that I had won. On the trailer was my prize, a Duck Sneak boat equipped with electric motor mounted on the stern, foot pedals to steer it, and a new twelve-volt battery. The little fiberglass boat was shaped much like a shoe, being eight feet long and about forty inches wide. It was carpeted on the inside and had a comfortable seat; it was painted camouflage. Winning the contest, the Sneak boat, and trailer was certainly a highlight during that period of my life. I was forty-five years old and the oldest to win the state contest. I was also given three hundred dollars for travel expenses to represent our state in the world duck-calling contest in Stuttgart the following month. That was a wonderful experience for me, going to Arkansas for the first time and meeting so many friendly people. Duck-calling week there is held during Thanksgiving and at the start of duck-hunting season. I managed to place nineteenth in the World Contest!

The Sneak boat I won opened up a new hunting world to me and allowed me to gain access to many places in the big swamp that I previously could not go. I had heard about the boat several years earlier and what a great rig it was for getting around in the flooded waters and across the flooded ridges. The design came from the small rural community of Pelion, South Carolina, and, I believe, was the brainchild of its manufacturer, Bobby Tindal.

As I write this, my little Sneak is twenty-two years old and is still one of my cherished possessions. My frequent use of it has required replacement of the electric motor twice. Although I hunted mostly in the upper reaches of the Santee Swamp, the Sneak was good for fishing protected waters also.

The Sneak has become widely known throughout the southeast, and is still manufactured today in Pelion. The unusual experiences afforded me while using my Sneak boat were numerous, and some were completely unexpected. The quietness and ability to maneuver in as little as six inches of water opened up areas where wildlife thought man could not go. With a 105-amp battery, the Sneak would perform all day on stop-and-go traveling.

The Sneak fit nicely into my fourteen-foot aluminum jon-boat, and when leaving Low Falls Landing, my 25-horsepower Johnson would quickly have us entering Broadwater Creek, where I did most of my Sneak boat hunting; then up Broadwater and past Broughton's Mound to Indigo Flat, I would turn right and through Gar Lake to what was known as the "T." At this point, Fuller's Earth Creek went left and on up toward the Sumter-Columbia Hunting Club, and the right fork was Tavern Creek. When leaving Low Falls, some days it might take an hour and forty-five minutes to reach my favorite spot up Fuller's Earth Creek; or if the water was high, not nearly that long. But I was always careful with my boats, especially since most of the time, I was by myself.

I did use the Sneak in other areas of the Santee, such as all the waters between Otter Flat and Pine Island Creek. I also visited the woods between Stump Hole Landing and Low Falls, where one January I had several scares from large alligators that had evidently been flushed out of their habitat by high water. The alligators were on the back side of the Santee River directly behind what is known as Pine Island, a small, high bank right on the river that was home to a dozen huge pine trees and many large alligators. I had no idea gators would be active during January, but they were. However, I never saw one move that day, even though some were sunning on the surface near saw grass, and some could be readily seen submerged in the clear water. Only their snouts were above the surface. All were longer than my Sneak boat, and I had no idea what they might do if spooked by my presence. There was a long, dry ridge in the area, and, months before, I had hunted it and noticed where alligators were dragging across the ridge in several places. After this day, I never hunted the area again. Others liked it better than I did and considered it their spot. The Santee held two demons that I respected highly—the American alligator and the cottonmouth moccasin. My experience with both was frightening, to say the least.

Sneak boat hunting was tailor-made for high water, and during years when the water wasn't high in the swamp, my visits were less frequent. The mallards didn't seem to come up from the refuge if they couldn't find acorns in shallow water. But when conditions were right, I loved the journey to Fuller's Earth Creek.

Many journeys up Fuller's stopped at an area where an old map showed Broughton's Quonset hut was located. But I never saw any evidence of a shelter of any kind way up there. It was here I would unload the Sneak and get it ready for the day's hunt. I always made sure the big twelve-volt battery was fully charged, and I always wore waders and carried my raincoat. The two would keep me comfortable if rain set in. The Sneak had a small dry compartment in its bow. That was where my tools, lunch, drinks, and small spotlight were kept. I took with me a camouflage life jacket, a full-length paddle, and the two small two-foot paddles that came with the boat. The little paddles were a necessity for moving the craft along slowly. Behind the battery was space enough for six small mallard decoys I had accumulated. They were just the right size for that space. My gun lay across my lap, and a full box of number sixes was open and directly between my legs on the carpeted floor. One item I always took with me, every time, was my trusty compass. It was a good one and helped me out on several occasions. I wore an old ski belt around my waist, just in case the boat, somehow, decided to dump me into the cold, swampy water— something that never happened, thank goodness! I had spray-painted the ski belt dark brown.

I chained the jon-boat each time, just in case, to a tree in a secluded spot, or sometimes hid it in the flooded canes on the bank. I would be gone for most of the day. The water level dictated my route, and I knew which ridges and flats the ducks used, and why. The Fuller's Earth Creek area I hunted had very little boat traffic, and most days it was rare to even hear another boat.

One of my productive and favorite spots was a hundred yards or so on up the creek, and on the right side. It was floodwater from a small, well-defined creek running through a stand of large cypress trees. High oak ridges abounded on the left, and on the right, a thicket of cover wood ducks liked. I could usually count on some action here. When traveling to spots like this, I ran the electric motor, but once there, it was pulled up and locked. I wore a bill cap, along with a camouflage face mask and brown cotton gloves. The little boat and I were hard to see, as we looked almost like logs and trees in the dark swamp we were visiting. I have gotten so close to squirrels when drifting and using the small paddles that I could have caught them with the landing net fishermen use. Once, I saw a raccoon feeding on clams he had gathered. He was so intent on getting the shells open that I moved to within five feet of him. He never sensed I was there until my Sneak boat bumped the log he was sitting on. I watched him as he swam away, unhurriedly.

On occasion, Doug Odom, a friend who owned a marine dealership in Orangeburg, would go hunting with me. He was a Duck Sneak dealer and loved the swamp as I did. He was an excellent woodsman and an excellent shot with a shotgun. We would use a wide jon-boat and transport both our Sneaks in it. He knew the upper Santee Swamp pretty well, and we would exchange information during duck season

When we hunted together, we would work opposite sides of a flat in hopes of moving ducks toward one or the other of us. The ducks might be swimming, or if spooked, might fly out over one of us. Doug and I made several trips together over the years. One morning, as I recall, when the temperature was below ten degrees, Doug, while running the motor, almost had a frozen face and hands by the time we got to Broadwater.

Mostly, though, I hunted by myself with the Sneak. As I grew older and was reluctant to get out of bed two or three hours before daylight, I would arrive at Low Falls about eight o'clock with my Sneak boat. Most of the hunters would be coming out of the swamp when I was going in.

The ducks would have settled down, and I pretty well had the swamp to myself.

Above the Quonset hut area was a small lake referred to as Pine Island Lake. I could get to it through two different creek beds, and when hunting up that way, I would go one way and come back the other. Going left on Fuller's Earth Creek would lead me to some productive floodwater and a deep creek that mallards frequented when the water was low. I recall one trip when I discovered a big flock feeding in the shallows on seed from a yellowish-colored plant. The mallards were all over the weedy area and very content with their feeding. I had pulled up the electric motor and was very slowly easing into where the greenheads were gathered. I was using the small paddles and moving a foot at a time by using just a stirring motion and creating no ripples. Even though the boat and I were camouflage in color, motion would flush the ducks if I moved too fast. I could not seem to get near enough for a good shot, but had made good progress into the feeding area.

It was always a mystery to me why wild creatures did certain things, and ducks seemed to have their peculiarities, too. This flock began to disappear into the flooded waters. I don't know whether they sensed my presence or what, as I had been very careful with my approach. For a few minutes, I could not see a single duck, but suddenly several appeared and were swimming my way. They passed my position as if they were not aware I was anywhere near. Suddenly, and I never knew why, it seemed that every duck in the area took flight and came out of their weedy protection in my direction. When sitting in my Sneak, I was limited to the amount of area in which I could swing my shotgun; but, lucky for me, the fleeing mallards were coming out straight overhead. I didn't have to do much swinging around with the gun and took two big mallards as they exited in my direction. They hit the water with a satisfying splash. Just why they took flight and came toward me was inexplicable. Maybe someone else was far back in the flat, or maybe a deer flushed the contented flock. I never knew.

Someone had painted a remarkable sign and attached it to a large pine on the bank of Pine Island Lake. I always thought Pine Island was on the Sumter-Columbia Club property; perhaps it was one of their caring members who put it up. The sign was sizeable, and I would make a point to read it every time I was up that way. I never knew whose words were on that sign, but they were evocative and appropriate for the area. The sign read, "This is one of the most beautiful places on earth. Please help us keep it that way." Evidently, someone else loved and appreciated the swamp, its animals, and its beauty.

My little Sneak boat was so sneaky that on occasion it would surprise me. Leaving Pine Island Lake late one afternoon, I was just drifting with the current and following the high bank on the way back to my boat. With a craft so quiet, I never knew just what I might come upon. That afternoon, a handsome buck deer in his prime was standing on the edge of the shallow little creek. He saw me drifting, but never stopped drinking the cool swamp water as I approached. He looked upstream with his wondering eyes, and I could tell his ears and nose were searching for the identity of the intruder into his world. The deer season was in, and I could have easily taken him from the great swamp, but to let him walk was his reward for coming my way. He slowly turned away and disappeared into the dense canes growing on the bank.

The animals of the great swamp are all unique and special to their environment. I certainly took a toll on the duck population that would come to visit each fall, but I never took advantage of others just to have something to shoot at. I was a duck hunter and that was about it, with the exception of a squirrel hunt or two before and after each duck season. Squirrel season lasted several weeks more, and I visited this same area to chase the bushy-tails through their giant oaks. This extended my enjoyment and appreciation of an area that existed long before I discovered it. Just to sit under the great oaks forming a canopy over the ridges was rewarding enough on some days. To eat my olive sandwiches and sip a Coke here was a peaceful activity I did countless times. And, when taking a guest with me, we sometimes cooked hamburgers on my small Coleman one-burner stove. Carolyn would fix the patties the night before, and we all thought the burgers tasted better when cooked in the cool swamp air. The tiny iron frying pan graced us with two patties at a time, and as we were enjoying the first two, two more were on the way. We hunted the squirrels in the morning and the afternoon; and, as it should be, midday was cooking and resting time.

I happened upon a pair of otters one afternoon, and with the Sneak I followed them through their home, the flooded swamp. Nothing in the animal world native to our swamps can traverse the water like an otter. This pair must have been mates, as they seemed to enjoy each other's company very much. As I followed them, not too closely, and watched their playfulness, they stayed together constantly. They knew their world well, and every log seemed to be a new adventure. They would run up and down, rub their handsome fur coats together in a childish fashion, and on to the next log. Even though a raccoon is a common swamp dweller, he is a poor swimmer in comparison to otters.

I once saw a swamp rabbit perched on a log jump from it and swim out through the flooded swamp. I'm convinced that in some fashion, though some better than others, all animals can swim when necessity calls.

Some hunts in Fuller's Earth Creek were full of surprises. After unloading the Sneak one Saturday morning, I headed to one of my better duck-holding spots. I was my usual careful self that morning, as conditions seemed to be right for a good hunt; and I was in no hurry, as the day was young and I was fresh with enthusiasm. I could hear a summer duck's whistle now and then as I stirred the little black paddles that kept my boat progressing toward the sounds. My face mask and brown gloves had completed my camouflage, and my 12-gauge lay across my lap. I proceeded carefully, and after about ten minutes I saw several ducks flush and leave in front of me, but to my left and near the acorn ridge I was following. I had not seen them, and thought maybe they somehow had seen me. But again, within the next fifty or so yards, several more wood ducks flushed. "What's happening here?" I asked myself. The wind was in my face, which was in my favor. Then, I heard on the hill the barking of running dogs. They were nowhere near the water's edge yet, but I figured some deer hunters had put them out on the Sumter-Columbia Club property. They must have jumped back a ways and had a deer on the move.

At first, I put this idea out of my mind and continued my progress farther into the cypress flat. I was staring harder than ever now, determined to locate some ducks before they located me. Then I saw what was happening and what was flushing the ducks before I got anywhere near. A small deer with maybe four points had eased out into the flat, apparently in an attempt to lose the dogs tracking him on the ridge to my left. The young buck, in his effort to lose the dogs, had decided that he could find safety in the flat. He was ahead of me and didn't have the slightest notion I was around. The wind was not right for him to catch my scent.

The dogs were closer now and sounded as if they would be at the water's edge shortly. The buck had made his way out into the flat quite a ways where the water was maybe a foot deep. I slowed my progress to see just what he was up to. He would stop and listen frequently as he made his way out in front of my projected path. Cypress trees were everywhere, and cypress knees showed all over the shallow flat. Finally, I saw him select his hideaway. It was a small knoll of swamp with cypress knees all around it, just out of the water; and I saw him lie down among the cypress knees. This was a perfect example of a deer outsmarting a pack of dogs by taking to an area of refuge. His instincts told him that the dogs could not follow his scent very well in water.

I had not seen this occur during my hunting years, and so I opted to see what the dogs' plan of action would be once the deer's trail ended abruptly at the water's edge. The deer was probably fifty yards upwind of my vantage point, and I could see his head move ever so slightly. The dogs never attempted to come out into the flat. They only ran the edge, hoping to pick up a trail. The barking quit and they backtracked into the swamp. What ducks that had been nearby had certainly taken leave by now, so I turned my attention to the buck hiding on the cypress knoll. Just how close could I get to him? I thought I'd like to see.

The wind would not betray my presence, since it was still blowing in my face, and there were big cypress trees I could use as cover while making my approach. The deer seemed settled, and I figured I could keep the trees between him and me as I moved forward. This was always my technique when moving toward feeding ducks; but this was a challenge I had not faced before under these conditions.

Every chance I got, I moved when the deer's head was down and he was not looking for the dogs anymore. Progress was slow, but sure. The cypress trees were my friends until they gave out, but by then I was within twenty yards of the little knoll hiding the young and, I'm sure, nervous buck. When he finally realized that I was something he didn't understand, he slowly stood, took a long look at me, turned away, and began a quiet walk through the shallow flat in a direction his instincts told him to go. His pursuers never knew.

This flat was very long and was very near the end of the Santee Cooper property. In other words, it was on the uppermost part of the Santee Swamp. The deer had interrupted my duck hunting in the first part, but the best part was farther down the flat. I wasted no time moving to undisturbed territory by running the Sneak's trolling motor. The trolling motor's steering controls were foot pedals attached by wire cables running through metal tubes and on under the boat's seat. I always marveled at the little boat's design. The motor's shaft had been cut and shortened to about twenty inches, and a six-inch round pulley had been mounted on the shaft. The foot control cables were attached to the pulley. The foot pedal idea worked beautifully, and a push-button switch was located on the right side and top part of the pedal. This switch cut the electric motor on and off. On the left side was the speed control in the form of a rheostat for variable motor speeds. It also had a reverse switch. When traveling from spot to spot, the twenty-four-pound thrust MinnKota pushed the Sneak as fast as I would want to go. Too fast, and a stump or cypress knee in the right spot could cause the boat to turn over. It was the very lowest speeds that worked the Sneak's magic in getting around so quietly. The boat was widest about where the seat was located, and this is where my weight was centered. The back of the seat was attached to a cross member of the boat's frame. It was comfortable for several hours, but getting out occasionally was a treat!

The only close call I ever had with it was grabbing a tree that I didn't realize was rotten, and trying to swing around it while still moving. The tree promptly broke and fell across the boat behind my head and on top of the steering cables. The weight of the tree almost pushed the back under. The water would have been over my head, but the little fellow was very stable all the while.

Several hundred yards down the uppermost flat was a shallow area, but very wide. Several acorn ridges were nearby, and I had been successful in locating mallards there. It had taken me years of exploring the swamp to find places ducks liked. I'm sure there were many such places I didn't find. That day, the water was mostly dark-colored and clear, but I began to notice a muddying effect in the water. Was this fresh water coming in, or had ducks muddied the water from their feeding activities? Many times I had seen the water cloud over the leafy bottoms as ducks stirred for acorns and seeds. I began to hunt more seriously and pulled the electric motor up and out of the water. It was paddling time. If there were ducks in the shallows, they hadn't made a sound! But I was checking every corner in sight and soon the water became cloudy again. My sharp vision caught the glow of several green, iridescent heads in the morning sunlight. I was in luck; a flock was feeding in the shallows. Upon coming a little closer, I determined that there were thirty to forty ducks scattered out in the shallow flat. Trees and my cover were thinning out, and the way things looked, I might not get a shot at these busy ducks.

My last concealment was a group of large cypress knees, and I decided to stay put and see if the ducks would feed closer. They were quiet and tipping up as they searched the bottom. If only I could be a little closer, but they had to move closer to me if that were going to happen. I was so involved with the mallards in front that I failed to notice a half-dozen swimming in from my right side. I had arrived before they had, and they were not aware of my presence. If they kept coming, they would be close enough for a long shot. I looked back at my flock still busy tipping up, and decided that I might as well try a shot at these newcomers. There were two drakes at the back of the flock, fairly close together, and I put the 12-gauge to work on them. The first shot covered the two drakes, the rest took to the sky and flew to my right. Their exit in that direction must have prompted the main feeding group to follow their route of escape. At least half of them were flying out under the tall cypress trees and giving me a side shot. I don't know where the others went. Quickly replacing the shell I had just fired, I shot the gun empty at those leaving, knocking down two hens.

Grabbing a handful of my number six shot reloads, I slid over the side of the Sneak. I really didn't know how many mallards were down, but at the ranges I was shooting, I didn't figure they would all be dead. And I was right; ducks were scrambling to get away, and if the water had been deep, I would have lost some. With the water no more than eight to ten inches, I trotted after the cripples, shooting as I went. I must have awakened the whole swamp as I shot a handful of heavy loads trying to finish off the cripples. I reached for my old duck strap in my coat, and strung the hens and the two drakes. I was panting from the run when headed back to the boat, only to see a half-dozen mallards arriving and settling in the flat to feed. They evidently had not heard the news a few minutes earlier.

––––––––––

It was late in the season and what I thought was a good idea turned out to be not so good. I had motored up close to Pine Island Lake with my new Winyah boat carrying the Sneak boat. Several trips before this, I had located what looked like a creek bed on the north side of the lake. I had explored it thoroughly and found two splendid, open holes, very near a high oak ridge. Sometimes there would be decoys in one, and feathers around, as if hunters had had some good shooting there. Behind this opening only twenty-five or so feet was a very deep creek bed that one day I pulled my Sneak boat to and spent several hours exploring. Wood ducks were plentiful around the small, deep creek. I enjoyed discovering new territory.

That day, I had a full charge on the Sneak's battery and had decided to slip the Sneak in just below the lake and see what I could find. Fuller's Earth Creek continued on and out the northeast end of Pine Island Lake. I had never gone past the lake, but I knew the Sumter-Columbia Club property was up that way. I felt floodwater was kind of public, so I didn't hesitate to look around. My usual hunting equipment was in the Sneak and the weather was good. I knew I would be in unfamiliar waters and swamp, so I had my compass along. Also, I kept a roll of bright orange ribbon under the bow for marking trails, or to help me find a particular checkpoint. Tying a piece of this ribbon on a limb here and there would be helpful on the return trip.

Midmorning, I left Pine Island Lake through the left side and headed, I thought, northwest. Checking the compass, I knew I would come back in a southeast direction. So off I went feeling secure about everything. I tried to remember how many flats and flooded oak ridges I crossed on the way away from the lake, and I did tie ribbon in a place or two that looked like trouble spots. I had no idea what the names of the creeks I found were, as I wasn't privy to maps of private land. I followed one rather large, flooded creek a long way in one direction; too far, really. I still did not think I would have any difficulty getting back to Pine Island Lake. Turning around and heading back on this same creek, it must have been about two in the afternoon. I had tied a ribbon on a limb overhanging the creek where I had entered it after crossing a flooded oak ridge. But, for some reason, I couldn't seem to find the ribbon. So, turning around, I backtracked, then back again the other way. Doing such things takes the life out of the Sneak's big battery unnecessarily, even though it felt plenty strong at that point. Getting close to where I thought I had entered the creek, I decided that I couldn't be too far wrong, so I crossed the oak ridge there. However, nothing really looked familiar; but I kept looking at my compass to make sure I was headed right, and I was. Sometimes, some ducks would get my attention, and I would spend a while working them, something that was unproductive in every sense. I finally quit fooling with the ducks and was getting a little worried that I needed to find something familiar, as I only had an hour or so before nightfall.

Looking at the compass again, I set a trail in the southeast direction, figuring that I would come out close to Pine Island Lake, then go downstream to my boat. I had left the boat on a high bank just below the lake. Identifying the lake area, or around it, shouldn't be a problem as I had been around there before; but I was unfamiliar with the area above the lake. On the east side of the lake, I knew the high ground existed because I had seen a road where trucks had driven in to the lake itself. How much high ground was above the lake, I didn't know. That area was all new to me.

Finally, with about thirty minutes left before dark, the Sneak brought me out to a creek that was flowing rapidly. I felt that since I was in the right direction, it was definitely Fuller's Earth Creek. But I must be above Pine Island Lake, because nothing looked familiar and the water was flowing to the right when I entered it. Checking the compass again, I turned right and figured I'd follow the creek down to the lake. I even saw high ground on my left going downstream. That comforted me considerably, and it looked just like the high bank where I had left my boat; but there was no boat to be found. I was truly puzzled and didn't like it a bit. The dark was coming, and I didn't know where I was. What had I done wrong? The little boat's battery was weakening rapidly, and I had maybe twenty minutes of light left. The lake should be ahead and not far, but how far? I thought I had gone far enough to find it, but no lake. Could I be on another unknown creek? How much longer would the motor run on the weakened battery? Whatever I did, I was not going to leave the high ground but a few yards. Something said to keep going downstream, and that's what I did. Hugging the bank as the last light faded, I stopped and hooked up the little spotlight that I kept under the Sneak's bow. On downstream another few minutes, and there it was—the lake! I was so relieved! Even though it was now dark, I knew exactly where I was and where my Winyah was. My mistake was I had come out the flooded swamp way above Pine Island Lake in completely unfamiliar surroundings. I had not come back down the swamp far enough before coming out on the southeasterly compass heading.

The electric motor had slowed, but it still had enough power to keep me in the right direction. On through the lake and out the creek on the left, and a few careful minutes later, the weak spotlight caught a glimpse of my lonely boat, patiently waiting in the dark. We were delighted to see each other!

# 25

## JAY AND CAJUN

My son, J. M. III, is a duck hunter, a regular chip off the old block. How do I know he's a duck hunter? Because he supports his duck-hunting addiction with an eleven-month job as an inventory auditor. He lets very little interfere with his duck hunting, and every year he prepares better than the year before. I'm proud that he loves the same sports I do, but his mother says I made one mistake while rearing him: instead of putting a baby rattler in his crib, I put a duck call in there. And, if you could hear him blow it today, you'd swear he'd been blowing it ever since. He sounds more like a mallard than a mallard does!

Jay has the best equipment his money can buy, and if something better comes out, he'll have that before long. His efforts are second to none. I've known him to drive the seven hundred miles to Arkansas and go straight to the duck blind, then scout ducks on the river the rest of the day. To him, success during those short weeks of duck season is everything. He shoots a huge Benelli shotgun that can reach beyond my best efforts, and sometimes he gives me the opportunity to shoot my three shells before he turns loose with his big Benelli. I've seen him chase a crippled goose for half a mile before being outsmarted in a muddy field. A dedicated hunter, that he is.

On March 5, 1982, a chocolate Labrador retriever was born in Baton Rouge, Louisiana, that would become a very special hunting companion for Jay, and for me, also. Jay named him Cajun at his mother's suggestion, and from the very beginning he showed great promise, not only as a retriever, but also in becoming a member of our family. He loved his family unconditionally for over fifteen years. He was Jay's dog, for sure.

I remember very well my first hunt with Cajun. Just the two of us went to Jay's open-water blind on the Santee. At that time, I wasn't sure just how far a Lab could swim. As a youngster, my hunting dogs were pointers and setters given to me by my Uncle Clyde, who always seemed to have a puppy available. I really can't figure why I never had a retriever, since duck hunting was always my favorite, but I didn't.

Cajun was about nine months old on our hunt that day, but he performed like a much more seasoned dog. He swam with great enthusiasm, and he retrieved as if he couldn't get his bird fast enough. I remember that day it rained some, and he would get under my knees as we sat together in Jay's blind. He retrieved my downed birds, some a good ways out, as I held my breath that the swim might be too far. But, over the years, it became apparent that none were ever too far. His endurance was amazing.

Once, I took Cajun on a dove shoot, and that day he showed me just how smart he really was. I had downed a dove and had sent him for it. When he was on his way back, I knocked another one down that fell between me and Cajun's route back to my stool. He saw it fall and slowed as he passed it on the plowed corn field. He delivered my first bird, and without a word from me and with no hesitation, returned to my second bird, delivering it to my feet as if to say, "Nice shootin', Grandaddy." Jay allowed me to take him many times over our years, and I enjoyed him so much.

As Cajun matured, Jay trained him in obedience, and his dedication to his master grew every year. When Jay took his vacation weeks during duck season, Cajun was his constant companion. He learned boat hunting quickly, and those two hunted from the Santee Swamp potholes and flats to the grass beds of lower Lakes Marion and Moultrie. Jay always said, "Cajun makes a good bedfellow," and they shared a bed often, both at home and in the bottom of Jay's boats.

One cute occasion each year was Cajun's birthday party with just his daddy, grandmother, and granddaddy. He seemed to sense it coming, and expected his vanilla ice cream cup and full pound of ground hamburger. He loved to lick the ice cream cup while one of us held it, and he never seemed to get his fill of the little hamburger meatballs we rolled for him. On his fifteenth birthday, we sent birthday announcements celebrating this special milestone in a Lab's career.

———————

Cajun's family, at times, thought he might have a little cat-breeding in him —that he might be a little bit "feline." It is said cats have nine lives, and on occasion we believed our Cajun had several, too. I can remember some close calls.

March 3, 1997
Orangeburg, S.C.

Mr. Cajun Reynolds of Orangeburg, S.C. announces his fifteenth birthday on March 5, 1997. During his illustrious career, Cajun has hunted fifteen seasons in South Carolina, and made special trips to North Carolina, Louisiana, and has "jetted" to Canada.

Cajun is now semi-retired and limits his hunting to an occasional duck and dove hunt. He looks forward to '97, his sixteenth season.

The Reynolds
Family

The first was during a hunt in the Santee Swamp, near an area known as Little Creek, a creek running northerly and bordering the Great Ridge. The day was typical duck weather, cold and very windy. On such a day, ducks usually seek shelter off the open water, and Jay felt the big flooded swamp was where he should be.

He and Cajun were set up over decoys and were hunting out of Jay's boat and blind of gunnery net. Some mallards were working the area, and on one occasion a mallard passed a bit too far for a clean kill, but Jay managed to shoot him down. He immediately sent Cajun after the crippled duck, which had fallen in a thicket of low bushes. Cajun had marked the duck and headed in its direction into the flooded swamp. The water level was high and had covered all the dry ridges in the Little Creek area.

Cajun was soon out of sight and in pursuit of the downed mallard. Not having visual contact, Jay could not know what was occurring. The duck gave the dog a merry chase through the flood, but somehow Cajun had caught up with the cripple and started back with his catch. But apparently Cajun became disoriented and lost his way back to the boat. Jay saw him swimming in the wrong direction with the duck tightly in his jaws. Jay called and attempted to get Cajun's attention, but the wind directed his calls away. Nothing seemed to change the direction the dog was taking, and soon he was out of sight again.

Jay became concerned that Cajun had not remembered his way and that there was not a place for a swimming dog to rest anywhere within hundreds of yards of their position. A long time went by, and Cajun had not returned to the decoys or the spot where he had left. Just how long could a Lab swim, particularly one that had lost his way? Fifteen minutes went by, twenty minutes went by, and not a sign of the dog. Thirty minutes, then forty-five minutes. Jay was truly concerned. Cajun was a very strong swimmer, but forty-five minutes was beyond any dog's endurance. Then, out of the swamp's muddy and flooded waters, came a brown head struggling toward Jay. No longer was he moving with any authority, but calling on all his reserve strength to move him forward in search of his master. Jay started the boat's motor and hurried to his cherished companion. Lifting into his boat a very exhausted Cajun was a very thankful duck hunter. Had Cajun been able to find a log or a tree fork to rest in, or had he swum the whole time? We will never know just how he survived such a swim.

---

Jay and Cajun often went boat riding on Sunday afternoons, particularly on the river near the Low Falls area. There was usually a group of boaters who would run their small boats up and down the river. They always seemed to want to see who had the best setup and were constantly working to gain a little speed on the others. Jay had come to try out a different propeller on his Yamaha outboard and had motored down the river from Low Falls. As usual, Cajun was his accustomed passenger that hot July afternoon, as they leisurely rode down the Santee toward Pine Island, a section of riverbank featuring a few huge pine trees. It was a popular camping area for both fishermen and hunters. There they met other boats and decided to run them up the river.

Jay made the decision to put Cajun out on the Pine Island campsite in order to race another boater with a like boat. He never dreamed what was in store for Cajun that afternoon.

Behind Pine Island lay a marshy area of shallow water, saw grass, and swamp that was the home of many large alligators. We had seen them often sunning on the riverbank, but we had never heard of any attacks or scary incidents, as they seemed to stay to themselves. But this day would be different.

Jay had assumed Cajun would stay close to the campsite, but instead, as Jay sped upriver, Cajun ran up the riverbank in the direction where his master had gone. Stopping upriver just a little ways to talk boats with a friend, Jay heard Cajun in the distance. At first his barking sounded like he was baying an animal, then his barks became more distinct and much louder, finally turning to yelps and screams.

Starting his motor instantly, Jay sped back down the river to where he thought Cajun might be. He knew then his decision to put Cajun out was a bad one. Judging from the yelps, his Lab must have stumbled upon a gator or something, and a confrontation must have occurred. His heart sank as he hurried toward Pine Island. "What have I done?," he thought. Arriving and securing his boat, he called for Cajun, but there was no response at all. The air was silent, and Jay could feel his heart pounding. Had he put his dog out on top of a gator? His calls were going unanswered, so he struck out walking the riverbank and continued to call his dog. Jay spent a half hour or more wandering all through the area, but not a sign of Cajun. What had happened? Had a gator gotten a hold on him and dragged him to the water? If so, Cajun would have no chance in such a situation. Jay returned to his boat and waited. A friend joined him, and they sat in their boats wondering what to do next. Jay was completely heartbroken, and when a large gator appeared in the river a few yards from their spot, he thought the worst. But if Cajun was not in the water, just maybe the powerful Lab had fought the battle of his life and had somehow escaped.

And that's just what had happened, for coming on three legs was a bloodied and muddied Cajun. Jay hurried out to gather him up in his arms. He had found his way back to his daddy.

As fast as the boat would go, Jay headed back upstream to Low Falls. Cajun seemed to be in shock as he lay on the boat's carpeted floor. He was bleeding badly from puncture wounds. Hurrying to the phone at the landing, Jay reached a friend in Orangeburg and told him to find a vet on call that Sunday, and when he got in town, he would call to find out where Cajun could be helped. The phone call worked, and soon Cajun was being cared for by his regular vet, who had treated him for years. The puncture wounds were deep, and the muscles in Cajun's haunches were torn badly. His vet put drainage tubes in the injured areas. He was in very bad shape and stayed with his vet for a couple of weeks. But, being the strong dog that he was, Cajun handled the treatment and slowly began his recovery. Carolyn and I took over after he left the vet by keeping him on our screened back porch the entire month of August.

Cajun was the talk of the town having won the fight of his life. His master always said to other Lab owners and friends, "You ought to see that gator when my dog got through with him!"

A week or so later, I took an acquaintance who, as a hobby, houses alligators in a fenced-in pond. He has studied them for years, and I asked him to accompany me to the area where Cajun had his encounter. So we took off to Low Falls and on down the big Santee to the Pine Island area. I had put my .38-caliber pistol in my pocket, just so, and my "alligator man" was armed with only a stout axe handle.

We walked the riverbank, constantly fanning a million mosquitoes, and then proceeded to roam farther from the river and out into the swampy area. There were a couple of dry ridges running back into the swamp. Both had water on both sides that definitely looked like alligator habitat. Leaves, small limbs, and an assortment of swamp ingredients covered the swamp floor on the ridges. We had not seen an alligator, nor did I cherish the thought, but suddenly my alligator man said, "Look there!" On the small ridge nearest Pine Island was a section of bare ground as if someone had used a leaf rake in the middle of the swamp. We could see where the leaves, decayed limbs, and vegetation had been raked and piled up on the ridge's high point. It was something I had never seen before—an alligator nest. Closer examination revealed claw marks in the soft swamp floor. A female gator had built the nest recently. After my expert explained to me that this mother-to-be wouldn't be far away, I was ready to move on! He wasn't ready, though, and told me to keep a sharp watch for the gator whose nest he was about to examine. He said she would charge us if she felt her nest was in danger, and the charge would be violent, to say the least, but that he had held off many gators with an axe handle. I certainly wouldn't have wanted to attempt that, but he said, "You must warn me if you see any movement on either side of the ridge." There was a tree nearby with easy access that gave me a better look at our surroundings, so with my pistol, I climbed up. The next thing I knew, he was on his knees and digging into the pile of nesting material before him. It didn't take long to uncover several white, elongated-looking eggs which he held up for me to see. And, after digging farther, he uncovered a total of twenty-four eggs.

Quickly, he returned them carefully to their incubation, and with more curiosity than good sense, we walked slowly on farther down the ridge. Coming to the end where we met the swamp, there were egg shells from the previous year's nesting. We were certainly in alligator country.

We measured some large gator prints in the mud on the way back to my boat. The mosquitoes had about licked all our repellent off by then, so we sat in the boat and diagnosed what we had found. Sipping a Coke, the alligator man theorized that Cajun, in his journey up the riverbank, had come upon a female gator protecting her nest, and that since females are considerably smaller than bull gators, she had only done what she needed to do. And that was just to protect her territory, as she was not hungry. A large bull alligator would have killed the dog immediately. Cajun had escaped with his life, and Jay, Cajun, and I had learned a lesson about the demons of the Santee Swamp.

―――――――

Hunting the Santee without Cajun was unthinkable. He could sense a trip in the making. I've seen him watch our every move, and smelling our clothes, he could tell what was up. We could see the wag of his tail, the look in his eyes, and his excitement before every trip. He always knew that the bow was his place in our boats. Pointing the way in the early morning darkness, his ears would stand out as we sped down the river. He had many good days with us, and Jay and I were always pleased when we could down our limit for Cajun to do his thing.

Jay had seen him go under the water to retrieve a cripple, but I had never seen a dog do that. One morning we had made the long trip up to the big swamp above Broadwater Creek. I had found quite a few wood ducks in a flooded area off Fuller's Earth Creek. Overall, the place was wadeable for the three of us, but some spots were much deeper.

The woodies came early and fast, and were a tough target coming in through the flooded cypresses and tupelos. Jay and Cajun had selected a spot not far from my brushy blind. The woody flight was over in fifteen minutes or so, but we knocked down several that had fallen close by. Cajun began his hunt upon Jay's command, and soon he was searching for ducks he had seen fall. We knew a couple were crippled, and our retriever would be the only hope of finding them. Cajun had a great nose, and even though a woody can hide better than most swamp ducks, they can't fool a good nose. I saw Cajun investigating a brushy log, when suddenly a duck burst from its cover with Cajun right on him. This woody knew his only escape was to dive in the two-foot-deep water, but he did not know the dog would go right with him. I was amazed to see Cajun almost disappear in the swamp vegetation and come up with the duck firmly between his teeth. As time passed, we found out he could outsmart most ducks, as very few ever got away.

When Jay hunted several days consecutively and would come by to chat, Cajun would always head for his big, round dog bed that he knew awaited him in the middle of our den. He would be quite a sight on his bed, covering its full width with head hanging off one side. Jay always said he was really "flaked out." But when the boat was launched the next morning, he was ready as ever!

# 26

## JAY'S BLIND

Leaving Low Falls Landing by the Santee River channel and downstream about two miles, the river enters Lake Marion. Across the river from Low Falls was a sizeable creek that fed a lake of about ten to fifteen acres and was called Bee Tree Lake by the locals. On through Bee Tree Lake was some of the uppermost part of Lake Marion, excellent fishing territory for bream and bass, and for stripers (rock fish) in the early spring.

In the early '80s, several varieties of grass appeared in this upper area and all the way over to the Elliott's Landing side. These grasses, over several years' time, took over a huge portion of the lake, from the uppermost part all the way down to where the Santee River enters. And what we called "grass ducks" began their feeding and loafing activities around the numerous grass beds. Where ducks congregate, duck hunters congregate.

It wasn't long before activity in this area of the lake picked up and what we called open-water duck hunting was born. John Jackson's houseboat was anchored in this area, and we were enjoying the shooting from it. The flight up the lake to the big swamp above flew on as usual, nearly every morning. These were mostly mallards that continued on over us and to the acorns above. But smaller ducks, such as wigeon, teal and ringnecks, came to these grassy areas.

My son, Jay, who had been introduced to my favorite sport even before his teen years, decided to build a blind in the upper part of the lake. It would be one of the few permanent blinds there, and getting to it from the river's end would be easy unless the wind was up. Jay's blind was located on the outside of a cypress tree line, and its foundation was built between a trio of sturdy cypresses. The water was probably eight feet deep around the blind. When completed, it gave the appearance of a moss-covered bush sturdy enough to hold three people, and his boat was just the right width and length to be hidden underneath. Toss overboard three or four dozen decoys, each having twelve feet of anchor line; drive the boat under the blind; tie the bow to a post underneath; cover the outboard and red gas tank with a burlap cotton sheet; step onto the boat's back seat and up into the well-camouflaged blind; and our set-up was completed. I enjoyed hunting with him and Cajun countless times in the open water.

Looking from Jay's blind down the open lake toward Persanti Island was special. The sunrise would appear over the island, and the flight from the refuge would appear just about as regularly. Ducks on the Summerton Refuge in those days numbered a hundred thousand or more. Some mornings the flight would last nearly all morning, and we called not only grass ducks, but mallards and black ducks to our decoys. Jay and his friends took countless limits from his setup, and the open-water hunting lasted for many seasons.

Upon arriving at the blind each morning, we quickly learned to count on a visitor's greeting—a beautiful and loyal kingfisher slept underneath the blind. He certainly called it home, and as we approached in the wee hours, we could expect him to fly from his roost more often than not. We always felt he was a male bird, and wondered why he never had a "queen-fisher" with him. Jay would leave Cajun down in the boat for retrieving. Cajun was a great swimmer and handled his duties with pride. No bird was too far for his swim, but sometimes we would have to rescue him from afar with the boat. Cajun's early training was at Jay's blind, and when it was time for a snack, we always helped him up from the boat into the blind and shared our "vittles" with him.

Cajun was special in so many ways. In our rides down the river before dawn, he pointed the way from the boat's bow, his ears standing out in the wind as if he might take to the air. He loved to drink Coca-Colas from the palm of my hand, usually without wasting a drop. When Jay and I went hunting, Cajun was always with us.

When Jay wasn't using his blind, and weather conditions were considered ducky, I would invite friends to hunt with Cajun and me. I had a business associate who lived in Columbia, South Carolina, and who was employed by the same insurance company that I was. After Kurt Cowan's transfer to South Carolina, we became friends, not only in business, but on the lake as well. Kurt fished with me several times during the spring bass-fishing seasons, and has a nice seven-pound bass on his wall to show for it. But he wanted a pair of mallards and a black duck to add to his trophy room.

It took a couple of trips to the open-water blind for Kurt to get the birds he wanted. On our last trip together in that blind, Kurt bagged his black duck, at last. They had become scarce on the Santee, but that morning a pair skirted the decoys, as blacks do. But the cautious blacks listened to my begging call, and after several passes finally set their wings for a landing on the outside of the decoy spread. I told Kurt this would be his chance, and his 12-gauge scratched and clawed until the big black drake splashed the decoys. We sent Cajun for the retrieve, and he caught the big duck just as it started to dive. Kurt met Cajun at the boat and was presented a "king" from the Atlantic Flyway. I don't know who was prouder, Kurt or Cajun! Cajun always got his pleasure from licking his ducks from head to toe. I told Kurt that Cajun was just smoothing the feathers and saving the taxidermist a little work.

A year or two later, Kurt went with me on a short hunt just off the diversion canal between Lakes Marion and Moultrie. I had located a corner of marsh and saw grass that was loaded with ringneck ducks. It was opening day, and my longtime hunting partner was recovering from surgery. So, I knew Kurt would get a kick out of shooting the elusive ringnecks as they sailed over my decoys.

We arrived at the little landing quite early in hopes of getting our decoys placed in the right spot. And we did, as other hunters had not found my ducks. Ringnecks are really ducks of habit, and until they are shot out of an area, will continue to use it more frequently than any other duck I've hunted. I felt confident they would pay a visit to our corner, and I had told Kurt to bring plenty of shells because we were going to do some shootin'! The limit on ringnecks that year was five per person. Shooting ten of the black and white speedsters would be fun.

My little Winyah boat was very steady for shooting, and my gunnery-net blind had covered it effectively for years. In addition, the water level allowed us to run the boat up into the tall saw grass on the edge of the little pothole we would hunt. The slight daylight breeze wagged the decoys as the first light made them visible. I knew the first ringnecks would be too early for legal shooting, and told Kurt not to load his Browning autoloader for another few minutes. And, as usual, the early birds sat in the decoys over and over. Inevitably, as the sun rises in the east, some duck hunters will shoot before legal shooting time, and this morning was no exception. Sounded like some hunters opened up back toward Cherry Grove, so I told

Kurt to load and to stand for our first shots in the semidarkness. I loaded too, and the dozen or so ringnecks on the dark water promptly left, in high gear! We waited our time, and in a few minutes fast wings were beating their way toward our corner. I blew a few low-pitched calls, and the birds sensed company was already in their spot. We had positioned the boat a little downwind of the two dozen decoys so the ducks would pass us close, just before putting their feet in the water. I told Kurt to "fire at will," knowing he had never had such a target as a ringneck in front of his gun barrel. And, as I expected, his first shots were well behind his targets. He suspected that right away, and after those few wasted shells, he began to swing his gun ahead of the fleeting ducks. He dropped a couple in the decoys, and realizing his newfound success, fired his Browning empty over and over. I was tickled that he was having a great time and making the ammunition companies happy! And shoot we did for maybe fifteen minutes or so. Many ringnecks came to our spot that morning, and many left. But, when the shooting was over, we had bagged our ten birds without leaving our little corner.

As we drove into my backyard, Cajun met us as excitedly as if he already knew we had ducks in the boat. He always came to greet me and to get his nose deep down in the feathers.

Kurt said, as he was leaving for Columbia, "That's the best duck hunt I've ever been on!" I thought it was a dandy, too!

# 27

# Duck Calls and
# Duck Calling

Duck hunting, duck calls, and duck calling go together. Most duck hunters discuss this subject all during the year in readiness for the coming season. Certainly I've had my share of discussions along these lines and have formed my opinions over a fifty-year period.

One of the first things I see when opening my trophy cabinet is my first duck call. I've managed to hold on to it over the years, and very carefully attached to it with an old piece of rawhide is my first duck band, one of many I would remove from the legs of several different species of unlucky ducks that happened to get in the way of my gun's shot pattern. The little call was made by Lohman, and its volume is very soft. It probably sold for a couple of dollars back then, but I was proud to have it. As they say, a dollar was a dollar in those days. I don't recall that the Lohman brought in many ducks, as my calling was anything but ducky then.

It wasn't long before I learned about the Mallardtone call and had one tied on the rawhide around my neck. I always made my lanyards, and made many for friends from the rawhide I'd pick up at hardware stores. The Mallardtone calls were pretty good back then, and I used one for a long time, not only in the Santee lakes and swamps, but also Pocotaligo Swamp and on the coastal marshes of St. Helena Sound. I still have one in my collection with my initials carved on it, but I lost several over the seasons. In comparing the Mallardtone to other calls later on, I realized it was not loud enough nor did it have a real ducky sound. Of course, it worked, and that's what counted.

My brother, John, loved duck hunting as I did, and he was constantly on the lookout for a better duck call. I believe it was some friends in Sumter, South Carolina, who introduced him to Chick Major's Dixie Mallard calls.

At first they were difficult to blow, but my system of calling had been elementary when using the Mallardtone. To blow the Chick Major calls, I had to learn to use a steady stream of compressed air, and to separate the air stream with my tongue placed behind my front teeth in order to sound the individual quacks. It took months to develop the system, but once this was accomplished, I could blow a thirty- to forty-note highball, if needed. And endurance was tremendous compared to my old system. John had acquired the new technique too, and sounded great on his Chick Major calls. He soon acquired a catalog, and we ordered calls made of special hardwoods, such as bois d'arc, coca bola, and walnut.

Chick Major and I became telephone buddies and talked quite often. I would phone him, and he would listen to my calling and give me some pointers. He not only made a great call, but he was a world duck-calling champion, and a great friend. Chick was up in years and had been a world champion caller. In fact, his entire family became champions; he had taught them well. His wife, Sophie, and daughters, Pat, Dixie, and Brenda, all became lady world champions. They were terrific callers, and I eventually got to meet them all, with the exception of Chick, as he passed on before I made a trip to Stuttgart. I visited with his wife, Sophie, in 1978 when I participated in the world duck-calling championship. I had used one of Chick's calls to win the South Carolina championship, which qualified me for the world championship. I saw the small shop at Chick's home where he had made my call. That special quacker now hangs on the cherished trophy I received for winning the South Carolina contest.

During my visit to Stuttgart, Mrs. Sophie Major arranged a duck hunt for me through the Chamber of Commerce. It was my first hunt in Arkansas and not only did I acquire a taste for their kind of hunting, I met some nice people who have remained friends these many years.

The South Carolina Duck-Calling Contest has always been a popular event in the state's sporting heritage. Most of our winners have been avid hunters, and to win the contest is special to them. I was lucky to have won in 1978 and to bring home the title and trophy, along with the new Duck Sneak boat.

In winning the state contest, I used a calling routine based on actually calling a flock of ducks. But contest calling is entirely different from calling ducks. In contests, contestants showcase their ability using various calls within a one-and-a-half-minute time period. And so, to consume the entire ninety seconds, they blow long and varied versions of the long distance, or hail call, the come back call, the feed call, and the lonesome hen call. I have found that good contest callers are also good duck callers, despite the fact that calls that interest ducks are different from those used in competition.

Good hunters call more sparingly and more softly, but accurately, with no "squawks." I have found that one of the most appealing calls for ducks a few hundred yards away is a hail call consisting of six to eight notes in decreasing pitch. It mimics a real duck and is not high pitched. My son and I have used it for years to our advantage. Jay has developed the six- to-eight-note call with an inflection that almost duplicates the live mallards on the pond where he lives. He has copied the raspiness of the hens that come to eat his corn offerings each day. Jay has the ability to work a flock of ducks better than most. He watches their reactions to the various calls he blows. Both Jay and I blow very little when the ducks are coming toward us, but, rather, call to them after they have passed over and are downwind from our position.

On windy days, a loud call is a help. On calm days, a softer call is best. Ducks that have had a shot or two fired in their faces will work best to less calling and sometimes just to a single quack. In my opinion, the feed call and its many variations are overrated. I've heard the tame ducks on ponds chattering their feed calls, and I have imitated them for years, but I've turned very few ducks to my decoys using it. The right pitch and raspiness, along with what I call a combination highball-comeback call, does the trick for me. Varying the speed of this combination of six to eight notes has worked over and over.

A realistic decoy set is also a great advantage to good calling. Today's decoys are so vivid in their colors, shape, and detail that they are great foolers. I remember many years ago they were not so lifelike. And the new innovations in moving decoys have tremendously increased the effectiveness of decoy spreads. The Robo Duck with its whirling wings is a prime example.

The Arkansas-style duck call is normally a single-reed design, invented many years ago; but, in my era, it is Chick Major's Dixie Mallard that seems to provide the basic design used today. There are many call makers using the models that Chick Major designed about seventy years ago. But many calls today are pitched too high for hunting, and meant to be used solely in competition, the reason being that duck-calling contests are very popular in duck country. And most contestants are using what I designate as "screamers." On most days, they will scare more ducks away than attract them to their decoys. Their pitch is very high and most are much too loud.

Several call makers have perfected plastic calls and have succeeded in making ducky-sounding, consistently good ones that are moderately priced. These are made in molds from polycarbonate. They are actually copies of a successful wooden call the designer fashioned and copied by careful measurements. Once the measurements are put into the molds, all the calls from that mold are consistent in sound and performance.

I am presently marketing a line of polycarbonate calls made by World Champion Rick Dunn, of Beebe, Arkansas. Rick has succeeded in copying his custom wooden calls using polycarbonate. They are excellent reproductions of the raspy mallard sound needed for hunting.

I have had the pleasure of visiting with Rick at his shop in Arkansas, and also hunting with him the last two seasons. He is a master at working ducks in flooded timber, as I have seen him on many occasions using the soft calls that will attract mallards down through the flooded oaks in the Arkansas river bottoms. The six-to-eight-note call and a short feed call are his specialties. And he won't stop using them until the ducks get their feet wet among his decoys. Making them come all the way down is part of his hunt. On a couple of occasions, I've seen him let a flock pass because they didn't sit, only to call them around again for their final approach through the big trees to settle among his decoys.

Rick works most of the year making and stocking thousands of Echo calls for the coming season. But, when hunting season begins, he likes to hunt every day. Calling the birds, not shooting them, is his enjoyment from duck hunting. Many times he has said, "You do the shootin', I'll do the callin.'" It is a pleasure to know him and to distribute his Echo calls throughout my home state of South Carolina.

My favorite quacker is the Echo Timber call in a single-reed and double-reed configuration. Most days, under all conditions, those two will put ducks in front of my gun barrel. But, on very windy days on open water, I use the larger version double-reed call that Rick makes.

I have hunted with fine Arkansas callers over these years, but South Carolina has its share of outstanding callers, too. Duck hunters like Wayne Davis, Tom Green, Thomas Welch, Mickey Lowder, Jack Lundy, Eddie Cribb, and other younger local hunters who compete in calling contests have had their day on South Carolina's waters. All have special memories about the great hunts we all have had. Several have won our South Carolina duck-calling championships over their hunting years, and most continue to step into a blind or two during our duck seasons.

Wayne Davis and I are Sumter boys who grew up hunting the Santee and chasing ducks from one end of the lakes to the other. Any duck hunter who has had the pleasure of listening to Wayne's mastery of a duck call usually envies and appreciates his ability. His calling, in my opinion, places him among the best South Carolina has to offer.

In 1997, I met some avid duck hunters who, also, have become special friends of mine. They hunt in northeastern Arkansas and have invited me to share their special places with them. They make me feel like family, and I look forward to visiting in their homes and blinds each season. Friends like Randy and Ricky Gable, of Blytheville, Arkansas; and Ken Westmoreland and Steve Ingram, of Gosnell, Arkansas, all make me feel at home when I visit. I can't put a price on their friendship. They share their sport with me as if we've known each other all our lives. I usually pull my little Winyah when I go, but when I don't, they make room for me in their boats. Their blinds are huge and can accommodate five or six hunters. One of their special treats is a big breakfast cooked right in the blind. One of their blinds even has toilet facilities and heat, just in case the day is icy. And if it should rain, that's no problem, either, as a section of the blind is completely enclosed.

Getting ducks to respond to my calling these many years has been a satisfying and enjoyable part of hunting them. Seeing them slow their wing-beat, look my way, and lose altitude over my decoys has been a thrill I won't ever tire of. My Uncle Johnnie saw to it that I was bitten real good by the big duck-hunting bug, the same one that found him many years before.

# 28

# RINGNECKS, REDHEADS, AND CANVASBACKS

When recalling my days of hunting ducks in the swamps and marshes, chasing mallards, woodies, and black ducks immediately comes to mind. Throw in the wigeon, teal, and gadwalls, and that about covers the puddle-duck family that migrated to South Carolina. And maybe a pintail or two fell to my efforts, but not many.

In the early years of the nineties, the puddle-duck hunting slowed drastically. The big Santee Swamp and the lakes themselves were changing due to infestations of hydrilla and other aquatic grasses; everybody just called it grass. Thousands of acres of shallow water became almost completely clogged with hydrilla. It grew from the bottom of the lake and spread easily. A small piece could take root and grow almost anywhere there was water. The coves became clogged, and entrances to many waterfront homes became impassable in several areas of the lake. It was weedy from bottom to top. Areas stagnated and became infested with the very small gnats that seemed to hatch anywhere there was hydrilla. On a still day, whether in winter or summer, the hydrilla gnats were present by the millions. They became such a curse that fishing hydrilla beds was almost a tormenting experience. The gnats would just rise up from the weeds and cover anything in your boat, including you. They would swarm your eyes, enter your ears and nostrils, and drive your pet dog or retriever insane.

For several years, when fishing the hydrilla beds, we fashioned head nets with plastic inserts to see through, in hopes of keeping the gnats away. I remember we had to fish facing upwind so that the swarms would stay behind us. They seemed to hide behind any windbreak, and if we tried fishing with the wind, the gnats would cover us easily. There have been so many on my boat's windshield that seeing through it was impossible. My tackle boxes changed color, they was so completely covered, and my big Yamaha outboard would inhale the gnats into the carburetor under the motor's hood. Eating a sandwich or drinking from an open cup was unthinkable. And, when I arrived home from the lake, my wife would think I had developed a disease or something, as many gnats would have stuck to my sunscreen-covered face and neck.

The lake went through the weed era with many complaints from lake-side homeowners and others. Some fishermen said the weeds improved the fishing, and that seemed to be the case. The hydrilla did provide protection for the smaller bait fish and, of course, the predator fish like largemouth bass knew this. Grass carp were introduced into both Santee lakes and controlled spraying was frequent. Today, finally, the thousands of huge grass carp have almost cleared the lake of the pesky hydrilla.

For seven or eight years, though, we had a plus from the grass; a seldom-seen group of ducks flocked to the hydrilla. Thousands of ringnecks came to the grassy areas of the Santee and, later, hundreds of redheads and canvasbacks joined them.

A different kind of duck hunting began in our lakes and lasted until 1997. We weren't shooting the big mallards much anymore, but it was great sport to swing the gun on the swift divers as they passed over our decoys at speeds we had not previously experienced. I put the camcorder to work during those years to record the hurricane of wings around the Rocks Pond area. It was thrilling to see the huge flocks that would raft up around the vast hydrilla beds, and on some days, flocks of ringnecks by the thousands, with wings clawing the air as boats came by, would settle in the safe haven of open water. In February, I made a trip to that area to film the beautiful redheads and canvasbacks. This video is now among the film treasures I have accumulated.

My son had told me about the grass ducks down the lake, and he had added them to his vacation duck hunts in the afternoons. Our upper-lake hunting had been reduced to half-day hunts, and going down the lake where the grass ducks were would insure him a full day of hunting. We didn't know just how to hunt the diving ducks, and only after several hunting trips were we able to figure out what system to use.

I recall the very first hunt on decoying ringnecks. John Jackson, who became my constant duck-hunting companion, and I had launched my little Winyah boat at Spires Landing, near Rocks Pond. We had fought the grass-clogged beds for hours, and were returning to the landing, when John pointed to several hundred ducks rafted up in shallow water near Cherry Grove. We thought, at first, they were coots, but when we turned in their direction, they began to run across the water to gain momentum so that their small wings could lift their heavy, compact bodies skyward. They were ducks, all right, and they liked what they had found in that shallow, grassy flat. They broke into smaller flocks and circled ahead as we neared. My 30-horsepower Yamaha had a much-needed shallow-water drive, and I soon put it back to work in churning grass and water. The only cover in the area was two or three lone cypress trees. I headed for one that had been close to the ducks' takeoff area.

As hurriedly as we could, we set our decoys and tied a rope around the cypress and to each end of the Winyah, with the nose pointed into the wind. My camouflage gunnery-net blind was up in minutes, and our guns ready for action. I dug out my duck call, just in case. Divers are not mallards, and I wasn't sure they would turn to the call. But hopefully some would return to the area and see our mallard decoys in the open water bordering the grass. Maybe they would like to visit a few larger ducks that now occupied their spot.

Within minutes, the ringnecks were circling out beyond our setup and I began to call in their direction. Then, from behind us, a tightly-packed bunch of about a dozen buzzed by. I hit the call as they banked to look at our mallard decoys. Skimming and low they came, making only one pass before skidding to a stop just on the outside of the decoys. They had landed so determinedly that we had not fired a shot. John and I stayed down to look over the black and white speedsters that had joined us so suddenly. A short glimpse in our direction, and off they went, running, with wings beating into a blur. Another small group passed and swung away. This time, we stood and swung our 12-gauges past their noses and out ahead with a good lead. I had let two pass my gun since they came in on my end. John and I had an arrangement on this for years. Two well-placed shots from John downed the first birds, and I splashed one as he climbed to leave. The limit that year was three ducks per day, and in a short while, we had collected our six. The grass was always a help in stopping downed birds from drifting off, as was the case in our spot. So we removed our expensive steel shotshells from the smoking guns and cased them. The little boat and blind didn't seem to bother the ringnecks, and they continued to skim our decoys, many getting their feet wet for a closer look. It was satisfying to find ducks that would cooperate and decoy! Flocks of all sizes returned to our spot. We had found some new duck hunting that would last for years. It made our season, and the black and white ringnecks made us forget that we had been puddle-duck hunters for so long. The grass ushered in some challenging shotgunning by its attraction of diving ducks.

When the South Carolina duck hunters learned of the multitudes of ducks that were working the grass of lower Lake Marion, they were lured to huge grass patches around the Rocks Pond area, Spires Landing, Church Island, Bass Island, and the many other islands and coves in that section of the lake. Anywhere grass grew, the divers favored, and the younger hunters came to stand by small cypress trees in hopes of getting a passing shot. They would put out their decoys, hide their boats, and wade back to the cypresses offering to break up their outline. Good shooting resulted, and many ringnecks, redheads, and a few canvasbacks were taken this way. Some used large decoy spreads along with lay-out boats, which offered low silhouettes on the weedy water. They almost looked like nearby logs.

John and I used my Winyah and Yamaha with the gunnery-net blind. We had arrived at an age where comfort in hunting meant a lot to the enjoyment of our day together. One of our systems was to cruise the lower part of the lake to see just where the ducks were set up that day, and particularly, smaller concentrations of birds. If we found twenty or more ducks using a corner somewhere, we would run them out and set up as quickly as possible. More than likely, they would return in minutes, or not long after that. We took countless limits that way. We also used the cypress trees to anchor the Winyah. It had a flat floor, and the little boat was very stable as we stood to gun our birds. I kept a machete and a handsaw in the boat's dry box to trim some lower limbs from the trees where needed, but never too many that would put the cypress in jeopardy.

We had our favorite trees to tie on to and favorite spots, for sure. For instance, there was a small body of water on the side of Chimney Island and between a smaller island nearby. Ringnecks loved to loaf there and feed in the grass. We used the several cypress trees that grew there to secure the boat and as added camouflage, and from there we could see the huge rafts of ducks between our spot and the mouth of Cherry Grove. We hunted here and other spots close by on the back side of Chimney Island many times. All during the day, the rafted ringnecks would move around, and some would visit the little grassy slough beside Chimney Island. We had many successful shoots there.

John and I eventually invested in some ringneck decoys in hopes of improving our chances of stopping these heavily hunted birds. We put up the mallard decoys and used only the two dozen ringnecks. We felt twenty-four was about right for the small water we were hunting. And we put them out and picked them up more than a few times.

Another spot that we liked was Harry's Landing, again, very near the Diversion Canal. In fact, we hunted almost exclusively around the canal, mainly because it was protected water. The landing was located on the Lake Marion backwater that was near the vast open area of the lake. Just down from Harry's and on the back side of the canal was a sizeable body of shallow, weed-infested water. Cypress trees were here and there and a couple of small open ponds were near. The Diversion Canal had several breakthroughs in its bank, and in running the canal, I often looked for ducks through the breaks. On several occasions, divers were visible near a group of cypresses and looked inviting.

So, one morning we planned to be there early, before other shooters who put in at Harry's Landing arrived. We were disappointed that there was no early flight, and we figured other hunters had probably shot them out. But as the morning lingered on, a bird or two would fly our way and on past our decoys. At least something was happening to keep us on our toes; but, nothing passed over the decoys close enough for the 1⅜-ounce load of number threes to scratch them down. Things were just not working for us, and our patience was running thin.

Then, a little excitement came our way. We had been hearing some very vocal dogs running on the hill in front of us, but all had been quiet for a while. We figured some deer hunters were driving the area and that a deer was on the move. Suddenly, a big buck hit the water and headed straight for our setup. The deer season was in, but we didn't have any buckshot shells with us. John had been an avid deer hunter for many years, but I no longer shot deer. A minute later, several deerhounds appeared from the wooded area and were running the water's edge in search of a trail. They soon spied the buck making his way toward us and swimming hard. Into the water the whole pack came, with all eyes and noses toward the buck, which was now swimming and fighting his way through the grass and our decoys. The buck, sensing the pursuing pack, really put on the steam and leaped his way past us and headed toward the bank of the canal. He disappeared in the canal foliage, and we presumed he had swum the canal and on to safety on the other side. Losing sight of their quarry, it didn't take much to convince the pack to turn back toward the hill, and in short order, they did. This deer had outfoxed that bunch!

Of all the spots we hunted, there were two we called our favorites. They were on opposite ends of the Diversion Canal. One was close to Black's Landing on Lake Moultrie, and the other was a short distance from Big Oak Landing on Lake Marion. The better of the two was at Big Oak, and we never mentioned it to anyone. We hunted there mostly on opening days of the split season. Leaving Big Oak, a boat could cut through to Cherry Grove through a creek bed. I had fished this cut-through many times for bass and caught many nice fish. A small cove with saw grass growing all the way around it lay to the right, and like everywhere else with shallow water, had much grass. The saw grass offered good concealment for my boat as well as the boat's blind.

To get this spot, John and I often went early, leaving Orangeburg around 4:00 A.M. At 5:30 we would be putting out decoys. We always hunted it when the lake level was full, as low water really hurt this spot. Many times I would carry my little gas stove and cook us a couple of hamburgers during the morning. They really hit the spot, along with a cup of cocoa from our steel thermos jugs. This little cove would come alive with ringnecks on opening day. Sometimes a hundred birds would come in during the morning. The bag limit on ringnecks had increased to five per day, and shooting ten of those speedsters would have these two old hunters really swinging our guns. We loved our ringneck hunts, though! John had great hearing and would always alert me in the early light that ducks were on the move. He was a great shot with his two 12-gauge guns, which he alternated shooting, using the Browning B-80 one time and his older Remington 1100, which he had named the "killer," the next time. I was using the 3-inch chambered Beretta 303 by then, and it was great on ringnecks.

We hunted Big Oak mostly by ourselves, but one morning two hunters had already set up right by the wood duck box that was visible in the saw grass. This was our favorite spot to put the boat. They were standing in the water next to the saw grass, something we never did. I eased over and asked them if they objected to John and me setting up on the other side and directly across the cove from them. They didn't object. We agreed there would be plenty of ducks that opening morning, but we would have to shoot only those up off the water a good ways. To shoot low would be dangerous, for sure. Something I don't ever want to see again is fire from gun barrels in my direction. I supposed those two were seeing the same from us.

The little cove was hot that morning, as the black and white visitors flew in early and stayed late. The early fire from four guns would have been quite a picture for my camcorder, and when the shooting slowed, and the sun was a little higher in the yet-early morning, we picked up ducks we thought were ours. But I'm sure some of ours fell on them. John and I had ten fat little ringnecks in our boat and were preparing to cook our burgers, when the fellows hollered across the fifty-yard stretch of cove and asked, "Have you got yours?" We hollered back, "We're okay." They had, we thought, done more shooting, and maybe they had picked up too many. Both of them were wandering around in the saw grass, something I won't do. I've seen too many dogs with cut-up feet from retrieving from saw grass.

We had pulled the Winyah up and a little out of sight and were enjoying the hot burgers, when I saw a man paddling a small boat toward the decoys on the other side. This fellow was sure sneaky, and I knew only one reason why. He must be the game warden! He never looked our way, but paddled his small craft straight across to the hunters there. We could hear a little bit of their conversation and could see all that was taking place. I feared for the guys as the warden checked their guns, boat, and ducks, after showing them his badge. I felt like we would be next, as we sat and watched. I've always appreciated the wardens doing their job, particularly with slob hunters. But, this cove held no slobs that day. The warden soon paddled on out of our spot and back toward Big Oak. He would have been welcomed on our side. We might even have served him a Lake Marion hamburger, cooked right on the water.

————

Bob Hammond has been a fishing partner of mine for a long time. Bob is a few years my senior, as was John Jackson. And, like John, Bob could really shoot a shotgun. He had heard me talking about duck hunting at Big Oak during our bass fishing trips there, and had mentioned that he had never shot ducks, but would like to. So, we made our plans to hunt Big Oak together.

This time I carried my camcorder, and my son's chocolate Lab, Cajun, went along. I was hoping a few ducks would honor us with a skim or two over my decoys, so we set up early. I got some good video of the sunrise over the canal and of Bob talking about this being his first and only duck hunt. Our guns were silent in the little cove that morning as not the first duck showed up!

Bob and I picked up the ringneck decoys and set out through the cut-through creek toward Cherry Grove. Coots were everywhere, but few ducks, as we checked spot after spot. I was thoroughly disgruntled with what we had found, so we sped the boat on toward Rocks Pond. Cajun pointed the way, as he usually did, by keeping Bob company up front.

I decided to check the Black Branch area just the other side of Rocks Pond. Between these two areas is a sizeable stand of small cypress trees bordering a couple of small islands. As we passed the first trees, just off the big water, I noticed a flock of ringnecks swimming in open water near a line of cypresses growing in the shape of a horseshoe. They immediately took to the air as we slowed the boat. I said to Bob, "There's our chance!" I figured that, as usual, they would come back shortly, and we had better get set up as quickly as possible. I spied a small double cypress with limbs just right to fit the boat under. With decoys out and blind up in a hurry, the first duck beat a path to our decoys bobbing in the slight breeze. He came to my side, and I splashed him with my first shot. Cajun was ready for the retrieve, as I grabbed my camcorder. After I pulled up the net toward the downed ringneck, he hit the water on command. The Sony rolled away, and I started recording the day's action.

The ringnecks, as expected, returned one or two at a time; and Bob, with his old Remington semiautomatic with cylinder-bore barrel, took only a short while to gather his first limit of ducks, all drake ringnecks. Cajun made some very long swims for birds that the wind quickly carried away. Luck had been with us this day, and as Bob always said, "All days are good days, some are just better than others." I never did ask him how he classified this one!

———————

Our Lake Moultrie favorite spot was so close to Black's Landing that John Jackson and I could have smelled the hamburgers, steaks, shrimp dinners, and small Santee catfish being cooked; only they weren't being cooked during duck season. And we could have spit to the parking lot there!

We discovered this ducky spot one day when coming back from a hunt on the other side of the canal, an area that we called the Hog Pen, which was a top spot for big bass. I remember one morning well, when John, fishing out the back of my Dyna-Trak, landed a huge bass on a very shallow-running plug called a One Minus. The fish must have weighed nine pounds or so, and from that point on, we called it the Hog Pen. By the way, John always took pride in releasing a healthy fish like that.

We had seen thirty or forty ringnecks sitting in the very middle of a little pond near the Black's Landing parking lot. The hydrilla grass was all over the Santee by then, and the little pond had its share, too. Seeing that many ducks that close to the landing reminded us of our Big Oak spot that had similar groupings. We decided to return for an early morning shoot the next day, and arriving very early, which was our habit in situations like that, we were surprised to be the first car and boat there. So we just sat until time was right to put out our decoys. We chose a spot on the opposite bank for the boat and blind, as the wooded bank gave the boat some breakup camouflage.

We were not disappointed that morning or many mornings in years that followed, as the ducks continued to use this favorite spot. As with our Big Oak spot seven miles up the canal, we kept this information to ourselves.

On one shoot there late in the season, John and I took ten of the fast flyers during a morning of slow shooting. We didn't miss a duck that came our way. Cajun was with us, and we enjoyed having him. He was in his last hunting years, and we did not allow him to swim for downed birds anymore. When it was time to pick up, we would ride him close to the bird, and he would lean over and pick up each bird, showing his continued pleasure in doing so. Even though his health was failing, we still took him along on most trips, as he was always ready and showed his loyalty by doing his part.

That day had started slowly, but a strong wind directly off Lake Moultrie had the big water areas whitecapping. We strung our decoys along a weedy edge on the calm end of the little pond with the wind at our back. Cattails helped cover the boat's outline. Singles and doubles would come in off the big water and over our heads. They sailed with great speed down the pond and turned and came back to our decoys. A little calling would help just as they turned to come back upwind and into the strong breeze. They flew near or over our cattail cover affording us a good shot.

By the time we had downed ten birds, seven were on the water and three were behind us on the wooded bank. We had cooked and eaten our burgers and had drunk our hot chocolate, while the winds had moved a few ducks in bit by bit. Cajun had slept curled up on burlap cotton sheets most of the morning, awakening long enough for his usual hamburger. Now it was time to see if we could pick up our ten-bird limit.

We could see our birds on the water, but those behind us in the thick woods might not be so easy to find. I told John that if they were on the ground Cajun would find them, and that he did. I pointed him in the direction of the downed birds, and in minutes he was back with one of the speedsters firmly between his teeth. I took the bird and he went directly back, as if he knew he was supposed to. John saw him coming and said, "He's found another one." Just maybe he could find all three. This time Cajun walked the grassy edge as if looking for a trail. He disappeared into the tangled underbrush, and for a while I was concerned for him. But retrievers are smart, and Cajun had always had a good nose. I was about to go look for him, when on the other side of a little drain, I spied him coming ever so slowly with the third ringneck in his mouth. The duck evidently had been crippled and had left where he had fallen. Cajun had trailed him as he had done so often in the past. Despite nearing his fifteenth birthday, he was still our favorite retriever.

The last day of the 1996–97 duck season arrived during a very cold spell. John and I were trying to get in our last hunt despite our mixed emotions for battling this cold. We didn't arrive at Rocks Pond, until after 8:00 A.M. The water level had been low for a while, and we had about depleted our good spots to hunt. Since no one seemed active around the campground, we drove John's Explorer slowly around, looking at this very windy section of the lake.

I had gotten out in the fierce wind a couple of places that we had driven to, and each time I would say to John, "I just don't have enough clothes for this." Even though I had my best hunting garments on, they didn't seem to protect me from the frigid conditions.

With the lake so low, which meant finding cover to hide the Winyah would be almost impossible, we felt good about being in the car and out of the wind. So we parked out by the end of the boat slip, and just sat and watched. There were a few ringnecks boldly swimming with some tame Rocks Pond mallards out by the dock in front of the campground. We sipped a little warm coffee and scanned the empty sky directly in front. The lake was whitecapping vigorously, and the wind continued to blow straight off the open lake and into the Rocks Pond area. Surely, if there were any ducks left on our lakes, they wouldn't be out there!

John and I were about ready to head home when I saw a ball of black and white ducks riding the wind and headed back toward the Black Branch area. There must have been thirty or so streaming their way over the cypresses that were standing almost dry between us and the Black Branch cove. I knew the area well, having fished it many times, and it wasn't very far, but was there enough water and grass back there to attract the ducks? We waited about fifteen minutes. The ringnecks must have found a protected area they liked, and we decided to investigate. We had plenty of good, hot coffee and hot chocolate, so we figured that we could stand the cold for a while if we could get out of the wind.

Going out the Rocks Pond boat slip and into the whitecaps soaked my hooded jacket even before we could get out in deep enough water to make a downwind left turn. The waterproof garments were worth their cost this day, and we eased on back to sheltered water going to Black Branch. The water soon became too shallow to run the motor, so I got out and pulled John along as I had done many times. He was about ten years my senior, and he had a heart condition.

Soon we would be rewarded for our efforts, as sitting in the entrance waters to Black Branch was a raft of ringneck ducks. They took to the air, and their rapid wings quickly had them all vacating their shelter. They had selected a spot that included a pair of cypress trees that seemed just right for our boat. We set the ringneck decoys alongside the grassy edge in front of the cypresses, and before we could erect the gunnery-net blind, ducks were coming back. The wind was so strong that it carried the ducks' flight in a pattern past our setup before they could control their turn. Even after we gathered our wits and readied ourselves, the black and white flyers were exceeding their speed limit as they bore downwind! If we risked a shot but scored a hit, the wind would carry them into unretrievable territory. So we waited for their wide turn back into the wind before taking a shot. Our position turned out to be almost perfect. The decoys were positioned just upwind from our boat, and the boat was steady against the cypress trees, enabling us to stand for the shot. I don't remember ever having a better setup for swinging on ducks. It was almost like shooting skeet on a skeet field.

The two of us missed only a couple of shots, as we seemed to be on our game that day. And luckily we didn't have to chase any cripples. By the time the hot drinks and sandwiches were gone, we had ten birds to pick up. We had spent maybe two hours in the calm corner at Black Branch. The last day of our season started late and slow, but our knowledge of the ringnecks' habits had afforded us another great day together.

We got to hunt only once more for the diving ducks of the Santee, and that occurred on the opening day of the second part of the 1997–98 split season. It was December of 1997, and we chose to put out our decoys in our favorite spot at Big Oak. The grass carp had done their job well, as there were few weeds left anywhere around the canal area, and only a few divers had migrated down our way that fall. Our hunt that last morning was slow. We managed to bag three ringnecks early. No flight to speak of, and John and I agreed that the diver hunting that began six or seven years before was coming to an end.

The puddle-duck hunting that began when I was a youngster and had lasted for fifty years was now practically nonexistent; the Santee Swamp had been toppled by Hurricane Hugo. The divers that had provided some exciting days for us those last years had now moved on and away from our waters, largely due to the absence of grass. I shot my last shotgun shell on the Santee that day. And now, several years later, most of South Carolina's duck population is concentrated on our coastal marshes and ponds.

---

John Jackson had been my hunting partner for more than thirty years. During that time, we enjoyed each other's company not only because of our close friendship, but also because we were equally avid duck hunters of the Santee. I remember saying to him one day with all sincerity, "John, I want you to know that I've enjoyed our many hunting years together, and I have valued your friendship more than you will ever know." He turned to me and said, "It couldn't have been better. We've come through a lot together and have taken care of each other for a long time. I've enjoyed it, too."

The Santee lakes had been my sporting paradise since childhood, and I am grateful to have shared the many wonders they provided. I've lived on both sides of the lakes and have roamed them from the forks of the rivers to the Pinopolis powerhouse on the lower lake. I look back with fondness to my many enjoyable years and, also, with sadness at the loss of one of the Atlantic Flyway's top wintering grounds.

In retrospect, man is shortsighted when it comes to conserving his world, but we learn from our mistakes. Now we must reverse the continuing destruction of wetlands and wildlife habitat. We, as hunters, must continue to lead in this respect, as we are consumers of our efforts.

The salvation of waterfowling is really up to us as we fight against pollution and drainage. We must have respect for each other, our environment, and the waterfowl we take from it.

Waterfowl migration will again come our way and grace our wetlands if we have the foresight to prepare our refuges on the Santee and oppose proposals that threaten our beloved lakes and swamps. I have learned of a new dedication to replant the now-barren refuge fields that once attracted our waterfowl. With efforts like this, perhaps the big greenheaded duck will return to the ridges and flats to eat acorns and frolic again on the Santee.

---

My era has passed, and another begins for those enthusiastic young duck hunters who will search for their favorite spots as I did when the great Santee was born. My many sunrises on the Santee were a wonderful part of my life, and as I have recalled them on paper, I have relived them again and again, some dim, but all cherished.

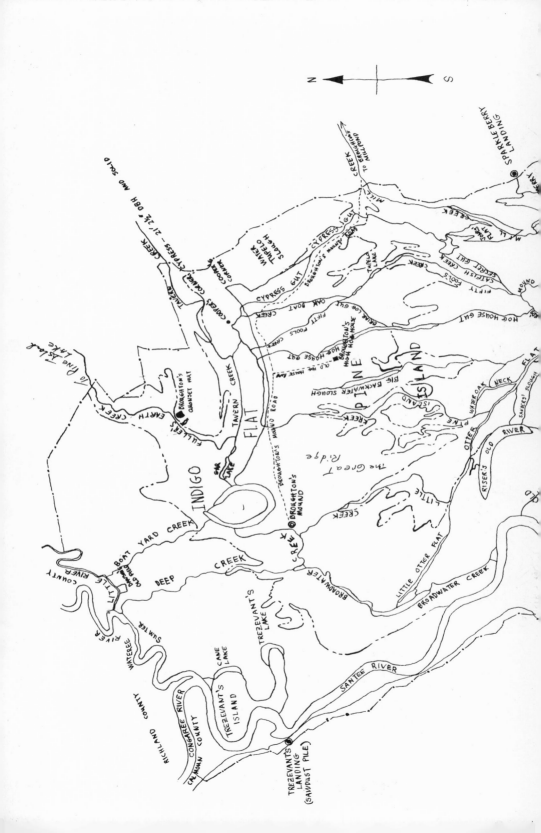